FARMING
THE
HOME
PLACE

FARMING THE HOME PLACE

A Japanese American Community in California, 1919–1982

Valerie J. Matsumoto

Cornell University Press

ITHACA AND LONDON

First published 1993 by Cornell University Press.

International Standard Book Number 0-8014-2074-1
Library of Congress Catalog Card Number 92-56774
Printed in the United States of America
Librarians: Library of Congress cataloging information appears on the last page of the book.

♾ The paper in this book meets the minimum requirements of the American National Standard for Information Sciences—Permanence of Paper for Printed Library Materials, ANSI Z39.48-1984.

Contents

Acknowledgments

Many people assisted me at every stage of this project, for which I am deeply grateful. I am especially indebted to the three generations of the Cortez community who generously shared their time, memories, personal and institutional records, and warm hospitality. I thank them all, including Robin Yuge Alexander, Gary Asai, Hiroshi Asai, Hisako Asai, Russell Asai, Shizue Asai, Asai Shizuka, Franklin Baba, Lena Date, Takashi Date, Shirley Baba Frice, Haruka Ishihara, Eugene Kajioka, Harry Kajioka, Kazumi Kajioka, Mae Kajioka, Mary Kajioka, Kajioka Masa, Kajiwara Hajime, Kajiwara Utako, Joe Kamiya, Marcia Kamiya, Mark Kamiya, Mary Kamiya, Grace Kimoto, Frances Kirihara, Christine Kubo, Daniel Kubo, Yoshi Kubo, Lucille Kumimoto, Florice Kuwahara, Sam Kuwahara, Kaoru Masuda, Yuriko Masuda, Ken Miyamoto, Takako Miyamoto, Albert Morimoto, Lois Morimoto, Mitsuko Morimoto, George Morofuji, Carole Narita, Haruko Narita, Leona Narita, Narita Saburo, Jack Nishihara, Takako Nishihara, Ada Nose, Alan Osugi, Ann Osugi, Sakaguchi Maju, May Sakaguchi, Rodney Sakaguchi, Yeichi Sakaguchi, Edward Sugiura, General Sugiura, Sugiura Suye, Grace Tanaka, Alice Taniguchi, Howard Taniguchi, Kumekichi Taniguchi, Candice Toyoda, Don Toyoda, May Toyoda, Edna Yamaguchi, Jim Yamaguchi, Lester Yamaguchi, Yamamoto Akio, Kiyoshi Yamamoto, Michael Yamamoto, Naomi Yamamoto, Ernest Yoshida, Ruth Yoshida, Sharyn Yoshida, Dennis Yotsuya, Edith Yotsuya, Ernest Yotsuya, Grace Yotsuya, Mae Yotsuya, Takeo Yotsuya, Umeko Yotsuya, and Yukihiro Yotsuya. Key

Kobayashi, Sandy Lofton, Matsushige Tsune, Caroline Nakashima, Tom Nakashima, Nakashima Kohei, and Lily Takahashi were also helpful. Scottie Hagedorn provided a vital link to the community at the outset of this project. I owe special thanks to Nobuzo and Miye Baba and to George and Helen Yuge, who welcomed me into their families and made the oral history interviews possible. I cherish their friendship and wisdom.

In the course of research I benefited greatly from the invaluable help of librarians at Merced College, the California State University at Stanislaus, the Merced County Library, the Green Library and Hoover Library at Stanford University, and the University Research Library at the University of California, Los Angeles. The staff at the Shields Library at the University of California, Davis, provided vital insights into agricultural history; I thank Axel Borg, Rafaela Castro, David Lundquist, Ted Sibia and John Skarstad. I wish to acknowledge the crucial support of Marjorie Lee and Brian Niiya at the Asian American Studies Reading Room at UCLA. Thanks also to Carlos Hagen-Lautrup and Eric Scott at the Henry J. Bruman Map Library, and to Betty Takahashi at the University Research Library at UCLA. Paul Bowman contributed a fine map of the early Cortez properties. I also thank the personnel at the *Turlock Journal* and the *Livingston Chronicle* for their help and good humor, and Seizo Oka for his kindness to researchers.

The Henry and Chiyo Kuwahara Memorial Scholarship from the Japanese American Citizens League made much of this research possible. A career development award from UCLA also facilitated the progress of this manuscript. My *orei* to Don Nakanishi, Director of the Asian American Studies Center at UCLA, for his support and example.

The incisive comments of many scholars helped to shape this manuscript. Mary Rothschild introduced me to new visions of history and inspired me to undertake this study. Estelle Freedman provided critical insight, encouragement, and a model of integrity. I cannot imagine surviving this process without the friendship of Peggy Pascoe and Vicki Ruiz, who read my manuscript countless times, always offering invaluable feedback and cheer. I am also indebted to Gary Okihiro and Roger Daniels for their thoughtful suggestions and expertise. I thank the members of the Women's History Dissertation Reading Group at Stanford, who, in the midst of their own pressing work, took time to improve mine: Dorothy Sue Cobble, Lizabeth Cohen, Gary Sue Goodman, Gayle Gullett, Yukiko Hanawa, Gail Hershatter, Emily Honig, Susan Johnson, Sue Lynn, Joanne Meyerowitz, Peggy Pascoe, Vicki Ruiz, Penny Russell, Linda Schott, Frances Taylor Anton, and Katherine Weinert. Thanks are also due the colleagues who generously contributed to this project in myriad ways: David Gutierrez, Judy Yung, Bruce Schulman, Miriam Silverberg, Alexander Saxton, Thomas James, Yuji Ichioka, Regina Morantz-Sanchez, George Sanchez, Ellen DuBois, Peter Reill, Scott Waugh, and Ronald Mellor. Lisa Joe and Lisa Mortimer deserve credit for their painstaking, efficient research assistance.

I am grateful to Peter Agree, Kay Scheuer, and Joanne Hindman at Cornell University Press and copyeditor Martin Stanford for their patience, fortitude, and hard work.

For their sustaining friendship I thank Victoria Marney-Petix, Robert and Ellen Brigham, Nikki Sawada Bridges, Frances Taylor Anton, Moira Roth, Shirley Oaks, Bernice Zamora, Becky Smith, and Craig Manning.

I thank Terry, Sachi, and Lori Matsumoto for their loving support throughout this endeavor.

V.J.M.

Los Angeles, California

FARMING
THE
HOME
PLACE

Cultivating a
Fallow Field

On a cool June evening in 1988, I sat with Dennis and Grace Yotsuya in the kitchen of their farmhouse in Cortez. The occasion was my first return to the central California community since I had carried out research there five years earlier. Over cups of hot green tea, we discussed life in the small Japanese American farming colony, established in 1919 by immigrants like Dennis's grandparents. At first glance, the Yotsuya home appeared to be a natural third-generation outgrowth of a rural tradition. Yet this was not the whole picture.

Why did Grace and Dennis, young college-educated urban professionals, decide to make their home in an agricultural settlement so small that it does not even appear on maps of California's Merced County? Our conversation gradually unfolded the historic factors and personal dreams that led them back to Cortez. The Yotsuyas' comments made clear the importance of community, not as an unbroken and unquestioned entity but, like history, a process of constant creation.

Dennis and Grace, third-generation (Sansei) Japanese Americans, share rural roots. Dennis grew up in Cortez; he went to school with Sansei peers and attended a Japanese American Presbyterian church. Grace came from a farming family in Tulare, California. As children, both darkened their fingers harvesting walnuts and helped with hoeing and weeding in the fields. Both were encouraged by their parents to attend college and to find an occupation more secure than farming. They met at the University of California, Berkeley, in 1972, in the

1

heady days of student activism. Both became involved in the Asian American student movement, working on community issues such as housing for elderly Issei (first-generation Japanese immigrants).

Like many young activists, Dennis and Grace learned that social service work provided more emotional gratification than monetary reward; other supplemental employment was necessary. Grace worked as a secretary and Dennis found employment in engineering. Still they cast about for a different means of making a living, seeking an occupation more attuned to their beliefs. Their two-year struggle to start up a commercial fishing business, however, left them with a deep respect for the forces of nature and a strong conviction that they were not suited for work at sea. In 1982 they decided to settle in Cortez.

A blissful rural welcome did not await them. The reaction of the senior Yotsuyas revealed the unsentimental practicality of concerned Nisei (American-born children of Japanese immigrant parents), who were all too aware of the rigors and uncertainties of farming, without any veiling of pastoral fantasy. As Dennis said, "They didn't think it was a good idea because they felt that I could make more money in the city; and why would I come back to such a hard lifestyle when it was so much easier in the city?"[1] Why, indeed?

Grace and Dennis's reasons for choosing to settle in Cortez illuminate the strong appeal of rural values joined with the desire to maintain ethnic identity. Both wanted to raise their daughters in the country. Although Grace had felt isolated as one of the few Japanese Americans in Tulare, she explained, "I still really liked the lifestyle, I liked the quietness of the country, and setting your own pace." In addition to the pressures of an urban work schedule, she worried about raising children in the Bay Area. "In the city they grow up so much faster. There are so many opportunities, but they're not always the best opportunities." In a rural setting, she felt, "we would be more at home and have the opportunity to grow up as a family. . . . And we thought maybe in the country, farming—especially farming—we'd be able to do things together."[2] Here Dennis interjected, laughing, "It hasn't worked out, but . . . ."

Rising land prices and the hegemony of large-scale agriculture in California have complicated the Yotsuyas' commitment to life on a

1. Dennis Yotsuya interview, Cortez, Calif., June 5, 1988.
2. Grace Yotsuya interview, Cortez, Calif., June 5, 1988.

small farm. The couple bought their thirty-five acres from Dennis's father and uncle in 1981. They had hoped to farm full time in a few years, but as of our meeting in 1988, Dennis still commuted ninety miles to an engineering job in San Leandro three days a week. Grace had found a niche providing childcare for seven local preschool children, including two Yonsei (fourth-generation Japanese Americans), a service for which there is a growing demand in Cortez as in the rest of the nation. For the Yotsuyas, then, other sources of income have been crucial to making small-acreage farming viable.

However unusual it may have seemed to their parents, the Yotsuyas' decision to move to Cortez illustrates two persistent American themes: the appeal of a return to the land and the attraction of life within a close-knit community. The Yotsuyas' desire to rear their children in the country might well have led them to some less developed, less costly rural area than the San Joaquin Valley. Yet Cortez offered several advantages. There they could draw upon family connections to make expensive land available; but just as important, Cortez offered the networks and interaction of a close-knit Japanese American community in whose history the Yotsuya family had deep roots. For many of the Cortez people, the community constitutes such an enveloping web of organizations, kin, work, and ways of thinking and acting, that they have difficulty describing it.[3] For the Yotsuyas and many others, community, as an all-encompassing notion, eludes definition. Although the ethnic community was rarely directly addressed in Dennis and Grace's words, its presence permeated our conversation as an understanding and a context.

In this sentiment, they are not alone. From the Puritans' "city on the hill" to the civil rights movement's "beloved community," the search for community has provided compelling motivation for American migrations and inspiration for utopian experiments. Scholars have been equally fascinated and frustrated in understanding this quest, which they have correctly taken to be an important key to comprehending the process of becoming American. Even today, in an age of anomie and much-debated diversity, when people are more transient than

3. Similar views of community have been analyzed in Kai T. Erikson, *Everything in Its Path: Destruction of Community in the Buffalo Creek Flood* (New York: Simon and Schuster, 1976), which deals with a West Virginia mining town and Elizabeth Rauh Bethel, *Promiseland: A Century of Life in a Negro Community* (Philadelphia: Temple University Press, 1981).

ever before, they are yet drawn together by communications technology. Previously unconnected lives are linked with stunning rapidity, while concerns loom ever larger about what a community is and how best to participate in it. In the postmodern world, communal ties take on even more importance than before, though perhaps in a different sense.

The recent work of anthropologists demonstrates the ways in which the definition of community has been stretched in our own time. As the growth of communication and transportation technology has made the world a smaller place, the geographic boundaries long associated with the delineation of a community have become more flexible. Shared meanings and relations may now span vast distances. As Roger Rouse posits, the melting of borders and the ability to connect instantaneously with kin and friends miles away have suggested an expanded notion of the "social space" shared by people.[4] Such redefinition calls attention to the common values and functions that bind community members together and the forces of both continuity and change that work upon communal ties.

Community studies, long the mainstay of the social sciences, have burgeoned in the garden of historical research since the 1960s. Questions regarding the nature of community and what might be uniquely American about such collectivities first appeared in an outpouring of research focused on the American colonial period. As scholars responded to social movements addressing issues of race, class, and gender, the 1970s saw the flourishing of East Coast community studies, centering on immigrant and urban groups.[5] More recently, scho-

---

4. Roger Rouse, "Mexican Migration and the Social Space of Postmodernism," *Diaspora* 1(Spring 1991):8–23.

5. The burgeoning of East Coast immigrant and urban history developed largely as a response to Oscar Handlin's 1951 landmark study *The Uprooted* (Boston: Little, Brown, 1973). This work claimed alienation to be the hallmark of the immigrant experience in the United States. Many historians took issue with Handlin's idealization of a rural peasant past and his emphasis on newcomer helplessness within the maw of industrialized urban society. Nevertheless, his scholarship placed on center stage the examination of the ethnic working class, and sparked a continuing dialogue on the nature of becoming American. Subsequent researchers pointed out the pitfalls of assuming that all new immigrants lost their ethnic heritage in an American melting pot; furthermore, one could not take for granted that they had all brought the same cultural baggage. In this vein, Rudolph J. Vecoli drew attention to the mutual aid societies and other vehicles of ethnic support—overlooked by Handlin—among Italian immigrants in Chicago and underscored the need for study of "the distinctive cultural character of each ethnic group and how this influenced its adjustments in the New World." (Rudolph J. Vecoli,

lars have turned their attention to white ethnic and African American communities. In this sense, the cultivation of the South as a research site paralleled the growth of studies of northeastern cities. At the moment, historians of the South are rendering the discussion more complex by exploring the dynamics of class and gender within African American groups as well as analyzing interracial relations.[6]

Thus, over the past two decades, the development of community studies reflects an important shift from an initial Euro-American focus to a broader concern with various ethnic communities; the historiography also evidences a gradual geographic expansion of scholarly attention beyond the East Coast. This literature is informed by a growing awareness of diverse ethnic American legacies rather than a monolithic "white American" heritage. Researchers have changed their tune. Unlike social scientists and reformers of the early twentieth century who lamented the backwardness of immigrants who clung to Old World customs, their counterparts who came of age during the civil rights movement have chosen instead to celebrate such cultural practices as wonderful spices in the American pie.

The earliest wave of ethnic community studies has broadened the panorama of U.S. history as never before and added new color and dimension by highlighting the themes of race, class, and gender. Yet this approach has two significant blind spots. For all its focus on community, it leaves largely unchallenged the previous assumption that

---

"*Contadini* in Chicago: A Critique of *The Uprooted*," *Journal of American History* 51 [December 1964]:417.) Under this rubric, scholars like John Bodnar, Kenneth Kusmer, and Virginia Yans-McLaughlin have investigated the community dynamics and mobility of a number of white ethnic and African American urban groups. Their research has suggested that, rather than being jettisoned at Ellis Island or on arrival in the city, ethnic culture has proved remarkably resilient. Yans-McLaughlin's work on Italians in Buffalo also placed gender in the foreground as a critical category of analysis in the assessment of immigrant adjustment.

6. Scholars, including Eugene Genovese, Herbert Gutman, Allan Kulikoff, and Lawrence Levine, have explored questions of racial and ethnic culture, the formation of support networks, and the extent of resistance or accommodation among African Americans. See Eugene Genovese, *Roll, Jordan, Roll: The World the Slaves Made* (New York: Vintage, 1972); Herbert Gutman, *The Black Family in Slavery and Freedom, 1750–1925* (New York: Pantheon, 1976); and Lawrence Levine, *Black Culture and Black Consciousness* (New York: Oxford University Press, 1977). For studies examining class and gender within black groups as well as analyzing interracial relations, see, for example, Darlene Clark Hine, *When the Truth Is Told: A History of Black Women's Culture and Community in Indiana, 1875–1950* (Indianapolis: National Council of Negro Women, 1981); Deborah Gray White, *Ain't I a Woman? Female Slaves in the Plantation South* (New York: Norton, 1985).

"culture"—whether "American" or "ethnic"—is static and unchanging, like a prized tablecloth handed down from mother to daughter. This approach is blind to the complex ways in which people retain, reshape, or jettison (sometimes temporarily) their ethnic customs; this view also tends to overlook the ambivalence people may feel about ethnic cultural practices and ideas. Thus, ethnic community is always dwindling as members "assimilate" or "acculturate." This perspective of gradual and unavoidable loss has led to an elegiac tone with regard to the future of ethnic communities, a sense of Atlantis inevitably sinking beneath the waves of postmodern capitalist society. Outmarriage and the loss of Old World languages are interpreted as the first harbingers of decline. Such a simplistic view denies the importance of historic context and the changing dynamics of individual, family and community strategies within that framework over time. As Micaela di Leonardo cautions, such falsifying of the past can lead to the creation of "misconceived nostalgia for worlds we have never lost."[7] The perception of the inescapable decline of ethnic communities has thus risen from static notions of ethnic culture and collectivity.

A second problematic perspective also underlies the first wave of ethnic community studies. These works, like much preliminary social and women's history, have been curiously limited in their treatment of race. They have narrowed their focus to two particular groups—European immigrants and African Americans—and yet these groups form only part of the racial and ethnic diversity of American history. Renato Rosaldo has pointed out that this view reflects regional patterns of thinking about race and ethnicity: "On the eastern seaboard, it seems, ethnicity and otherness really mean race and race really means black. Out here in the West, ethnicity and otherness really mean race and race really means Native American, Chicano, Puerto Rican, African American and Asian American."[8] In this vein, Ellen DuBois and Vicki Ruiz have critiqued scholars' continued reliance on a biracial model under which "the historic emphasis is on white power and people of color have to compete for the role of 'other.'"[9]

7. Micaela di Leonardo, *The Varieties of Ethnic Experience: Kinship, Class, and Gender among California Italian-Americans* (Ithaca: Cornell University Press, 1984), p. 135.

8. Renato Rosaldo, "Others of Invention: Ethnicity and Its Discontents," *Voice Literary Supplement*, no. 82, February 1990, p. 29.

9. Ellen Carol DuBois and Vicki L. Ruiz, eds., *Unequal Sisters: A Multi-Cultural Reader in U.S. Women's History* (New York: Routledge, 1990), p. xii.

Such limitations in perspective have obscured the rich multiplicity of the American past. As Ronald Takaki charged, in a 1990 work pointedly titled *Strangers from a Different Shore,* the tendency to omit the historic roles of Asian and other racial–ethnic immigrants has "shrouded the pluralism that is America and that makes our nation so unique, and thus the possibility of appreciating our rich racial and cultural diversity remains a dream deferred."[10] Not only have Asians largely been ignored in U.S. immigration history but, as Roger Daniels has asserted, there has been more emphasis on those who sought to exclude them than on the immigrants themselves; few scholarly works have conveyed a sense of their own agency within the parameters of their social and economic situations.[11]

In order to deal with these issues, recent scholars who have produced what might be considered a second wave of ethnic community studies have increasingly turned attention to the American West as a research site. Like George Sanchez they assert the importance of the West as "the locus of one of the most profound and complex interactions between variant cultures in American history."[12] The West is particularly important to the examination of Asian American, Mexican American, and American Indian cultural processes. The investigation of western migration and immigration, settlement, work, and family has contributed to a growing sense of racial–ethnic and multicultural communities as an integral, revealing part of the American social landscape. The long history of racial diversity as well as the economic and cultural issues played out in places like Santa Clara, Monterey, Los Angeles, San Francisco, Seattle, and Albuquerque have made them sites of both creative interaction and uneasy adaptations— sites that are quintessentially American.[13]

10. Ronald Takaki, *Strangers from a Different Shore: A History of Asian Americans* (Boston: Little, Brown, 1989), p. 7.

11. Roger Daniels, *Asian America: Chinese and Japanese in the United States since 1850* (Seattle: University of Washington Press, 1988), pp. 4–6.

12. George Joseph Sanchez, "Becoming Mexican American: Ethnicity and Acculturation in Chicano Los Angeles, 1900–1943," Ph.D. diss., Stanford University, 1989, p. 4.

13. For example, see Albert Camarillo, *Chicanos in a Changing Society: From Mexican Pueblos to American Barrios in Santa Barbara and Southern California, 1848–1930* (Cambridge: Harvard University Press, 1979); Mario T. Garcia, *Desert Immigrants: The Mexicans of El Paso, 1880–1920* (New Haven: Yale University Press, 1981); Richard Griswold del Castillo, *The Los Angeles Barrio, 1850–1890: A Social History* (Berkeley: University of California Press, 1979); Timothy J. Lukes and Gary Y. Okihiro, *Japanese Legacy: Farming and Community Life in California's Santa Clara Valley,* Local History Studies, vol. 31 (Cupertino:

Through their examination of communities in the West, anthropologists such as Micaela di Leonardo and Sylvia Yanagisako and historians such as George Sanchez, Dino Cinel, Albert Camarillo, and Mario Garcia have illuminated the continuous transformation undergone by ethnic enclaves since their inception. They have been concerned to recognize the limits placed on, as well as to celebrate the achievements made by, the agency of ethnic Americans.[14]

These scholars have mounted a major challenge to the portrayal of ethnic culture as static and unchanging. In analyzing the transformation of Japanese American kinship in Seattle, Yanagisako criticized the assumption of "the mechanical transmission of culture from one generation to the next through a near-mystical process of socialization within families."[15] These studies noted that the disruptive nature of migration/immigration militates against the wholesale re-creation of "village life" and suggested that newcomers have the opportunity to influence their own culture, shaped by their concepts of tradition and the demands of the new environment. Indeed, di Leonardo argued that, far from being a fixed artifact, ethnicity is a "cognitive resource chosen and altered."[16] This process of alteration—manifested in such areas as religion, music, courtship, and marriage—is compellingly delineated in Sanchez's study of Mexican immigration to Los Angeles between 1900 and 1945.

Recent analyses of the complicated relations of gender roles and ethnic culture among Chicanos, Italian Americans, and Japanese Americans make visible another field of largely unacknowledged work done by women: the work of sustaining "ethnicity" through the careful maintenance of family ties and cultural practices. New scholarship clarifies both the strength and conflict involved in this highly charged

---

California History Center, 1985); Sandy Lydon, *Chinese Gold: The Chinese in the Monterey Bay Region* (Capitola, Calif.: Capitola Book Company, 1985); S. Frank Miyamoto, *Social Solidarity among the Japanese in Seattle* (Seattle: University of Washington Press, 1939, 1984); John Modell, *The Economics and Politics of Accommodation: The Japanese of Los Angeles, 1900–1942* (Chicago: University of Illinois Press, 1977); Victor G. Nee and Brett DeBary Nee, *Longtime Californ': A Documentary Study of an American Chinatown* (New York: Pantheon, 1972); Ricardo Romo, *East Los Angeles: History of a Barrio* (Austin: University of Texas Press, 1983).

14. See, as well as works by these scholars already cited, Dino Cinel, *From Italy to San Francisco: The Immigrant Experience* (Stanford: Stanford University Press, 1982), and Sylvia Yanagisako, *Transforming the Past: Tradition and Kinship among Japanese Americans* (Stanford: Stanford University Press, 1985).

15. Yanagisako, p. 18.

16. Di Leonardo, p. 23.

arena and investigates the transformation of gender roles in an American framework. Yanagisako, for example, sets forth the importance of siblings and women-centered kin networks rooted in a U.S. context, though they are claimed as "traditional." Similarly, Sanchez asserts that a crucial key to Chicano culture lies in understanding the process of claiming certain family practices as traditional in a new setting.

In the second wave of ethnic community studies, the ambiguities confronting immigrants and their American-born children have been drawn powerfully. In his book on Italian immigration to—and re-migration from—San Francisco, Cinel boldly links the ambivalences of nineteenth-century newcomers with those of twentieth-century postmodern Americans: "We strive for a better life, only to find that the changes it entails are not always welcome. Like the immigrants, we seek to achieve success without paying too high a social and personal price."[17] For Chicano youth in the 1930s and 1940s, as Sanchez relates, the keen awareness of social inequalities led to an "ambivalent Americanism" characterized by "duality in cultural practices and marked adaptability in the face of discrimination."[18] The Nisei's feelings of vulnerability as racial-ethnic Americans parallel the Los Angeles Mexican Americans' sense of the fragility of their social position. Given the barriers Nisei and Mexican Americans faced in the dominant society, it is not surprising that an ethnic enclave might be, on the one hand, narrow and constraining and, on the other, a haven.[19]

As helpful as the works of scholars like Cinel, di Leonardo, Sanchez, and Yanagisako are, they have mainly centered on urban populations in San Francisco, Los Angeles, Santa Barbara, El Paso, and Seattle. Their metropolitan focus is shared by many Japanese American community studies. It is the Nikkei enclaves in Seattle, San Francisco, Sacramento, and Los Angeles that have received the most attention from researchers concerned with analyzing institution and kinship network formation, generational change, and the degree of ethnic cultural persistence.[20]

17. Cinel, p. 261.
18. Sanchez, p. 6.
19. Ibid., p. 199.
20. See Christie W. Kiefer's San Francisco study, *Changing Cultures, Changing Lives: An Ethnographic Study of Three Generations of Japanese-Americans* (San Francisco: Jossey-Bass, 1974), as well as the books cited earlier by Miyamoto and Modell. Yanagisako's study, *Transforming the Past*, is also based on research in the Seattle Japanese American community. The term "Nikkei" refers to any person of Japanese descent.

My study of Cortez directs the social and cultural questions raised by urban researchers to a Japanese American farming settlement in the San Joaquin Valley of California. Indeed, it is only in a rural setting that one can confront another major theme of the American romanticization of community life: the pastoral ideal that fueled the dreams of Dennis and Grace Yotsuya. Careful examination of a rural environment contests the assumptions that underlie perennial academic mourning for a lost Eden—assumptions of autonomy and choice linked with visions of a golden past inhabited primarily by Euro-American settlers. In this mythical yesteryear, no Indians were driven from ancestral homes and massacred, no Mexican populations were cheated of their lands, and no Asian laborers were recruited by corporate barons to the dismay of working-class whites. A sense of historical perspective threatens such glorious imagery; it forever draws back the curtain behind which we glimpse the Cherokees treading the Trail of Tears and the Chinese workers omitted from the official pictures of the completion of the transcontinental railroad. From this vantage point, exaggerated notions of racial–ethnic autonomy and choice are problematic and ahistorical. Understanding this historical context—the acknowledgment of real aspirations, real limitations, and resultant strategies and adaptations—undermines the idealized past and with it the idea of ethnic decline.

Cortez provides an ideal site at which to examine these themes. In this book I pay particular attention to the dynamics of external and internal forces that shape an ethnic community and, within a rural setting, reflect on the meaning of community and its changing function. My research in Cortez disclosed the complexity of choices and limitations faced by three generations as well as the resources with which they met these challenges. Tracing the development of the settlement casts light upon the strategies that community members used to maintain cohesiveness despite their removal to a concentration camp during World War II. My research also reveals the interplay of work, gender, intergenerational dynamics, and interracial relations in the postwar period. Rather than presenting a picture of ethnic community decay, the history of the Cortez Colony bears out the axiom that community is not an end in itself[21] but that it serves human needs, and as needs change, so, too, can the collectivity. Examination

21. A point made by di Leonardo, p. 135.

of Cortez's many networks reflects both the pervasive and flexible nature of ethnic community.

Despite the crucial role Asian immigrants and their children have played in the development of the billion-dollar agricultural economy of the West—particularly in California—only in the recent past have scholars investigated their contributions as farm laborers and operators. As Gary Okihiro has pointed out, the "ascendancy of the urban model and tyranny of the city" have obscured the "rural dimension of Asian American studies," which remains a fallow field, "uncultivated yet rich with possibilities."[22] Pioneering historians, including Okihiro, Sucheng Chan, Sandy Lydon, Yuji Ichioka, John Modell, and Ronald Takaki, have analyzed the agricultural economic structure and the ways in which Asian workers have sought to maneuver advantageously within it, in spite of discriminatory laws, manipulative landowners, and racial hostility. As Chan, Ichioka, and Takaki have noted, agriculture constituted a critical arena of the immigrant Japanese economy. In 1925, 46 percent of the employed Japanese worked in farming.[23] Their entry into California farmwork as it shifted to intensive agriculture ultimately facilitated the development of urban Japanese settlements. The demographic strength and breadth of this literature have laid the groundwork for the cultural questions posed by more focused studies like my own.

Several factors make Cortez—as a rural Japanese American community—a particularly rich site for exploring questions of ethnic support networks, gender role development, generational change and continuity, and the functions of community. In its origin as a planned colony, its weathering of World War II internment, and postwar reconstruction, Cortez illustrates the cultivation of ethnic community and culture as a choice reflective of shared history and changing needs.

In 1974 the people of the Cortez Colony celebrated their fiftieth anniversary, honoring the vision of the colony's founder, Abiko Kyutaro, and the first Japanese immigrant pioneers, as well as the endurance of the institutions and networks they forged. Cortez was the third Japanese Christian farming settlement started by Abiko, one of

22. Gary Y. Okihiro, "Fallow Field: The Rural Dimension of Asian American Studies," *Frontiers of Asian American Studies: Writing, Research, and Commentary,* ed. Gail M. Nomura, Russell Endo, Stephen H. Sumida, and Russell C. Leong (Pullman: Washington State University Press, 1989), p. 7.

23. Takaki, p. 193.

the most influential Japanese immigrant leaders of northern California. While its unusual beginning as a planned community commands interest, the experiences of the Cortez farm families parallel those of the many other Japanese Americans in rural areas before 1942. Although conceived as a Christian enclave, Cortez hosts both Buddhist and Christian churches, as is common in Japanese American communities. Although its small size—approximately forty-five families—limits the utility of quantitative analysis, Cortez does possess a three- and four-generational continuity rare among Japanese American settlements. Thus it offers a valuable opportunity to examine the creative adaptations of a community beset by hardship from its inception. The difficulties of establishing farms in an inhospitable land were compounded by the hostility of the surrounding white society, expressed in the anti-Japanese movement of the early 1920s. In 1941, after the lean years of the Great Depression had passed and the farms had begun to prosper, the bombing of Pearl Harbor unleashed war between the United States and Japan. The ensuing internment of Japanese Americans uprooted the Cortez Colony to the Amache Relocation Camp in Colorado and blighted the hopes of many farmers just as their dreams of economic success approached fruition. The postwar return to California meant a long, arduous struggle to reestablish the community and its institutions.

How did the Cortez Colony survive these trials, including the wartime internment to which Leonard Bloom and John Kitsuse have attributed the destruction of the prewar Japanese American community? The answer lies in the maintenance of the effective economic cooperative association that has constituted the backbone of Cortez agriculture, in conjunction with a constellation of social groups that have provided material assistance and cultural affirmation since the 1920s.

During World War II, like many Japanese Americans, the people of Cortez drew upon support networks of friends and relatives, formed before and during the "evacuation," to sustain morale and to channel aid. These informal ties particularly aided the Nisei as they left the relocation camps for work and education in the Midwest and East and for military service abroad. In addition, the Cortez Colony—together with the two other Abiko colonies—negotiated a unique formal arrangement to preserve their communities. Shortly before the internment, they jointly hired a white manager to operate their farms during their absence and thus were able to maintain their landholdings. After the war, in contrast to many other uprooted Japanese American enclaves, the people of Cortez returned together to rebuild their community.

In general, the internment of World War II accelerated earlier trends that differentiated the Nisei from their parents. Already influenced by mainstream middle-class values of love and marriage, the Nisei in the camps moved away from the pattern of arranged marriage. There, increased peer group activities and the relaxation of parental authority gave them more independence. In addition, the structure of camp life hastened the transfer of leadership from the Issei to the Nisei.

The influence of the wartime experience, generational transition, and the influx of newcomers marrying into Cortez families significantly altered the structure of the postwar community. By the 1960s and 1970s, a more favorable social climate and farm prosperity facilitated increasing interracial activities and enabled the third generation to have the higher education of which most Nisei had only dreamed. These broader academic and economic opportunities, as well as increased interaction with mainstream society, have also contributed to significant change in gender roles, to an increase in interracial marriage among the Sansei of Cortez, and to their pursuit of careers in urban areas. Such developments in both Cortez and the surrounding society call attention to the interplay of historical context and individual agency in cultural processes, and the related shift in the meaning of community.

The primary sources for exploring these historical themes included community institutional records, local newspapers, World War II concentration camp publications, and other wartime memorabilia. In addition, I conducted eighty-three oral history interviews with three generations of men and women: nine Issei, fifty-eight Nisei and sixteen Sansei.[24] By 1982, when I began my research in Cortez, only a handful of Issei remained, most of them women who were considerably younger than their late husbands. The earliest pioneers and the majority of the Issei male community leaders who had dealt with Abiko and who had conducted colony affairs in the early settlement

24. For a listing of the men and women interviewed, please refer to the Bibliography under "Unpublished Sources."

period had already died. Therefore, my perceptions of the Cortez Issei were largely filtered through the eyes of the second generation by memory and translation. In my interviews with the Issei, I was fortunate to have the interpretive assistance of their children and friends; even in the best of circumstances, however, something is inevitably lost in translation. The Nisei themselves are limited in their command of the Japanese language and not always aware of the nuances and vocabulary familiar to a native of Japan.

As important as the written records were in providing windows on a sometimes painfully shadowed past, it was the process of interviewing which gave me the richest sense of the complex dynamics of the communal ties that connect the people of Cortez within a web of support, obligation, and cultural location. I am deeply grateful to the generous women and men like Dennis and Grace Yotsuya who welcomed me into their homes, fed me in many ways, and shared their perceptions of the past and present as well as their hopes for the future.

As a researcher, I was both an insider and an outsider. While I did not grow up in Cortez or in a Japanese American community, my background as a Sansei woman whose parents had raised tomatoes in southern California gave me some familiarity with Japanese American culture and the rhythms of rural life. At the beginning of each interview, I was asked where my family came from and in which camp they had been interned. I replied that my grandparents came from Fukuoka-ken in southern Japan, that they and their children had farmed in northern and southern California, and that they had spent the war years in the Poston Camp in Arizona and the Topaz Camp in Utah. These facts enabled the Cortez people to locate me within the Japanese American cosmos and to confirm the presence of common bonds of understanding between us.

My status as a young, single woman with only the briefest acquaintance with orchard and vineyard agriculture doubtless influenced the kinds of questions I asked and the responses received. Sometimes my partial understanding led people to assume that I knew more than I did, necessitating later backtracking and patient explanation on their part. The process of interviewing also made me aware of the varying degrees to which one can be, simultaneously, an insider and an outsider. Even individuals who had long histories within Cortez felt in some respects like outsiders, particularly women who had married into the community. Such feelings and a strong sense of affiliation were not mutually exclusive; as Dino Cinel has remarked, human life is marked by complexity, ambivalence, and contradiction, and scholars should expect no less of history.[25]

Each person I interviewed could easily have been the subject of an entire book. The greatest challenge of this project has been to choose what material to incorporate. Certainly everyone who talked with me contributed to the sense of community ambience that (I hope) infuses this work.

When referring to Japanese immigrants, I have used the Japanese order of address, giving the family name first and the given name second. With the American-born Nisei and Sansei I have followed the American style of address. Because often more than one member of a family is mentioned, I have frequently referred to men and women by their first names to minimize confusion. The practice of first-name address also reflects the warmth and informality with which I met in Cortez, and I hope that it in no way conveys disrespect. I have also used the terms "white" and "Euro-American" interchangeably; whenever possible I have referred to specific ethnic and racial ethnic backgrounds.

Throughout this work I refer to Japanese Americans by the generational terms "Issei," "Nisei," "Kibei," "Sansei," and "Yonsei." These have become key identifying markers for Japanese Americans—including the people of Cortez—as well as for the scholars studying them. However, Gary Okihiro has rightfully drawn attention to the problematic aspect of such categories which, while valid and useful, can obscure diversity of behavior and attitudes. Given the age spread within each generation (e.g., the majority of the Nisei were born between 1910 and 1940), it is important to be aware of the potential for stereotyping and to allow latitude for variation.

The nomenclature of the World War II internment also demands consideration. The terms most used by government officials, journalists, and, subsequently, Japanese Americans and the general public are, as Yuji Ichioka has pointed out, euphemisms. "Evacuation," "assembly center," and "relocation center" carry more benign connotations than "internment" or "concentration camp." Researchers must grapple with the previous categories that are embedded in the primary

25. Cinel, p. 13.

documents and secondary literature. My work reflects this tension in terminology.

The organization of this book is both chronological and thematic. The two chapters that follow examine the prewar history of the Cortez Colony; they focus on the dynamics within the community and its relations with the larger surrounding society. The next two delineate the World War II experiences of the Japanese Americans inside and outside the concentration camp. The last two chapters focus on the postwar resettlement and development of Cortez. Chapters 2 and 6 follow a primarily topical structure that centers on key elements in family and community life: work, education, gender roles, marriage, and interracial interaction.

The men and women of Cortez shared with me a richly textured past woven from the sturdy threads of their lives. Major themes in Japanese American studies took on greater dimension when examined through the range of their experiences. Their stories revealed the presence of human toil behind the shining fruit in the supermarket, and illuminated the benefits and tensions of participation in a close-knit ethnic community. I hope my research can affirm the significance of this history and that it will stimulate further exploration by the third and fourth generations whose choices even now are shaping the future of the community.

CHAPTER 1

Taking Root in
a Harsh Land

The United States that Sakaguchi Maju encountered as a twenty-one-year-old Japanese picture bride was not what she had expected. Born in 1894 in a coastal village in Kumamoto Prefecture, where her family grew soybeans and *sato imo* (sweet potatoes), Maju had heard wonderful stories of America and in 1915 came with high hopes to join her husband, Sakaguchi Chokichi. Her expectations met with a rude shock. She cried every day and longed to return to Japan.

For Sakaguchi Maju, as for many Japanese immigrants, arrival meant adjustment to unfamiliar foods and customs as well as immediate immersion in a grueling round of labor. After staying two days at the immigration station on Angel Island, she began her new life in San Jose, California, entering a household composed of her husband, parents-in-law, and sisters-in-law. She spent her honeymoon working in a strawberry field. Her mother-in-law did the cooking for the family, while the young *yomesan* (daughter-in-law) went out to weed and tend plants with her husband. She bore six children between 1918 and 1932.[1]

Under the discriminatory California land laws aimed at restricting Asian farmers, the Sakaguchi family could not lease property for more than three years; thus, periodically they had to move to a new place and replant the strawberries that were their mainstay. The hardship of perpetually cultivating new land and then having to leave just as it

---

1. Sakaguchi Maju interview, Cortez, Calif., March 11, 1982.

became productive made financial security an elusive dream. Then they learned of a Japanese community in which they could own property. In 1926 they bought their first twenty acres in the Cortez Colony in the San Joaquin Valley of central California.

The threads of many such lives and dreams have together woven the fabric of the Cortez community as well as the larger tapestry of Japanese American history. Tracing the early development of Cortez makes clear the external and internal forces that shaped the settlement as well as the resources and institutions of the immigrant pioneers. Who were they? What values and expectations did they bring here? Why did they choose to settle in Cortez? What strategies did they use to counter legal and social discrimination? What kinds of organizations did they construct, and to meet what needs? What was the texture of their daily lives?

The growth of the agricultural industry and the long history of California nativism form the backdrop for the inception of the Cortez Colony. The Japanese men and women who settled there faced the challenges of primitive living conditions, grueling labor, and the hostility of the anti-Japanese movement. Community organizations played a key role in their survival.

Oral history interviews proved especially important in illuminating the workings of these institutions as well as the everyday routine of Cortez residents. Although thousands of Japanese immigrants toiled in California fields and orchards before World War II, farm life has become the stuff of family legend to their grandchildren and great-grandchildren. In the course of my research, I was overwhelmed by the wealth of detail that poured forth from the Issei and Nisei, gradually delineating the growth of a farm, the rooting of a family, and the developing web of social relations in a rural ethnic community.

The modern imagination is more apt to see the urban face of California, with its burgeoning technological industries and Hollywood dream factories, than the agricultural bounty of its heartland. And those who cast an appreciative eye over glowing oranges and eggplants in the supermarket, who select raisins, nuts, and fruit juice for camping trips, who buy canned peaches for winter baking or choose a wine for dinner seldom bother to learn the history hidden behind labels like "Sunkist," "Del Monte," "Blue Diamond." The hegemony of large-scale corporate farming and the style of cooperative marketing

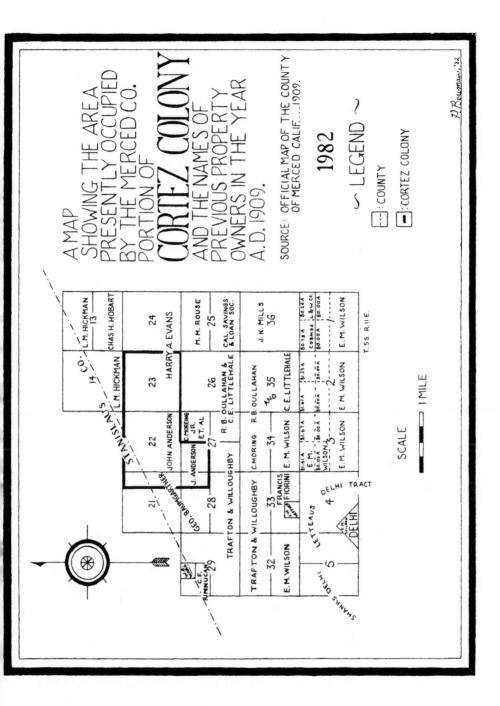

A MAP
SHOWING THE AREA
PRESENTLY OCCUPIED
BY THE MERCED CO.
PORTION OF
CORTEZ COLONY
AND THE NAMES OF
PREVIOUS PROPERTY
OWNERS IN THE YEAR
A.D. 1909.

SOURCE: OFFICIAL MAP OF THE COUNTY
OF MERCED CALIF...1909.

1982

~ LEGEND ~

[::]: COUNTY

[■]: CORTEZ COLONY

P.J.Bowman '82

SCALE

■ 1 MILE

L.M. HICKMAN 13
CHAS. H. HOBART
24
HARRY A. EVANS
M.M. ROUSE 25
CAL. SAVINGS & LOAN SOC.
J.K. MILLS 36
STANISLAUS CO.
L.M. HICKMAN 14
L.M. HICKMAN 23
26
R.B. OULLAHAN & C.E. LITTLEHALE
R.B. OULLAHAN 35
C.E. LITTLEHALE
22
JOHN ANDERSON
C. MOREING JR. ET. AL.
27
J. ANDERSON
C. MORING 34
R.B. OULLAHAN AND E.M. WILSON
GEO. BAUMGARTNER 21
TRAFTON & WILLOUGHBY 28
FRANCIS FIORINI 33
TRAFTON & WILLOUGHBY
E.M. WILSON 32
C.F. KINNUCAN 29
E.M. WILSON
LETTEAUS
DELHI TRACT
DELHI
SHANKS DELHI

T.5S. R.11E.

80.78A | 80.28A
COSM68. L&W CO.
80.00A | 80.00A
31.61A | 81.25A
80.00A | 80.00A
81.61A | 81.67A
E.M. WILSON
80.00A | 80.00A

have also obscured the vital role that Asian immigrants and other racial ethnic people have played—and continue to play—in the cultivation of California's billion-dollar agricultural industry.

Dramatic change characterized California agriculture throughout the nineteenth and early twentieth centuries. In the wake of the Mexican War, the vast Mexican *ranchos*—later mythologized in Western movies—became the fragmented spoils of Euro-American settlers. Many fortune hunters, first lured by the Gold Rush, discovered that a better living could be made feeding the miners, and they settled down to cultivate what Sandy Lydon has termed "green gold." Wheat became the first major export crop in the 1860s, its production facilitated by the completion of the railroads and the selling of railroad land grants; viticulture also thrived on the miners' demand for alcohol. However, bread and wine alone would not satisfy California's fast-growing population. In the last three decades of the nineteenth century, specialty-crop agriculture flourished,[2] producing a dazzling array of fruits, nuts, and vegetables.

From its inception, commercial farming in California had been shaped by the railroads, banks, and large-scale landowners who relied on hired laborers and tenant farmers. After the completion of their work on the railroads, many Chinese found employment in agriculture. They harvested wheat and other crops, reclaimed the swampland of the Sacramento–San Joaquin delta, and tended vineyards, orchards, and vegetable fields throughout the state. By the time of the Chinese Exclusion Act in 1882, they constituted more than half of California's agricultural labor force, and from one-half to three-quarters of its specialty crop workers.[3] The predominantly male Chinese workers were indispensable to large farmers and feared as competitors by

2. There are several definitions of "specialty crops." The oldest categorization of specialty crops developed in tandem with what the U.S.D.A. considered "basic commodity" crops (e.g., wheat, corn, sugar, cotton, potatoes, tobacco); all else falls into the category of "specialty crops." They include citrus, deciduous tree crops, and vegetables. In this vein, a 1986–87 study group on marketing California specialty crops, sponsored by the University of California Agricultural Issues Center, defined specialty crops broadly as "the state's fruit, vegetable, and tree nut crops." Certainly, the Cortez farmers' main crops—almonds, grapes, and peaches—fall into the category of specialty crops. In recent years, some agricultural experts have used the term to refer to unusual or "exotic" crops (e.g., radicchio and daikon), many introduced to the United States by immigrants and grown on a limited scale, or to uncommon varieties of common crops like lettuce and apples.

3. Lawrence J. Jelinek, *Harvest Empire: A History of California Agriculture*, 2d ed. (San Francisco: Boyd & Fraser, 1982), p. 52.

Euro-Americans who owned small farms. Organized labor and the Hearst press rallied public sentiment against the Chinese immigrants. Vigilante violence drove many Chinese from the rural areas and into the relative security of urban Chinatowns. After 1882, as bachelor laborers who were unable either to marry locally or to send for wives in China grew older, the number of Chinese workers in agriculture dwindled.

At the turn of the century Japanese immigrants followed the Chinese into California's fields and orchards. Some adventurous students in search of a Western education had begun to arrive in the 1880s. On their heels came increasing numbers of male workers. They journeyed abroad to pursue economic opportunity and to avoid military conscription as Japan loosened its restrictions on emigration. Severe economic dislocations after the Sino-Japanese War (1894–1895) and the Russo-Japanese War (1904–1905), compounded by rapid population growth, spurred the exodus. Many Japanese first traveled to Hawaii, in response to the demand for plantation labor; others flocked to the mainland to build railroads and take the menial jobs formerly held by the Chinese. Between 1891 and 1900, 27,440 Japanese came to the West Coast, from both Hawaii and Japan, to work in agriculture, canneries, logging, and mining, in domestic service, and in the meatpacking and salt industries.[4]

Within a relatively brief period, from 1898 to 1908, agriculture eclipsed both domestic service and railroad construction and became the leading enterprise of the Japanese.[5] Scholars have delineated several factors in the steady influx of Japanese into West Coast agriculture. First, farming had long been a respected occupation in Japan, and many of the immigrants, coming primarily from the economically distressed rural prefectures, had some experience in it. When they met with obstacles to entering urban manufacturing industries—partially because of animosity against the Chinese who had preceded them and also because there was a sufficient pool of white labor to fill these positions—agriculture became increasingly attractive.[6] As Ichihashi Yamato observed, the Japanese gradually left the "railroads, mines,

4. Harry H. L. Kitano, *Japanese Americans, The Evolution of a Subculture*, 2d ed. (Englewood Cliffs, N.J.: Prentice-Hall, 1976), p. 16.
5. Yamato Ichihashi, *Japanese in the United States: A Critical Study of the Problems of the Japanese Immigrants and Their Children* (Stanford: Stanford University Press, 1932), p. 163.
6. Masakazu Iwata, "The Japanese Immigrants in California Agriculture," *Agricultural History* 36(April 1962):27.

and lumber mills, where they found little opportunity to rise and at the same time were subjected to rule of thumb and close supervision," and turned to farming, which offered the best chance for economic independence and mobility.[7] By 1909, more than 30,000 Japanese worked in California as tenant farmers or farm laborers.

The Japanese easily adopted the contract labor system of the Chinese and were soon in great demand as farm laborers because they would accept lower wages than non-Asian workers. As young rootless bachelor males, they were well suited to the seasonal harvest needs of growers engaged in intensive farming, and they were more willing to migrate from district to district than the established white workers.[8] As the Japanese gained familiarity with U.S. laws and agricultural practices and began to amass some capital, a growing number moved from farm labor to tenant farming.

Like many European immigrants, the majority of Japanese workers initially intended to make their fortunes and then return to their homeland. They considered themselves *dekasegi* workers, only going away temporarily. However, few attained the success of which they dreamed. Reconciling themselves to more modest gains, a substantial number who developed stakes in small businesses and farming sent for wives and established families. This transition in orientation to the United States, Yuji Ichioka has suggested, marked the turning point between two major periods of Japanese immigration history: an initial phase (1885–1907) of *dekasegi* influx, and a subsequent phase (1908–1924) during which the Japanese, influenced by immigrant leaders advocating permanent residency, began to put down roots.[9] These immigrants termed themselves the "Issei," the first generation of Japanese in the United States.

Japanese American communities grew as female immigrants arrived, mainly between 1908 and 1924. In 1907, the Gentlemen's Agreement had curtailed the flow of male laborers from Japan but had left a loophole permitting the families of men already resident to join them. Urged by Japanese leaders to establish permanent settlements, many men returned to their homeland to find wives. Some were reunited with the women they had married prior to emigration. A sizable

7. Ichihashi, p. 177.
8. Jelinek, p. 68; Iwata, pp. 27–28.
9. Yuji Ichioka, *The Issei: The World of the First Generation Japanese Immigrants, 1885–1924* (New York: Free Press, 1988), pp. 3–4.

number eagerly awaited the arrival of picture brides. Marriage in Japan at this time was arranged by families rather than individual couples, and the *shashin kekkon* (picture marriage) deviated from usual practice only in the absence of the bridegroom from the wedding ceremony. The union received legal recognition when the wife's name was entered in the husband's family registry.[10] The picture brides arrived clutching photographs and scanned the faces of the men on the dock, hoping to find the one that matched. They came for a variety of reasons. Like Sakaguchi Maju, most had heard stories of the bright prospects of life in America and were desirous of earning money to help their families. Some perhaps hoped to escape hometown scandals, or had dutifully acquiesced in parental decisions; others came motivated by a spirit of adventure or a wish for independence. Whatever their motives or backgrounds, they found many challenges to their dreams in a variety of locales: the urban Little Tokyos where their families ran small shops and boardinghouses; the lumber mill and salmon cannery towns of the Pacific Northwest; the fields and orchards of the West.

Lawrence Jelinek has stated that the California Japanese, both as laborers and farmers, "were responsible for developing the commercial importance of rice and potatoes, while they dominated the vegetable and berry regions of the Sacramento, San Joaquin, and Imperial valleys as well as of Los Angeles and Orange Counties."[11] They also played a major role in cultivating orchards and vineyards in these areas. According to an Immigration Commission report, by the summer of 1909, half of the Japanese labor force in the United States—roughly 39,500 out of 79,000—worked in agriculture, three-fourths of them in California. Approximately 6,000 may have been independent farm operators.[12]

The era of the most extensive Japanese involvement in farming—1900–1941—coincided with and facilitated the rise of industrialized

10. For further information about the picture brides and Issei women in general, see Emma Gee, "Issei Women," *Counterpoint, Perspectives on Asian America*, ed. Emma Gee (Los Angeles: Asian American Studies Center, University of California, 1976), pp. 359–64; Mei Nakano, *Japanese American Women: Three Generations, 1890–1990* (Berkeley: Mina Press, 1990), pp. 24–29. Also helpful is Yoshiko Uchida's novel *Picture Bride* (New York: Simon & Schuster, 1987).

11. Jelinek, p. 69.

12. Robert A. Wilson and Bill Hosokawa, *East to America: A History of the Japanese in the United States* (New York: Morrow, 1980), pp. 64–65.

agriculture in California. The consolidation of landholdings gradually displaced many small farmers. They found it hard to compete with large-scale owners, who hired Mexican and Japanese workers to tend their vast acreage. The growing polarization between small and large farms reflected the uneven tug-of-war between corporate and family agriculture.[13]

Hostility to Asian farmers and laborers served as a potent organizing tool for politicians and labor unions, as Alexander Saxton and Roger Daniels have made clear. Campaigns for the exclusion of the Chinese in the nineteenth century and the Japanese in the twentieth found widespread support in California. Fears of economic competition, coupled with Euro-American beliefs in the inferiority of racial-ethnic peoples, fueled agitation against Asian immigrants. They met with harassment, violence, and social and legal discrimination. Denied the right to become naturalized citizens and to exercise related civil rights, Asians constituted a particularly vulnerable segment of the labor force. While they faced a battery of restrictive municipal, state, and national laws,[14] the immigration and land laws most affected rural community development.

The passage of a series of immigration laws shaped the contours of Asian settlement in the United States. The Chinese Exclusion Act of 1882 effectively ended the influx of all but merchants, scholars, and diplomats. Despite the clamor of exclusionists to extend such prohibitions to other Asians, the United States exercised more caution in dealing with Japanese immigrants. Japan's status as a rising world power had been confirmed by victory in the Russo-Japanese War. In 1907–8, President Theodore Roosevelt negotiated the Gentlemen's Agreement that barred the immigration of further male workers, but admitted the wives and family members of Japanese already living in this country. In 1910, of the 72,157 Japanese on the United States

13. Jelinek, p. 62.

14. Roger Daniels traces the passage of anti-Japanese legislation in *The Politics of Prejudice: The Anti-Japanese Movement in California and the Struggle for Japanese Exclusion* (Berkeley: University of California Press, 1962). Yuji Ichioka examines the conditions of Japanese immigrant settlement and resistance to exclusion in *The Issei*. For a discussion of the legal restrictions faced by Asian immigrants, see Sucheng Chan, *Asian Americans: An Interpretive History* (Boston: Twayne, 1991), chap. 3; Megumi Dick Osumi, "Asians and California's Anti-Miscegenation Laws," *Asian and Pacific American Experiences: Women's Perspectives*, ed. Nobuya Tsuchida (Minneapolis: Asian/Pacific American Learning Resource Center and General College, University of Minnesota, 1982), pp. 1–37.

mainland, 5,581 were married women and 4,502 American-born children. By 1920, out of a population of 111,010, the number of married women had risen to 22,193, accompanied by an increase to 29,672 Nisei.[15] Anti-Japanese leaders like California Senator James Phelan noted with alarm the emergence of Japanese families and denounced the loophole that had made this possible. The Immigration Act of 1924 heralded the triumph of the exclusionists by cutting off all Asian immigration to the United States.

Asian farmers met with frustrating restrictions in land use in California. The Alien Land Law of 1913 prevented them from purchasing land or from leasing it for more than three years. This law did not go far enough in the eyes of anti-Japanese forces. A harsher law, passed in 1920, barred "aliens ineligible to citizenship" from leasing land or from acquiring it through corporations or in the names of their American-born children.[16] Nevertheless, as Roger Daniels has suggested, these laws may have had greater psychological than economic impact since by 1920 many Issei had already acquired the title to land in the names of their Nisei children. It appears that the laws were not consistently enforced, especially in regions where such strictures ran contrary to the interests of large landowners. For example, many landlords in Santa Clara County circumvented the laws by making verbal agreements with the Japanese tenant farmers to whom they leased property.[17]

In 1919, against this larger backdrop of California agricultural development and a long history of anti-Asian nativism, a handful of Japanese families settled in the Cortez Colony. The first to arrive found a bleak pocket of the San Joaquin Valley, scoured by sandstorms, abounding in voracious jackrabbits, and holding little promise of the fertile Eden they envisioned. Yet Cortez made attainable the cornerstone of the dream: landownership. By the 1930s, around thirty families, each operating a twenty- to forty-acre farm, constituted a tenacious community with strong collective bonds.

The seed from which the colony grew was the dream of Abiko Kyutaro. An energetic idealist, Abiko wore many hats—village ped-

---

15. U.S. Census, 1920.
16. Daniels, *Asian America*, p. 145; Chan, p. 40.
17. See Lukes and Okihiro, pp. 19–33, 45–53, 55–62.

dler, banker, newspaper publisher, businessman, immigrant leader. His eventful life (1865–1936) spanned two countries and two centuries. Abiko was born to the Kobayashi family in the town of Suibara, in Niigata Prefecture, Japan. Shortly after his birth his mother died, and Kyutaro was brought up by the family of his scholarly maternal grandfather, Abiko Taido. Because of straitened family circumstances, Kyutaro assisted from childhood in the family business by peddling candles and paper in nearby villages.[18] At the age of seventeen, he secretly set out with friends for Yokohama, planning to stow away on a ship to America, where he hoped to make his fortune. This proved more difficult than he had expected, and for several years he worked in Tokyo at odd jobs and attended classes, including English.

In Tokyo Christianity played a major role in determining the course of Abiko's life. He had first encountered Christian beliefs in Suibara through an English missionary who influenced his decision to journey to the United States. In Tokyo he was baptized and, under the guidance of a Presbyterian minister, Okuno Masatsuna, Abiko began to develop the religious commitment that would shape the rest of his life. Like the majority of the earliest Japanese immigrants to the United States, Abiko came as a student, in 1885. He traveled under the auspices of the Fukuinkai (Gospel Society), the first Japanese immigrant organization in San Francisco. Founded by Methodist and Congregationalist converts in 1877, the Fukuinkai provided members with fellowship and spartan lodgings, and subsequently gave rise to other Christian groups.[19]

During the late nineteenth century, and for decades after, San Francisco was the major port of entry for Japanese into America as well as the largest population center of Japanese in the nation. Only in San Francisco did the U.S. Census of 1890 find enough Japanese to constitute an ethnic community, as measured by a distinct census category. By the turn of the century, other sizable enclaves coalesced in Sacramento, Fresno, Portland, Seattle, Tacoma, Salt Lake City, and Vancouver, British Columbia. In 1904, 10,000 Japanese, or one-fourth

---

18. Seizo Oka, "Biography of Kyutaro Abiko: Issei Pioneer with a Dream," *Pacific Citizen*, Holiday Issue, December 19–26, 1980, p. 61. For more information about Abiko, see Ichioka, *The Issei*, especially pp. 146–50, and Kesa Noda, *Yamato Colony: 1906–1960* (Livingston, Calif.: Livingston–Merced JACL Chapter, 1981), pp. 1–15.

19. Ichioka, *The Issei*, pp. 12, 16–19.

Abiko family portrait, 1925. Left to right: Kyutaro Abiko, Yasuo Abiko, and Yonako Abiko. Photo courtesy of Lily Abiko.

of the Japanese in the United States, lived in San Francisco.[20] Nearly one-third of the San Francisco Japanese were employed in domestic service, followed in number by keepers of boardinghouses and hotels, employees in white-owned stores, and factory workers. Many found work in businesses that catered to the ethnic community: restaurants, employment agencies, grocery stores, bathhouses, shoe repair shops, and laundries. The growing Japanese community was able to support fourteen prefectural associations (*kenjinkai*), eight schools that taught English, and a number of religious organizations that, like the Fukuinkai, were primarily Christian.[21]

As the oldest Japanese organization in the United States, the Fukuinkai offered immigrants the opportunity to socialize with their countrymen as well as to receive religious training. With characteristic zeal, Abiko became an influential leader and instructor of the Methodist Branch Fukuinkai while he simultaneously pursued studies at the University of California at Berkeley.[22]

In the 1900s, imbued with Christian idealism and possessed of leadership skills gained in his Fukuinkai work, Abiko turned his energies to the advancement and guidance of Japanese immigrants in the United States. A powerful advocate of permanent settlement in the United States, he became one of the most influential figures in the Japanese American community. He answered nativist calls to exclude the Japanese by mounting a critique of both the dominant society and the immigrant workers. Beyond the factors of racial discrimination, economic fear, and political maneuvering, he believed that ignorance about the Japanese lay at the heart of the exclusion movement; the answer, he felt, rested in education. Abiko also decried the *dekasegi* mind-set of the Japanese, which he saw not only as a spur to gambling and unscrupulous behavior but as the major obstacle to founding a stable immigrant community.[23] Unflinching in his ideals, he took a bold and unusual stance in favor of the *shashin kekkon* (picture marriage) practice, sensationalized by the exclusionists as a reason to

20. Wilson and Hosokawa, pp. 58, 106–7. As Hosokawa and Wilson point out, it was not until 1910, following the devastating San Francisco earthquake and the heavy concentration of anti-Japanese activity in northern California, that Los Angeles began to eclipse San Francisco as the major population center of Japanese in America, a position it has maintained to the present day.

21. Ibid., pp. 58–60.

22. Oka, p. 61.

23. Ichioka, *The Issei*, pp. 146–47.

curtail Japanese immigration. Abiko roundly criticized both the Japanese Association of America and the Japanese Foreign Ministry for the decision to stop issuing passports to picture brides in 1920.[24] This, he foresaw, would impede the progress of community formation—his lifelong commitment.

Abiko's views reached a large audience through his first enterprise, a Japanese newspaper purchased in 1897, merged with a second paper in 1899, and renamed the *Nichibei Shimbun* (*Japanese American News*). The *Nichibei Shimbun* ultimately became the most widely circulated of the Japanese immigrant newspapers.[25] Through his paper, Abiko continued to assist Japanese students by providing part-time newspaper jobs for those who needed sponsorship to study in the United States. Most importantly, however, the *Nichibei Shimbun* constituted a powerful instrument for nurturing cohesiveness in the immigrant Japanese community. It confronted issues such as educational discrimination in San Francisco, restrictions on Japanese immigration, the Alien Land Law, and the debate over picture brides.[26] In the first edition of the *Nichibei Shimbun*, Abiko stated his belief that such a newspaper could strengthen relations among the dispersed immigrants and "establish spiritual ties of the Japanese living on the West Coast."[27] Among the newspaper's long-term aims were the protection of the rights of Japanese in America, the exploration of new fields of enterprise for urban and rural Japanese, and the encouragement of further Japanese immigration to the United States.[28]

The goals enumerated in the *Nichibei Shimbun* were close to Abiko's heart. From the time of his involvement with the Fukuinkai, he had dreamed of establishing permanent Christian colonies of Japanese immigrants, whose numbers steadily increased. To this end, he organized several other businesses. In 1902 he founded the Nichibei Kangyosha (Japanese American Industrial Company) which handled

24. Ibid., p. 174; Daniels, *Asian America*, p. 132.

25. Ichioka, *The Issei*, pp. 20–21.

26. A number of the *Nichibei Shimbun's* reporters later pursued notable careers in the United States and Japan. Among them were Yamada Minoru, who joined the *Asahi Shimbun* in Japan, and Ichihashi Yamato, who became a professor of Japanese history and government at Stanford University.

27. Oka, p. 65.

28. Ibid. In addition to the *Nichibei Shimbun*, Abiko published an English language newspaper, *Pacific Press*, intended to enhance American understanding of the Japanese and thus to foster more harmonious interracial relations.

Japanese contract labor for the railroad, mining, and sugar-refining industries, and the acquisition of farmland in central California. In this period, Abiko also set up and managed the Nichibei Kinyusha, a savings and loan company. Through his earnings from these concerns Abiko was able to set up in 1906 the Beikoku Shokusan Kaisha (American Land and Produce Company) which purchased land in Merced County to be subdivided and resold to become his first settlement, the Yamato Colony in Livingston, California.[29] These organizations and the *Nichibei Shimbun* provided the bases for the realization of Abiko's dream and the hopes of those drawn by it.

The Japanese who pioneered Abiko's three colonies in Livingston, Cressey, and Cortez were among the fortunate minority to make the transition from farm laborer to farm owner. In 1907, Issei families settled on the first piece of land Abiko purchased in Livingston, California. This was the beginning of the Yamato Colony, which by 1920 covered 2,450 acres, and had developed a close affiliation with the nearby Cressey Colony, another Japanese settlement begun in 1918. In 1919, Abiko established the 2,000-acre Cortez Colony, thirteen miles northwest of Livingston and seven miles south of Turlock. Through his liberal terms, Abiko made it possible for these Issei to become landowners, but the full realization of his vision and their dreams was not easily or quickly accomplished. In fact, Abiko's first land acquisition company folded in 1913, overextended by purchases, and in the early years, the colony settlers, like most of the Issei farmers, endured great hardship in transforming sandy wasteland into what the California State Board of Control would later include with "the best in the State."

As the mobility and numbers of Japanese immigrant workers increased, so did the anti-Asian sentiment that had led to the barring of Chinese immigration in 1882. In 1908, under pressure from the small farmers, urban groups and journalists who resurrected the specter of the "Yellow Peril," the United States and Japan concluded the Gentlemen's Agreement that limited immigration to the wives and relatives of Japanese workers already present in America. In 1913, seven years after the Yamato Colony settlers bought their farms, California passed

---

29. Ichioka, *The Issei*, p. 149. For an account of the beginning of the Yamato Colony see Noda, pp. 1–15.

an Alien Land Law that barred "aliens ineligible to citizenship" from owning land and limited their leases to three-year periods. Despite the severity of this law, the Japanese—including the Cortez and Cressey pioneers—circumvented it by buying land in the name of their American-born children and by forming corporations to hold title to their land.

During World War I, hostility against the Japanese waned and their fortunes improved. As non-Asian farmworkers flocked to urban areas to meet the wartime industrial labor demand, the need for farm tenants and laborers rose. It was during this second decade, Masakazu Iwata has asserted, that the Japanese made their most notable advances in agriculture, realizing high wartime profits and enlarging their operations.[30] The Yamato Colony members had by this time achieved a solid footing and were able to prosper from the wartime demand for their produce. By 1920, 5,152 Japanese farmers held 361,276 acres in California and produced crops valued at $67 million.[31]

With the end of World War I and the return of veterans and workers in the war industries, however, economic competition and anti-Japanese sentiment resurged. A formidable anti-Japanese movement emerged from a number of California organizations: the Native Sons—and Native Daughters—of the Golden West; the American Legion; the California State Federation of Labor; and several farm groups, particularly the California State Grange. Their efforts spawned several exclusionist organizations, such as the California Oriental Exclusion League, led by State Senator J. M. Inman, and the Americanization League of the San Joaquin Valley.[32]

Founded in 1919, on the eve of the renewed nativism, the Cortez Colony faced a complex web of hostility, ambivalence, and fear from its inception. Even before the pioneers arrived, the local newspapers devoted much attention to the anti-Japanese crusades of Valentine S. McClatchy, publisher of the *Sacramento Bee,* and U.S. Senator James D. Phelan. In July 1919, Phelan described California as a tributary colony of Japan, declaring, "The rats are in the granary. They have gotten in under the door and they are breeding with alarming rapidity." His

30. Iwata, p. 30.
31. Jelinek, p. 69. According to Masakazu Iwata, in 1910 the Japanese in California "owned 17,035 acres, leased by cash 89,466, by share 50,400, and by contract, 37,898. By 1920, the corresponding figures were 74,769, 192,150, 121,000, and 70,137." Iwata, p. 30.
32. Daniels, *Politics of Prejudice,* pp. 84–85.

focal concern was the stipulation in the Gentlemen's Agreement of 1908 that permitted the entrance into the country of the wives, especially picture brides, of Japanese workers. These women, he argued, circumvented the agreement by toiling in the fields as laborers and giving birth to children, thereby "increasing the horde of nonassimilable aliens who are crowding the white men and women off the lands. If this is not checked now," he concluded, "it means the end of the white race in California, subdivision of American institutions and the end of our Western civilization."[33] To combat this perceived peril, exclusionist leaders called for stringent measures. McClatchy advocated cancellation of the Gentlemen's Agreement, the exclusion of picture brides and all Japanese immigrants, and the passage of a law barring Asians and their American-born children from holding U.S. citizenship.

These proposals were matters of growing concern in the San Joaquin Valley. The timing of the development of the Cortez Colony would have done little to allay the fears of exclusionists. In December 1919, shortly after the first settlers arrived, the alarmed Merced County Farm Bureau directors formed a special committee of delegates from fraternal organizations and boards of trade within the county to oppose further Japanese colonization.[34] In January 1920, this committee officially became the Merced County Anti-Japanese Association, electing as president Elbert G. Adams, a Farm Bureau representative and editor of the *Livingston Chronicle*. Farm Advisor J. F. Grass was voted secretary and Major Harry Thomas of the Fruitland Farm Center and the American Legion was elected vice president. Representatives from the Odd Fellows, Lodge of Elks, Knights of Pythias, Native Sons, and local farm centers agreed to launch a twofold campaign of "moral persuasion against persons who attempt to sell or lease property to Japanese" and "pitiless publicity" against those undeterred by the former method.[35]

In Turlock, the town closest to the Cortez Colony and the Stanislaus County "Melon City of California," the anti-Japanese issue was complicated by the cantaloupe growers' reliance on Japanese laborers during the harvest season. Local exclusionists succeeded in obtaining

33. *Merced County Sun,* July 11, 1919.
34. *Merced County Sun,* December 19, 1919.
35. *Merced County Sun,* January 16, 1920.

pledges from many residents of the white community not to sell or lease their land to Japanese, but the question of labor remained a thorny one. Growers protested that they could not afford to pay the 38 cents to 40 cents a crate for picking and packing melons demanded by white workers, as opposed to the Japanese rate of 26 cents, nor could they rely on American workers to stay in the field until the end of the harvest.[36] As the melon harvest drew near, the editor of the *Turlock Journal*, Winfield Scott, bitterly noted:

> hundreds of Japanese flocking to Turlock, and ready to scatter out over the broad and fertile acres comprised in this great irrigation district, while white men, also in hundreds, and many of them ex-servicemen, are here for the work which should rightly be theirs, and at a living wage—a wage sufficient to enable the worker to live like a white man; but the Japanese, as ever, are ready to underbid the American and take the work at what he can get.[37]

The Turlock Board of Trade appointed a committee to investigate the matter and to recommend a course of action for growers, laborers, and contractors, for shippers and distributors. At a July 1920 meeting that endorsed white labor and a fixed contract price of 35 cents per crate, growers were conspicuously absent.[38]

During the harvest season of the following year, these unresolved, long-simmering tensions erupted in vigilante action and violence. Masked white bandits, who were never caught, robbed a number of Japanese ranchers in the Turlock area. On July 13, masked white

36. *Turlock Daily Journal*, July 22, 1920. Yuji Ichioka's data shows somewhat lower wage rates: The investigator sent by the Japanese Association of America reported that the standard rate of pay for Japanese harvesters was 20 cents per crate. Ichioka, "The 1921 Turlock Incident: Forceful Expulsion of Japanese Laborers," *Counterpoint, Perspectives on Asian America,* ed. Emma Gee (Los Angeles: Asian American Studies Center, University of California, 1976), p. 197.

37. *Turlock Daily Journal*, July 16, 1920. The *Turlock Daily Journal* added a small tantalizing paragraph at the end of an article, on July 21, 1921, stating: "The first symptom of the trouble became manifest two weeks ago when the unionists, pickers and packers in their meetings touching the wage scale to be asked here denied Japanese representatives seats in the meetings." The white unionists and non-unionists also adopted a new policy of refusing to compete with the Japanese in cantaloupe harvesting.

38. *Turlock Daily Journal*, July 17, 1920. The *Turlock Daily Journal* may have misreported the wage-scale demanded by white workers; Yuji Ichioka has cited a petition circulated by the white workers which sets the wage scale at 25 cents per crate. Ichioka, "The 1921 Turlock Incident," pp. 196–97.

men expelled ten Japanese laborers from Livingston. And in the early morning hours of July 20, armed white raiders awakened fifty-eight Japanese laborers in cantaloupe ranch bunkhouses and at the Iwata Store. The vigilantes deported the workers from Turlock on trucks, unloaded them at Keyes, six miles north of Turlock, and warned them not to return.

The Turlock deportation, as Yuji Ichioka has asserted, represented more than the action of a group of transient white harvesters—it was planned and sanctioned by a sizable proportion of the Turlock community. Of the 150 people involved, half were local residents. The extent of their complicity was evidenced by the use of trucks and cars—beyond the means of migratory workers—and the fact that when Japanese called the Turlock police station for assistance during the raid, the two officers on duty had absented themselves to avoid involvement.[39]

This expulsion, one of several such vigilante incidents to occur in rural California during the 1920s, sparked national outcry; newspapers expressed public indignation from coast to coast. Even exclusionists like California Governor William Stephens and Senator Inman deplored the deportation, fearing that such actions would serve to discredit the Japanese exclusion movement.[40] Stanislaus County Sheriff Dallas, backed by state and federal authorities, assured protection of Japanese harvesters enroute to Turlock, and growers, anxious over the harvest, kept shotgun vigil on their ranches at night.

Despite the efforts of the vigilantes, the white community in Turlock did not reach a consensus on Japanese immigration. A division of opinion was clear when the local chapter of the Japanese Exclusion League of California fell short of its 1921 fund-raising goal of $2,000; by the end of the drive in March, Turlock had raised $420, and the rest of Stanislaus County gave $10. "General apathy," was the disapproving verdict of the *Turlock Journal*.

In Livingston, the other city close to Cortez, the situation of the Japanese settlers was even more complex. The record of events not only reveals the ambivalent attitude of Livingston whites and the fine line of acceptance trod by the Yamato Colony members, but also

39. Ichioka, "The 1921 Turlock Incident," p. 197. Ichioka's article provides a thorough examination of the deportation of the Japanese. Only six of the raiders were arrested and brought to trial, and all received a "not guilty" verdict.
40. Ibid., p. 198.

suggests a deep-rooted factor in the long prewar rivalry and social distance between these two Japanese communities. The mounting pressure of anti-Japanese sentiment and organization formed a wedge that split ethnic loyalties along class lines.

By the time of the influx of the Cortez settlers, the white Livingston community and the Japanese Yamato Colony had reached a delicately balanced state of peaceful coexistence. With the settlement of Cortez, however, the Livingston newspaper separated the Japanese into two categories: "the Japanese" and "our Japanese." The editor of the *Livingston Chronicle*, Elbert G. Adams, reflected this contradiction—he was the friend of a number of Japanese in the Yamato Colony and recorded their social events as amiably as any other local affairs; he was also the president of the Merced County Anti-Japanese Association. Although Adams was vocal in the campaign to halt further Japanese immigration, the term "Jap" which was printed in most California papers of the 1920s, including the *Turlock Journal* and the *Merced County Sun*, did not appear in his paper. Adams made it clear that, while vehemently opposed to the influx of Japanese, he did not support the other exclusionists' aim of denying citizenship to the American-born children of Japanese already settled in the United States. Frequent mention of interracial social affairs, the actions of local institutions such as the Farm Center and the Board of Trade, and letters to the editor indicate that quite a number of Livingston whites besides the editor of the *Chronicle* held an ambivalent view of the Japanese.

In November 1919, E. G. Adams announced the arrival of "the Japanese Problem" in Livingston. The Yamato and Cressey colonies were continuing to attract newcomers, and in the fall of 1919, the first pioneers began to settle the Cortez Colony. Adams wrote:

> Probably nowhere in California did the people of a community dread the issue more than here in Livingston, for our conditions, with relation to the Japanese, are or, rather, have been different than elsewhere. Here we had a score of families of high class, high type immigrants, nationality Japanese. They made good neighbors, good farmers, good patriots. They helped this district prosper and improve and they were admired by their fair minded American friends and observers.[41]

41. *Livingston Chronicle,* November 21, 1919.

Adams's tone shifted ominously as he continued, citing differences in class background to distinguish the first Yamato Colony members from the recent arrivals:

> But all that was the situation as it existed here up to a few months, if not only a few weeks ago. . . . We could not blind our eyes or deaden our senses to the fact that more Japanese were coming in here; Japanese not of the type of the original twenty-one families.[42]

In fact, the first group of Livingston Japanese (the Yamato Colony) had included a number of highly educated and accomplished men—a wealthy civil engineer, a college agriculture professor, a high school teacher, and a divinity school graduate.[43] The Cortez settlers in general did have less education and they were primarily working-class people. Historian Kesa Noda has also found significant social and economic differences between the Yamato and Cressey colonists as well as between the earlier and later Yamato settlers.[44] Regardless of the Issei's perspective on this class difference, Adams viewed it as a clear separating line. His warning to the Livingston Japanese was equally clear:

> For years the Japanese who first located here seemed to be keeping the situation locally well in hand, but of late it has become apparent that control over their newly arriving brothers was being lost. It has become a matter that our Japanese friends here, too, must worry over.[45]

It is impossible to ascertain the extent of the control of the Yamato Colony members over the influx of other Japanese into the area. However, the uneasy climate of the times and the veiled threat of retaliation for noncompliance may have exacerbated the contrasts between the two colonies—the Yamato Colony, founded in 1906, had by 1919 attained a degree of economic well-being and social acceptance by whites, while Cortez was a newly established, struggling venture of greenhorn pioneers.

It is likewise difficult to assess the degree to which class consider-

---

42. Ibid.
43. Noda, p. 21.
44. Ibid., p. 93.
45. *Livingston Chronicle*, November 21, 1919.

ations really affected anti-Asianism. Even highly successful immigrants like George Shima, the "Potato King," confronted barriers to social acceptance. Urban studies have stressed the racial basis for anti-Asianism, particularly among Euro-American workers. As a rural community, Livingston presents a different, highly unusual scenario due to factors of religion, language, and timing as well as class. As an all-Christian settlement with a number of educated middle-class pioneers fluent in English, the Yamato Colony in its early days had been able to forge positive ties with the larger Livingston community. Given the heat of anti-Japanese sentiment in the late 1910s and early 1920s, it does not seem likely that middle-class status would have improved the reception of the Cortez settlers (many of whom were also Christian). However, shared bonds of class, religion, language, and history clearly made a difference in how the Yamato colonists were perceived and treated at a crucial point. And it appears that intraethnic class divisions, exacerbated by anti-Asianism, did discourage the formation of a strong ethnic alliance between the Cortez and Yamato Colony residents. It would take another manifestation of anti-Asianism—the World War II internment that drew no distinctions among Japanese Americans—to heal the rifts between them.

As in the rest of Merced County, anti-Japanese feelings ran high in Livingston in 1920. With the sanction of a vote taken at a mass meeting attended by "practically every resident of this town and people from the surrounding country," signs appeared at the highway entrances to Livingston, stating, "No more Japanese wanted."[46] Senator J. M. Inman of Sacramento, president of the California Oriental Exclusion League, praised these signs to a crowd of several hundred in Merced and expressed the wish that this message be copied and placed over the Golden Gate in letters "large enough for the Japanese to see all the way from Hawaii."[47] Livingston businessmen applied pressure to block the sale of local property to Japanese. The Merced County Anti-Japanese Association circulated pledge cards among landowners in the Livingston district exacting a "morally binding" agreement not to

---

46. Hearings before the House Committee on Immigration and Naturalization on Japanese Immigration, July 19–21, 1920, 66th Cong., 2d sess., pt. 3 (1920), p. 851. It is significant that the signs in Livingston read "No more Japanese wanted," rather than "No Japanese wanted." This, too, reflects the unusual situation of the Yamato Colony members.

47. *Merced County Sun*, January 30, 1920.

sell or lease land to Japanese.[48] The exclusionists also resorted to more direct means: On twenty-four hours' notice, a banker, G. H. Winton, and a merchant, T. H. White, bought a forty-acre ranch south of town for $12,000 to keep it from falling into Japanese hands.[49]

The exclusionists failed, however, to prevent two major land sales in Cortez—the Sunny Acres tract adjoining the state veterans' colony on the north, and the 1,250-acre tract owned by Harry Evans along the Santa Fe Railway on the north side of the Merced River. In both instances the *Livingston Chronicle* detected that "the engineering is being done by Mr. Obika [*sic*], a Japanese editor of San Francisco, who is well known in Livingston and Merced where he has done much realty business of late."[50] In the case of the latter tract, the *Chronicle* alleged, Evans was said to have sold to a Merced banker but the real purchaser in the transaction was Abiko.

Amid the controversy over the efforts to settle Japanese in Cortez, the position of the Yamato Colony members was quite precarious. They were caught between issues just as, on a single page of the *Livingston Chronicle*, an article blithely reporting that "K. Okuda is having a nice new home erected on his ranch" was sandwiched between a recruitment notice for the Anti-Japanese Association and a photograph of a man hanged in effigy for selling land to a Japanese. Just as ironically, at the peak of exclusionist activity, a chaperoned group of predominantly white youth surprised two young Nisei women, Rose and Mary Naka, with a midnight feast of ice cream and cake, on the occasion of Mary's return from Mills College. Such an interracial event would have been rare for Japanese Americans anywhere at this time.

Constrained most likely by coercion, the Yamato colonists became involved with the Livingston Anti-Japanese committee. According to E. G. Adams, three of the Yamato leaders—Naka Kiyoichi (father of Rose and Mary), N. Satow, and M. Minabe—composed a subcommit-

48. Hearings before the House Committee on Immigration and Naturalization on Japanese Immigration (1920), p. 850.

49. Ibid., p. 853; *Livingston Chronicle*, March 19, 1920. As Kesa Noda has stated (p. 85), while the *Livingston Chronicle* may have reported Winton's involvement in buying a ranch to keep it from being sold to Japanese, a number of Yamato Colony members remembered receiving his assistance in buying land. She has suggested that the whites who befriended the Livingston Japanese maintained two positions, one public and one private.

50. *Livingston Chronicle*, January 16 and 30, 1920.

tee to work toward halting the arrival of more Japanese in the area. Naka, as colony representative, conferred with Adams on an average of three times a week for four months.[51] In May 1920, the *Chronicle* noted approvingly that no land in the Livingston District had been sold to Japanese since January 1, and expressed confidence that the Yamato Colony would "continue to cooperate with the whole community in keeping out in future the lower class of Japanese who are still reaching out for land in many parts of this state."[52] By this time, the "No more Japanese wanted" signs had been replaced by another slogan: "Livingston, the community with a destiny."[53]

The vulnerability of the Yamato Colony in their relationship with the larger Livingston community—and their corresponding cooperation with the local Anti-Japanese committee—may have driven a partial wedge between them and Abiko during this time. In his testimony at a July 21, 1920, congressional hearing before the Committee on Immigration and Naturalization regarding Japanese immigration, E. G. Adams criticized Abiko for not having "done the right thing toward the [Japanese] people residents of Livingston." As Adams explained, "They asked him to cease bringing in Japanese from other places, and he persisted, and it was the cause of an internal fight between the Japanese, and I understand that they notified him that he should lay off."[54] Adams also reported to the committee that in "February or March Mr. Naka lived here actually in danger for the attitude he took in attempting to solve the problem locally in Livingston; and also in Oakland and San Francisco."[55] The record does not make clear from precisely whom Naka was in danger nor the substance of his efforts to resolve the matter. However, the congressional testimony of Adams and Naka does suggest reasons for friction between Abiko's sister colonies, given the way in which interracial relations complicated intraethnic dynam-

51. Hearings before the House Committee on Immigration and Naturalization on Japanese Immigration (1920), p. 851. These three men appear to have played key leadership roles in the Yamato Colony. For more information on Naka Kiyoichi, see Noda, pp. 21–22. "M. Minabe" was probably Fred M. (Umetaro) Minabe; "N. Satow" was probably Nobutada Satow. For more information on Minabe and Satow, see Noda, pp. 10, 35, 87–88.

52. *Livingston Chronicle*, May 14, 1920.

53. Hearings before the House Committee on Immigration and Naturalization on Japanese Immigration (1920), p. 852.

54. Ibid., p. 852.

55. Ibid., p. 854.

ics. Indeed, the Livingston-Cortez rivalry persisted until after World War II.

The fragile position of the Livingston Japanese, and the care they exercised to maintain the difficult balance, found illustration in the testimony given by Naka Kiyoichi before the congressional committee on July 21, 1920, and in his related essay printed in the *Livingston Chronicle* on July 23. The record of the hearings included both Naka's answers to questions from the committee and a written report he submitted on religion, society, education, and farming in the Livingston Japanese settlement. Although the Yamato Colony members lived in a segregated enclave—which Naka attributed to their lack of fluency in the English language—he emphasized that they considered themselves a part of the American community. "In order to urge upon ourselves the best training of our children for future good citizenship in this country," he asserted, "we feel and believe that we need the kind cooperation of our American friends, and we, in return, are willing to do anything that we can."[56] As an indication of the Yamato Colony's community spirit, Naka pointed out that, "Since we have come here several Japanese business men have wished to start a business in Livingston, but we have refused to allow them to do so, because we are satisfied to do business with the American stores and wish to cooperate with them."[57] He concluded his oral testimony by expressing the desire for "a splendid American community here and not a large Japanese community here."[58]

Naka's newspaper essay, published on the front page of the *Chronicle* two days after the hearing, displayed not only his eloquent command of English, but also a plea that could be extended beyond the Japanese in Livingston. Naka's painstakingly worded appeal presented a careful rebuttal to the denial of citizenship and the labeling of Japanese as "upper class" and "lower class" by the dominant society:

> When it is stated that the Japanese of Livingston are a higher class than elsewhere I reply without hesitation that if they are, it is because they are living under more favorable conditions and not because of difference in class. The Japanese of Livingston are, for the most part, Christians, and

56. Ibid., p. 855.
57. Ibid., p. 855.
58. Ibid., p. 854.

because of this they have had the help of the American Christians of this community. . . . However, the prime reason for their advancement here has been the fact that they owned their own homes.[59]

Naka stressed the Yamato Colony members' commitment to their homes and community: "We love these little farms as if they were our children. They are our sweethearts. They reflect in tree and shrub and vine the hardships and trials through which we passed in bringing them to such a state of perfection." He bypassed the question of further Japanese immigration to discuss the reasons why he felt Japanese were not easily "Americanized."[60] This he attributed to the immigrants' initial intentions of returning to Japan, their lack of Christian background, the isolating effect of the racial prejudice they encountered, and most importantly, the denial of American citizenship. The remainder of his testimony presented a plea that the American-born children of the immigrants not be denied the rights of citizenship, and called for mutual respect and understanding between the races.[61]

At the end of 1920, E. G. Adams praised the Livingston Japanese as "the only [Japanese] group in the state who have maintained independence from their strenuously objecting and fighting countrymen" and have abstained from battling the Asian exclusion initiative. Adams declared the Japanese question settled in Livingston, and his projection for the city's future included several generations of American-born Japanese. The problem would be one not of antagonism or defense, but "one of helpfulness, of social and community assimilation." Social boundaries were clearly defined, however, when he hastened to add, "No one—American or Japanese—wants or expects physical assimilation here." There is also no missing the warning in his concluding bouquet to the members of the Yamato Colony:

Anything published in the *Chronicle* in future in relation to the Japanese question will be so intended as to not include the Livingston Japanese if present circumstances locally are perpetuated. So far as we will be concerned, there will be no Japanese in Livingston. That is a consideration

59. *Livingston Chronicle*, July 23, 1920.
60. Hearings before the House Committee on Immigration and Naturalization on Japanese Immigration (1920), p. 854.
61. *Livingston Chronicle*, July 23, 1920.

that our Japanese have earned. It is up to them whether they make a change necessary, and we think they will not.[62]

Adams and the exclusionists had additional reasons for optimism. In 1920, they succeeded in passing the California Alien Land Law barring the transfer or lease of land to Japanese nationals. In addition the law prevented lease or purchase of land by any corporation in which Japanese held a majority of the stock, thus undermining Abiko's method of acquiring land. Finally, the law attempted to halt the practice of alien Japanese serving as guardians for their minor American-born children. Under the Fourteenth Amendment, however, this key measure concerning guardianship was not enforceable. Allied with other nativists who had long opposed Southern- and Eastern-European immigration, the anti-Japanese exclusionists carried their campaign to a national level and testified before the Senate in 1924. In that year, Congress passed the Immigration Act, which established a two percent quota system and also prohibited the entry of any "alien ineligible to citizenship," thereby cutting off all immigration from Japan. However, the exclusionists were unable to gain a proposed constitutional amendment stripping Nisei and other Asian Americans of U.S. citizenship.[63]

In spite of the efforts of exclusionists in the 1920s, settlers continued to arrive in Cortez. Who were these men and women, attracted by advertisements in the *Nichibei Shimbun* and by word of mouth, who struggled to realize their dreams in an uncultivated land and hostile society? They came from a variety of areas and backgrounds, and not all had extensive experience in farming, or in farming the kinds of crops suitable to the Cortez soil. A few of the men came to America with parents or brothers, but most—like the majority of the first Japanese immigrants—came to the United States as single transient workers hoping to make a fortune that would enable them to return to Japan with wealth and status. Instead, they developed interests in agriculture and small businesses and put down roots. The few who were married were joined by their wives. Single men often returned to

62. *Livingston Chronicle*, December 3, 1920.
63. Roger Daniels has thoroughly chronicled the exclusionists' legal battles in *The Politics of Prejudice*, pp. 80–104.

their homeland to find wives, or resorted to the practice of marrying a picture bride. The Cortez colonists represented a number of prefectures, including Hiroshima, Kumamoto, Yamaguchi, Fukuoka, Fukui, Shiga, Kanagawa, and Yamanashi; the first six of these prefectures rank high among those that scholars have identified as the most economically distressed agrarian prefectures at the turn of the century, which suggested that Cortez settlers came primarily for economic advancement.[64] Unlike the entirely Christian Yamato Colony, a sizable portion of the Cortez Colony maintained the Buddhist faith—a religious division common in most of the large Japanese American communities. The individual histories of the Cortez Issei illustrate the patterns and variations of Japanese immigration. The following three examples are representative in many ways of the thousands of Issei who came to California.

The movements of the Kuwahara and Yuge families exemplify one pattern in which Japanese immigrants to the United States continued to migrate within the country. They fanned out from the port cities and moved through rural districts in search of work.

Kuwahara Yonekichi, born in 1877, came to the United States in 1898 and was joined in 1905 by Fujii Den, a twenty-two-year-old picture bride. Both came from farming families in Fukuoka Prefecture. Despite the low status of Western religion in Japan—derogatorily called *"yasukyo"*—the Kuwaharas became staunch Christian converts in America. They first lived in Alameda, California, and then in Berkeley, where they both did domestic work. During his stint as a "houseboy," Yonekichi learned how to cook and to bake cakes, a novel accomplishment which he later shared with his Issei women neighbors in Cortez. Yonekichi at one time ran a small florist's shop, and then acquired an Asian art store. In 1919, attracted by Abiko's Christian ideals and the prospect of owning land, he and his wife purchased a farm in Cortez. At first, only Yonekichi moved there to work it with their oldest son and daughter, while Den continued to do domestic work in Berkeley. In 1924, Den and their youngest daughter also moved to Cortez.[65]

Two of the other early pioneers came from quite a different background. Yuge Zenshiro was the educated youngest son of a family that

---

64. Wilson and Hosokawa, p. 49.
65. May Sakaguchi interview, Cortez, Calif., March 10 and 11, 1982; Sam Kuwahara interview, Cortez, Calif., January 25, 1982.

raised silkworm eggs in Shiga Prefecture. When he arrived in the United States in 1902, his intention was to investigate the possibilities of raising silkworms in Florida, but he never traveled beyond the borders of California. He and Ikeda Yei, the daughter of a rice broker, had been married before he left Japan. In 1904, she came to join him in America. Here their four children were born, and, like the Kuwaharas, they embraced not only a new country but also a new faith—Christianity. Despite their lack of farming experience, they took what work they could find in the rural communities of Watsonville, Castroville, and San Juan Bautista, where Zenshiro cleaned a saloon in the winter. Like Kuwahara Den and many Issei and Nisei women before World War II, Yei did domestic work for a white family in Watsonville, and there she learned to read and write English.[66] In 1919, the Yuge family moved to Cortez.[67]

Fukagawa Suye came to Cortez a few years after the Kuwaharas and the Yuges. She was born in 1905 to a farming family in Fukui Prefecture, the youngest of six children. Following her sixth-grade education, she went to a sewing school where she learned to make *nihongi* (Japanese clothes) by hand. When she was eighteen, her parents arranged her marriage to twenty-six-year-old Sugiura Yonehichi, whose family was from the same community. Yonehichi had been living in the United States with his parents from the age of seventeen and returned to Japan to be married, as many single men preferred to do if they could afford the travel expenses. Suye first saw her husband during the wedding ceremony, at the moment when she raised a ceremonial cup of rice wine to her lips and lifted her modestly downcast gaze.[68]

In February 1923, a month after the wedding, the Sugiuras set sail from Yokohama to San Francisco. Among their shipmates on the *Tenyo-maru* was another couple, Hawaiian-born Kumekichi Taniguchi and his wife Sugano Chitose, who were destined to be their neighbors in Cortez as well as fellow members of the Buddhist church. Upon their arrival in March, the Sugiuras spent several trying days while

66. Evelyn Nakano Glenn examines the domestic service work of Japanese American women in "The Dialectics of Wage Work: Japanese-American Women and Domestic Service, 1905–1940," *Feminist Studies* 6(Fall 1980):432–71. For a more comprehensive work, see her study *Issei, Nisei, War Bride, Three Generations of Japanese American Women in Domestic Service* (Philadelphia: Temple University Press, 1986).

67. George Yuge interview, Cortez, Calif., February 8, 1982.

68. Sugiura Suye interview, Cortez, Calif., February 9, 1982.

awaiting clearance at the immigration station on Angel Island. Then followed a shopping expedition, in which Suye doffed her kimono and sandals to don layer upon layer of Western clothing: "unda shiatsu" (undershirt), beaded blouse, bloomers, corset, several petticoats, and high-heeled shoes.

The couple moved directly to Cortez where they lived with Yone-hichi's parents, not an uncommon practice. Contrary to the accepted assumption of the nuclear Japanese immigrant family, a number of Cortez Issei lived with parents (also considered to be Issei) or siblings. Therefore, not all Japanese immigrant brides escaped the dreaded fate of living with in-laws.

Like many new wives of Japanese workers, Suye quickly had to learn to do cooking as well as farmwork, from which she had been exempt in Japan as the frail youngest child. In April, on the occasion of a welcome party to celebrate her arrival, her mother-in-law told her, "Make yourself presentable, and put a little powder on," but Suye was so sunburned from staking grape plants that the powder on her face, she recalled, looked like frost on a mountain.

These Cortez settlers, like the majority of the Issei, migrated through several jobs, as domestic workers, farm laborers, and tenants. They joined a landowning minority, however, when they bought their twenty- and forty-acre farms from Abiko. Purchasing the land was only the beginning of their commitment to establishing a community with a cooperative structure. From the time of their arrival in Cortez, they faced continual challenges to their endurance and morale.

The development of the Cortez Colony exacted years of arduous struggle and adaptation. The settlers had to deal with hostility from outside the community and from hardship within. Primitive living conditions, isolation, intensive farm labor, and disease made life extremely difficult. The first to arrive erected simple board-and-bat houses that provided little protection from sandstorms and winter chill. Nisei children like Ernest Yoshida could see stars peeping through the roof at night. The pioneers carried water in buckets from a well or hand pump, and lit their homes with kerosene lamps because there was no electricity until 1925, and even then not all families could afford it. Life—especially for the women, who shouldered field duties as well as domestic chores—was one long round of work.

Like the Yamato colonists, most of the Cortez pioneers initially planted, and replanted, grapes, primarily Thompson seedless. But sandstorms and the ubiquitous jackrabbits destroyed the first series of plantings. Rabbit drives to rid the fields of the voracious animals became annual community events. Several years passed before the grape vines began growing and then producing fruit. In the meantime, the Issei hired themselves out as grape pickers in the nearby towns of Turlock, Denair, and Hughson. By the time their vineyards started to bear good crops, the Great Depression had begun, killing the market for grapes.

While their vineyards were maturing, and during the depression years, the Cortez settlers turned to raising labor-intensive "truck crops" like strawberries, eggplants, onions, and carrots.[69] Producing annual row crops has always been more time-consuming and worrisome than maintaining vineyards and orchards, but in the days before farm mechanization, the work was taxing and endless. With hand shovels, men and women dug irrigation ditches; horses and mules pulled the ploughs. There were always weeds to hoe, crates to nail, animals to feed, and produce to tend, pick, and pack.

This kind of intensive labor required the energy of every family member, regardless of age or gender. Only by the exercise of spartan frugality and the participation of all family members in the work force could the Japanese farmers eke out a living and maintain their precious hold on landownership. This practice of family wage economy,[70] especially with regard to women, was a focal point in the rhetoric of anti-Japanese exclusionists like Senator Phelan. He declared emphatically, albeit inaccurately, "White women will not and no woman should work in the fields. There is no necessity for it and if we allow the Japanese to come to this country, it will be very difficult for the white man alone to compete against the entire Japanese families, both men and women."[71] For the Japanese, as for earlier immigrant pioneers, this intensive work was a matter of survival.

69. By 1940, Japanese farmers controlled 40 percent of California's truck crop production. Jelinek, p. 69.

70. Two historians, Louise Tilly and Joan Scott, have used the term "family wage economy" to refer to the practice of working-class family members in the nineteenth and early twentieth centuries combining their limited earnings in order to sustain their household. This pattern, Evelyn Nakano Glenn points out, has occurred in urban families in the nineteenth and twentieth centuries, and among working-class racial–ethnic families in the present. Glenn, *Issei, Nisei, War Bride*, p. 207; Louise A. Tilly and Joan W. Scott, *Women, Work, and Family* (New York: Holt, Rinehart, and Winston, 1978), pp. 15, 104–6.

71. *Merced County Sun*, September 24, 1920.

The work of Japanese women stretched from dawn to dusk. In addition to fieldwork, they scrubbed laundry on washboards, cooked meals on wood stoves and over outside fires, washed dishes, drew and heated water for the *ofuro* (Japanese bath), tended babies, and waged a constant battle against the sand and rain that invaded their homes. The children born in the early years of the colony were delivered at home. Kajioka Masa recalled giving birth unattended, cutting the umbilical cord herself, bathing the baby, and then calling a doctor to sign a birth certificate. Most women were attended by local *sanbasan* (midwives) like Mrs. Yotsuya and Suye Sugiura's mother-in-law. The popularity of Mrs. Tsuruda, a Cressey *sanbasan*, indicates the existence of some ties to the Yamato Colony.

In those lean early years, the settlers' diet was limited; meals often consisted of *miso* soup and rice, or tomato-*juri*. The Cortez Issei remembered eating large quantities of rabbit. Many children took bread and jam to school for lunch and wistfully eyed those students whose families could afford meat sandwiches.

Because of the arduous toil, primitive living conditions, and poor nutrition, tuberculosis took its toll in the community. A number of Nisei recalled friends and neighbors struck down by the "white plague" and the local newspapers mentioned some of the sufferers who went for treatment to the county hospital or the Tri-County Sanitarium at Ahwannee. In the 1920s the treatment for tuberculosis consisted of fresh air, rest, and nourishing food—sometimes only a stopgap respite for the overworked and underfed.

Confronted by such serious internal and external problems, how did the Cortez Colony manage to survive? The key to their endurance lay in the development of the vital economic, religious, and educational institutions that fostered their economic independence and cultural cohesion. Through their agricultural cooperative association, their two churches—Presbyterian and Buddhist—and an educational society, the Cortez Japanese were able to overcome isolation, to market and ship their produce, and to maintain social support networks and cultural traditions.

One institution has encompassed the lives of every member of the community—the Cortez Growers Association (CGA), officially established as a nonprofit corporation on April 18, 1924, by Kuwahara Yonekichi, Morofuji Nenokichi, Yoneyama Seitaro, and Yuge Zenshiro. Following a policy of Abiko's, the Cortez Japanese—like the Yamato Colony—had side-stepped some early economic hostility by confining themselves to farming and by avoiding competition with the Euro-American businesses in town. However, in shipping and marketing their produce, interracial contact was inevitable. Here they were handicapped by a language barrier, racial prejudice, and lack of familiarity with American legal and business practices. In addition, by the time their vineyards and orchards began to bear fruit, the boom period of World War I had ended and the produce market was depressed. Like other Japanese farmers of the 1910s and 1920s, they turned to the organization of an agricultural cooperative to meet their needs. They had to look no further than the Yamato Colony for a working model.

The formation of cooperative farm organizations, as Masakazu Iwata has suggested, contributed significantly to the prewar success of the Japanese farmers. These groups, called *nogyo kumiai*, were most widespread in southern California, where they were often linked with marketing associations in Los Angeles. Such associations provided a range of services, from agricultural publications to assistance in marketing produce and buying supplies.[72] By joint purchase, the Japanese were able to obtain much better prices for fertilizer, insecticide, and supplies. Selling their produce collectively enabled them to compete with much larger farmers.

In forming their cooperative association, the Cortez Issei used a legal tactic to which a number of immigrant Japanese resorted. Like the Yamato colonists, they first consulted with the San Francisco law firm of Guy C. Calden and Albert H. Eliot, known for assisting Japanese farmers to acquire property through a legal loophole. To avoid the strictures of the Alien Land Law of 1913, a Japanese alien could form a corporation in the name of a minor American-born child, and, as guardian, become an officer of the corporation. As the American-born Nisei came of age, the corporations were dissolved and the farm titles were transferred to their names. The early records of the CGA reflect this strategy, in both the lists of "corporation" members—like Yoneyama Seitaro's Sunny Acre Farm Co., Morofuji Nenokichi's T.

72. Iwata, p. 33. To my knowledge, the Japanese American communities of Cortez, Livingston, and Cressey were the only ones able to maintain their farms collectively through the vehicle of their cooperative associations during the evacuation of World War II.

and M. Vineyard Co., and the Aloha Farm of S. Ogata—and in the by-laws:

> RESOLVED: That this association shall be composed of citizens of the United States and aliens ineligible for citizenship under the laws of the United States and corporations engaged in agricultural pursuits; that corporations shall be represented by one or more of their officers, and it shall be immaterial whether said officers are citizens of the United States or aliens who are ineligible to citizenship.[73]

Membership in the CGA was, and still is, contingent upon approval of the Board of Directors and payment of a fifty-dollar fee, a sum that has not been raised since 1924. Although the membership fee is now a matter of custom, in the early years it constituted a vital source of the organization's working capital. By the end of its first year, the CGA had gained seven more members: Kubo Kasaku, Narita Suetaro, Nakayama Gentaro, S. Ogata, Shiono Tetsuzo, T. Tomoeda, and H. Yamazaki. At this time the CGA had constructed a packing shed at a cost of $757, and decided to charge each member one cent to two cents for each crate of grapes shipped through the California Fruit Exchange, to raise funds for the $535.25 still due the contractor. In the following year the fledgling association continued to grow: it enlarged the packing house to accommodate more produce, dug a well on the CGA property to provide water for domestic use, and installed a telephone system.

The California economy had slumped even before the Great Depression. Grape and fruit prices plummeted, forcing the Cortez farmers to turn to other crops for subsistence. Many of the growers drew upon previous experience as berry growers and truck gardeners.[74] The importance and size of the berry crop, primarily strawberries, is evidenced by the formation of the Cortez Berry Growers Association on December 28, 1928. This organization, modeled on the CGA, shared its office, manager, and staff, and worked in conjunction with the older cooperative, but remained a separate entity with its own board of directors and banking until the CGA subsumed its operations in 1933. The change in produce marketing also led to the establishment of a Vegetable Department in the CGA, as members raised truck crops

---

73. Cortez Growers Association, *Minutes* 1(April 22, 1924):7.
74. George Yuge, *History of the Cortez Growers Association*, pamphlet, 1974.

Sam Kuwahara, the first full-time and Nisei manager of the Cortez Growers Association, in the office of the Association, ca. 1933. Photo courtesy of Florice Kuwahara.

of onions, carrots, and eggplants. Carrot shipping in particular continued to grow until World War II.

The 1930s marked not only a shift in crop production but also the entrance of the Nisei into CGA leadership. In 1933 Morofuji Nenokichi retired as the CGA's first president, and his son was elected to the Board of Directors. George Morofuji was the first Nisei to hold such a position. This generational shift also occurred in the position of the CGA manager.

The association had hired different part-time managers each year in rapid succession until 1932, when Sam Kuwahara, a Cortez Nisei, became their first full-time and American-born manager. He was initially appointed as a bookkeeper, at a salary of $125 per month, but his duties included management. Under his supervision, the rifts that had led to the formation of splinter groups of growers were mended, and the CGA began to assume the form it now holds as a modern cooperative association. Sam oversaw the purchase of a truck, which enabled the CGA to transport profitably its own produce to the San Francisco Bay Area. Also under his auspices, the Association constructed a dehydrator system to produce Golden Bleach raisins from Cortez-grown seedless grapes. This dehydrator was the CGA's largest investment to date, costing $10,303.86 for machinery, trays, boxes, and land.[75]

From its beginnings, the CGA enabled its members to surmount the language barrier and to obtain better terms by commonly marketing their produce; it also provided a measure of economic security. Although there has never been complete security in farming, the Cortez growers could draw sustenance from the collective endeavor that made them allies instead of competitors. They also gained a bargaining strength beyond the means of most farmers who cultivated parcels of twenty to forty acres.

Religion provided another crucial source of support for the Cortez settlers. Although the Cortez community, unlike the Yamato Colony, was not solely composed of Christians, the majority of the Issei drawn by Abiko's plan had embraced the Christian faith as part of their new home. Many had converted soon after arrival in the United States, having found fellowship and orientation in the churches and meeting places established by missionaries for new immigrants. Others were

75. Ibid.

introduced to Christianity by relatives or in-laws who had preceded them in America.

Soon after their arrival in Cortez, the Issei organized a Christian church school. Their first worship service was held in the Kajioka Hachizo home on December 12, 1920. Yuge Zenshiro recorded this occasion—"a fellowship gathering of almost everyone in Cortez"—at which guest Reverends F. O. Bergstrom and Fujii Jiryu of Livingston spoke and prayed "for the physical and spiritual well-being of the immigrants to Cortez." Yuge's closing sentiments echoed those of Abiko Kyutaro: "May the Cortez Colony expand and may the colonists find unity in Christ and be able to move forward in faith, hope, and love to accomplish God's will."[76] A makeshift bamboo shelter served as a meeting place for the early congregation, composed of several Christian denominations—Free Methodists, Methodists, Holiness Church, Presbyterians, and Episcopalians. In 1922 they built a church on a parcel of land set aside by Abiko specifically for that purpose. Four years later, members donated their labor and funds to add a kitchen and sleeping quarters to the church. In the same year a seminary student, Sekiguchi Kumekichi, came to Cortez to preach on Sundays and to work at the CGA during the week.

Within six years, delinquent taxes had accumulated on the church land, threatening the church with foreclosure. The congregation decided to seek the sponsorship of an established church through a mission program. Since the majority of the members were Methodist, they would have preferred that affiliation, but the Methodist Mission was already sponsoring the Japanese American church in Livingston and could not accept another. The Presbyterian Synod, however, agreed to accept the Cortez congregation as a sponsored mission. With the election of church officers and under the ministry of Reverend Sekiguchi, the church officially became the Cortez Presbyterian Church in 1927.[77]

As the community grew, the congregation contributed their talent, labor, and money to improve the church. In 1928 they built a manse to accommodate the family of Reverend Watanabe Renpei and dug a well. In order to raise funds to provide a car for Reverend Watanabe,

76. Cortez Presbyterian Church, *Fiftieth Anniversary*, pamphlet, p. 40.
77. Ibid., p. 7. The church officers were Elders Kajioka Hachizo, Kajioka Otokichi, Kuwahara Yonekichi, and Yuge Zenshiro; and Deacons Shiono Tetsuzo, Yoshida Yonezo, Yamaguchi Tomoichiro, and Yamamoto Rokutaro.

the congregation put on a theatrical production. Yoshida Yonezo, who had a reputation as a skilled *benshi* (theater narrator) wrote a play based on the life of the Christian martyr Saint Stephen. The elaborate *kabuki*-styled play was staged in the Santa Fe Railway shed behind the CGA offices on Christmas Eve and raised $500 for the minister's new Chevrolet. This was an early indicator of the complex overlay of Japanese and Christian cultures that would come to characterize Cortez.

In the late 1920s, Nisei Kenneth Mayeda became concerned with building a church program that would meet the needs of the American-born second generation. He sought the assistance of white Christian leaders in training Cortez Sunday School teachers, and initiated the involvement of Cortez teenagers with Christian Endeavor, a statewide organization for young people. Christian Endeavor gave them not only spiritual education but also opportunities to travel to conferences and participate in interracial activities. The Cortez Nisei entered Bible competitions, held positions as county officers in Christian Endeavor, and broadcast religious messages and music over the Merced radio station KYOS.

The growing round of church activities—prayer meetings held in Japanese, the English-language Sunday School, and holiday festivities—provided social occasions for families on isolated farms and cemented the bonds of friendship and support among the peer groups of Issei women, Issei men, and their children. The church also enlarged the Nisei's social horizons by giving them, through Christian Endeavor, a vehicle for interaction with other Nisei and non-Japanese American youth.

Christianity was not, however, the unifying force in Cortez that it was in Livingston, the site of Abiko's first colony. A number of Cortez pioneers remained devout Buddhists in spite of the missionary fervor of the Presbyterian Church elders. By 1934, there were twelve Buddhist families in Cortez.[78] They sent a delegation to the Stockton Buddhist Church to request that monthly services be held in Cortez, as a division of the Stockton church. The Reverend H. Mikami was the first of their visiting ministers. Because they had no church building, the members took turns having the services in their homes and hosting the minister overnight. In 1939, the Buddhists rented the Educa-

---

78. The families were those of Asai Seiichi, Baba Nobuyoshi, Kajiwara Junjiro, Kubo Kasaku, Miyamoto Matsuichi, Nakagawa Yusuke, Nishihara Umetaro, Shimizu Tokuitsu, Kumekichi Taniguchi, Yenokida Utaro, Yoneyama Seitaro, and Yotsuya Eisuke.

tional Society Building, and there the Reverend E. Hojo conducted their monthly services until World War II.

The Cortez community had constructed the Educational Society Building, the Gakuen, in 1928 on another piece of land designated by Abiko for educational purposes. The Gakuen housed the *nihongakko*, or Japanese school—a shared experience of most second-generation Japanese Americans. There the Nisei were sent after public school hours to learn the language of their parents from a series of teachers.[79] It was also at the Gakuen that boys and girls learned the Japanese art of bamboo-stave fighting when the Educational Society formed a kendo club. Teenagers took advantage of a new social outlet with the founding of the Young People's Club in 1933. Here, as in the Japanese school and the kendo club, Nisei from both churches met to plan outings, parties, and sports activities.

By the eve of the turbulent 1940s, Abiko Kyutaro's vision had taken form in a stable community of some thirty families. A constellation of social, economic, and religious institutions enabled them to weather the early years of hardship. Through their two active churches and a Japanese school, they gained emotional support and affirmation and maintained as much as they could of the Issei's cultural heritage. By this time the Cortez farmers were beginning to see the end of the long struggle for financial security, as their ranches produced good crops for welcoming markets. The CGA had grown into a diversified concern, handling the marketing and shipping of produce, the purchase of farm supplies, and the dehydration of fruit.

The residents of Cortez also found an increased degree of acceptance in the surrounding society. Passage of the 1924 Immigration Act had stemmed both the influx of Japanese immigrants and the most virulent agitation against them in the West. Over the course of two decades, the Cortez settlers had become part of the rural cosmos as familiar neighbors and fellow farmers. The Japanese, who had been warned away from Turlock in the early 1920s, now received invitations to participate in the annual Turlock Melon Carnival parade. The Cortez Colony made a float for the parade, and the local chapter of the Japanese American Citizens League carried a giant American flag. This

79. The Nihongakko teachers were Mr. Ideno, Mr. Kobayashi, Mr. Kubota, Mrs. Uno, and Mr. Uchimura.

process of change was most visible in the lives of the second generation who had gradually found a place in the larger community via the public educational system. The Nisei became mediators between their parents and the surrounding society. In the local public schools they learned English and gained a reputation as diligent students, participating in athletic events and the 4-H Club. They began to move into some of the social circles from which their parents and the older Nisei had been barred by a language barrier, economic circumstance, and prejudice. For example, Nisei Ernest Yoshida and Nobuhiro Kajioka worked on the Merced County Fair Board—an impossibility for the Issei less than two decades before. The social climate had changed to such an extent that, in the words of one Nisei, "We thought we were accepted."

CHAPTER 2

Growing Up in Cortez:
The Prewar Years

The second-generation Japanese Americans who grew up in Cortez have vivid memories of waking early to walk the two and three miles to the Ballico Grammar School and kicking wild pie melons on the way. Meanwhile, their parents set off to work in the fields of strawberries, eggplants, and grapes. After school, the young Nisei returned to pick berries, bunch onions, and nail crates; in the evening, they ate rice cooked outside over a fire and submerged themselves to the chin in a steamy Japanese bath. It was in these early years that the people of Cortez developed the family stability and community networks that enabled them to survive both the Great Depression and the chaotic years of World War II.

The experiences and expectations of the Nisei provide a key to understanding their integration of both Japanese and American mainstream culture, as they forged crucial bonds of community solidarity. Their negotiation of intraethnic and interethnic roles within the rural prewar environment reflects both adaptability and endurance. The arenas of family, work, education, recreation, and marriage offer overlapping contexts within which to analyze the internal dynamics of Cortez. External elements also increasingly played a role in the Nisei's lives. Their entry into the public school system reveals not only the parameters of interracial relations but also the tensions of class differences between the Japanese American teenagers of Cortez and Livingston.

The new developments and exigencies of the two decades before World War II framed the formative experiences of Nisei youth in Cortez. In the 1920s, rapid change transformed California's physical and social landscape. New technology entered everyday life in the form of automobiles and radios. The popular imagination found a catalyst in the latest entertainment, the movies, and the burgeoning film industry made southern California a mecca for the starstruck. The population mushroomed as close to two million migrants headed west, drawn by the siren call of Hollywood and the southern California oil boom, as well as the general promises of health and job opportunities promoted relentlessly by state booster groups and the railroads. At this time, California emerged as the leading example of industrialized agriculture in the United States. It produced a dazzling array of two hundred commercial crops, a diversity unsurpassed by any other state.[1] Many midwestern farmers gambled on a new start in the fertile valleys depicted enticingly on produce crate labels. The cultivation of this Edenic bounty, however, increasingly reflected not the prosperity of small-family farms but the rationalization of agribusiness: crop specialization, growing consolidation of landholdings, new methods of irrigation and transportation, and reliance on a low-paid migratory labor force.

Swift change produced anxiety as well as elation. As the corporate framework of business and agriculture solidified, many found themselves—despite their expectations—jockeying for footing on the lower rungs of the ladder to success. Nativism, never far from the surface of California history, found expression in the rise of the Ku Klux Klan and anti-Japanese agitation in the 1920s, soon followed by Mexican repatriation drives.

As heady growth characterized the decade of the 1920s in California, the Great Depression indelibly stamped the 1930s. In the wake of the stock market crash of 1929, real estate developers, construction companies, oil firms, service industries, moviemakers, and farmers all took a nose dive along with the national economy. As Americans tightened their belts and cut back on frills, the market declined for the specialty crops that had commanded such high prices a few years

---

1. Richard B. Rice, William A. Bullough, and Richard J. Orsi, *The Elusive Eden, A New History of California* (New York: Alfred A. Knopf, 1988), p. 380.

earlier. California's agricultural profits plummeted from $750 million in 1929 to $327 million in 1932.[2] As the jobless roamed city streets and countryside alike, competition for even menial work exacerbated interracial tensions. Forced repatriation campaigns decimated Mexican American communities, deporting tens of thousands to Mexico. Their place in the California harvest labor force was soon filled by the first sizable group of white fieldworkers, as almost 300,000 midwestern farmers—the migrants immortalized by John Steinbeck—flooded into the state. A measure of relief came from a number of New Deal public works projects that began to provide employment as well as to further sculpt the California terrain, with the building of dams, bridges and canals; one of the most ambitious undertakings, the Central Valley Project, transferred water from the Sacramento River to the San Joaquin Valley, opening thousands of acres to cultivation. However, in spite of New Deal efforts, the economy did not fully revive until the advent of World War II.

The San Joaquin Valley reflected in microcosm the growing cultural diversity of California's population in the two decades before the war. The Japanese settlers of the Yamato, Cressey, and Cortez colonies were only one of a number of ethnic minority groups in the Livingston area (within Township 5) of Merced County and the Turlock area of Stanislaus County. The success stories of the Central Valley's immigrant agricultural royalty enticed many of their countryfolk. What might be possible in a place where men with names like Koda and Arakelian could become "rice kings" and "melon kings"?

Demographic patterns in these two overlapping locales convey a sense of the rich cultural mozaic of central California.[3] A variety of peoples began to arrive after the turn of the century. In 1903, a local land promoter, Nels O. Hultberg, began enticing Swedish settlers from the East and Midwest to take advantage of low prices for land and promises of plentiful irrigation water. Before long, an agricultural community called Hilmar, after his oldest son, took root and flour-

2. Ibid., p. 396.
3. Mapping demographic changes in the Cortez area posed challenges because it was for so long a sparsely settled area on the fringe of larger official locales. Cortez has tangled affiliations with both Turlock—the nearest city, seven miles away in Stanislaus County—and Livingston, thirteen miles away, with which it shared location in what was previously Township 5 in Merced County. Most Cortez residents have a Turlock mailing address. They and their children attended the Livingston High School.

ished near Turlock. A number of Portuguese—predominantly farmers and former seamen—also came as part of a secondary migration in this period. Many adopted the strategy of raising sweet potatoes while gradually developing the dairy herds for which they became known.[4]

Economic opportunity was not the only motivation for early settlers. In 1911 a group of forty-five Assyrians came seeking religious freedom as well as a temperate climate in which to farm. Similarly, the upheavals of World War I spurred an exodus of Armenians, many of whom settled in the Central Valley; those in the Turlock area gained prominence as melon growers.[5]

Mexican workers have long played an important role as the core of the region's farm labor force. As early as the 1910s a few families settled in Turlock, drawn primarily by railroad work; this community dwindled during the years of the Great Depression and did not begin to grow until the 1940s. The majority came as migrant field hands, arriving for the harvest season and then returning to homes in Brawley and El Centro in southern California. This pattern persisted in the 1970s and 1980s, as family groups from the Southwest and men from Mexico continued to follow the crops north.[6]

By the eve of World War II, the Livingston area of Merced County boasted a highly diverse population. No official ethnic composition breakdown exists for this small sector, but Betty Frances Brown obtained an estimate from the local census takers for 1940. According to them, the English-Irish-Scottish-Germans formed the largest proportion of the population at 45 percent. They were followed in turn by the Portuguese (10 percent), Mexicans (8 percent), and Japanese (6 percent). Five percent identified themselves as Mennonites of Russian-Belgian-Dutch extraction; Swedes and Italians each made up four percent of the area's population. Livingston was also home to smaller numbers of Germans, Armenians, Greeks, Filipinos, Slavs, African Americans, and Indians. An estimated 70 percent of the local popu-

4. Carolyn Larson and Geraldine Johnson, "Turlock: A Center of Swedish Settlement," in *Streams in a Thirsty Land: A History of the Turlock Region,* by Helen Alma Hohenthal et al., ed. John Edwards Caswell (Turlock, Calif.: City of Turlock, 1972), pp. 72–86; Helen Hohenthal and Helen Manha Miguel, "The Portuguese: An Important Element," *Streams in a Thirsty Land,* pp. 87–97.

5. Sarah Sergis Jackson and Victoria Yonan Nevils, "The Assyrians: Settlers from the Near East," *Streams in a Thirsty Land,* pp. 98–107; Helen Hohenthal, "Other Ethnic Groups," *Streams in a Thirsty Land,* pp. 126–29.

6. Ernestine Rojas, "Original Mexican Settlers," *Streams in a Thirsty Land,* pp. 120–25.

lation was engaged in agriculture: dairy farming, fruit and vegetable production, and related work in packing sheds and dehydrating plants.[7] By 1940, Livingston boasted a population of 1,000 within city limits and approximately 2,500 in the surrounding farm area.

Economic conditions varied between the ethnic minority and white populations of the Livingston area. Providing a comparison of living conditions of several local ethnic groups, Betty Frances Brown suggested that the most recently arrived peoples—the Japanese, Portuguese, and Mexicans—lived at a lower economic level than the longer established white groups. In addition, the populations of the new immigrants had grown more rapidly in the 1920s and 1930s than those of the Northern European stock residents. Although no job markets had developed locally in the two decades prior to the war, the construction of more canals made possible the irrigation of greater acreages and drew increasing numbers of farmers. By 1940, the Portuguese had prospered as dairy farmers, reaching a higher economic status than Mexicans, most of whom worked as laborers for Japanese and white farmers.[8] The majority of the Japanese owned or were buying their own land. The economic difference between the Mexicans and the Japanese may have derived in part from the fact that many of the Mexicans were initially drawn to the area as railroad and vineyard workers, whereas most of the Japanese came specifically to settle in the Abiko colonies. The proximity of the United States–Mexico border and the greater ease of return to their homeland perhaps encouraged the Mexicans, more than the Japanese, to view their work in "El Norte" as temporary. Also the anxieties and population fluctuation caused by the repatriation drives aimed at Mexican immigrants in the 1930s may have affected the development of the local Mexican American community.

The increase in the number of Japanese significantly altered the composition of the local elementary and high school populations. By 1942, of the 414 students from Livingston High School, 97 were Japanese American, as were nearly half of the 98 pupils from the Ballico Grammar School in Cortez.[9] Although the Yamato Colony was the

---

7. Betty Frances Brown, "The Evacuation of the Japanese Population from a California Agricultural Community," Master's thesis, Leland Stanford Junior University, June 1944, p. 71.

8. Ibid., pp. 27–28.

9. Ibid., p. 29.

largest of the three Japanese settlements, there were more Nisei in the Cortez elementary schools than in Livingston's, as might be expected considering the thirteen-year gap between these two settlements and the related differences in age. Even within the Cortez community, the experiences of the older Nisei differed somewhat from those of the younger, reflective of more than two decades of change within and outside the community.

In general, during the 1920s and 1930s, town life meant more modern conveniences than those found at farm residences, but there emerged considerable variation in rural living conditions. Thirty percent of the homes in the Livingston area of Merced County were without electricity in the 1940s; the local branch of the San Joaquin Light and Power Company only extended service to rural homes with a minimum number of electrical appliances. Homes were frequently heated by natural gas or wood and coal stoves.[10]

In the city, all homes had running water and indoor baths and toilets; in the rural area, a number of families, as did those in Cortez, pumped their water by hand, bathed in tin tubs, and had wooden outhouses built apart from the main house.[11] The condition of rural homes by the 1940s varied broadly, from "country estates replete with swimming pools and tennis courts to the many one-room shacks with no electricity or sanitary facilities."[12] According to Betty Brown, some of the Japanese and Portuguese homes were "modern, well-painted, and landscaped," but the majority were "barren, unpainted, and in complete contrast to the beautifully pruned and tended orchards and vineyards surrounding them." Brown added that on such ranches, often "the barns and poultry pens were in much better repair than the home."[13] By contrast she described Swedish houses as immaculate and well built, with flower gardens; Mexican homes, while unpainted and small, also usually had flower plots and goat pens.

Within the range of variation, the average Japanese home was a practical structure composed of a kitchen, front room, and two bedrooms. Outhouses were always separate and most families also had a separate Japanese-style bath (*ofuro*) in which a "metal tub was affixed to a platform raised over an oven in which fires could be built,"

10. Ibid., pp. 37, 44.
11. Ibid., p. 42.
12. Ibid., p. 44.
13. Ibid., p. 40.

enabling a whole family to bathe in one tubful of water.[14] The Japanese soaped, scrubbed and rinsed themselves before soaking in the *ofuro,* the precursor of the popular California "hot tub." Most of the Japanese, like their rural neighbors, had gas refrigerators and radios, usually equipped with shortwave apparatus to receive broadcasts from Japan. By the eve of World War II, three Cortez families had telephones.

The general cost of living in this rural area was somewhat lower than the state and national average, for a variety of reasons, including the low rental rates and the large proportion of owned homes. The practices of canning fruit and raising vegetables, of slaughtering poultry and wild game, and of gathering one's own fire wood also contributed to family independence. Certainly the Cortez families relied heavily on such economical measures.

Sociologists such as S. Frank Miyamoto and Harry H. L. Kitano have stressed the importance of the family as the basic unit of Japanese— and Japanese American—society. Kitano has characterized the traditional Japanese family as one marked by "strong solidarity, mutual helpfulness and a patriarchal structure," emphasizing filial piety, respect for age and authority, and a preference for male children.[15] This kind of family unit, he maintains, survived in a modified form during the early period of Issei settlement.

In addition to the family, the ethnic community became an important reference group in sanctioning and reproving individual behavior.[16] Central to social organization, according to Miyamoto, was a code of duties defining the roles and responsibilities of each member of that society. These obligations were enforced by the "Japanese belief in the superiority and greater importance of the group over the individual."[17]

Indeed, the key to the persistence of Japanese American ethnicity, according to Stephen S. Fugita and David O'Brien, lies in both group orientation and the long history of voluntary associations through which the immigrants structured social relations. In contrast to many European groups, the Japanese, like the Jews, arrived in this country with organizational networks extending beyond family and village.

14. Ibid., p. 41. Several Cortez families still enjoy soaking in their outdoor *ofuro.*
15. Kitano, p. 33.
16. Ibid., p. 36.
17. Miyamoto, p. 7.

Fugita and O'Brien suggest that participation in such associations has maintained community cohesiveness even while more visible features of ethnicity have waned.[18]

The children of Cortez, like their Nisei contemporaries, grew up with a strong sense of family and community ties, reinforced by overlapping institutional participation—in church, public school, Japanese school, the Cortez Growers Association, and the Cortez Young People's Club. These organizational networks, combined with the variable factors of age, gender, economic situation, and birth order in the family, shaped the individual's sense of identity and expectations.

Within the family, the Issei's values, labor, dreams, and frustrations molded the early lives of their daughters and sons.[19] The commitments and beliefs of the first generation in Cortez have in many ways continued to bind their children: to a farm, to a community, to ways of acting in the world. According to most Nisei, the Issei were strict parents. Stanford Lyman has argued that the Issei's child-rearing practices were "harsher than in Japan," partially because the Nisei lacked "the presence of an indulgent grandmother to counterbalance the severity of parental authority."[20] Second-generation women often recall their parents as being more strict than do their brothers, which reflects the somewhat narrower parameters of acceptable behavior for girls. Although the Nisei's lives were bounded by the demands of work and school, the boys had relatively more freedom than the girls, who had tasks within the home in addition to field labor and were often responsible for supervising younger siblings.

As Christie Kiefer has pointed out, in the society from which the Japanese immigrants came, mothers bore primary responsibility for the socialization of sons and daughters.[21] This pattern continued in the United States. Most of the interviewed Nisei (including those not

18. Stephen S. Fugita and David J. O'Brien, *Japanese American Ethnicity, The Persistence of Community* (Seattle: University of Washington Press, 1991), pp. 95, 104, 180.

19. Because the earliest Cortez pioneers had passed away and only a handful were left by the time I began my research, my perceptions of the Issei were largely filtered through the eyes of the Nisei, by memory and translation. In my interviews with eight Cortez Issei—six women and two men—and an Issei man from Livingston, I was fortunate to have the interpretive assistance of their children and friends. Even in the best of circumstances, however, something is inevitably lost in translation. The Nisei themselves are also limited in their command of the Japanese language and not always aware of the nuances and vocabulary familiar to a native of Japan.

20. Stanford M. Lyman, "Japanese-American Generation Gap," *Society,* January–February 1973, p. 60.

21. Kiefer, pp. 119–20.

reared in Cortez) felt closer to their mothers than to their fathers. It was the Issei women who interacted most with the children, exhorting, delegating, disciplining, and also sharing precious moments of leisure. Issei fathers tended to be more formal, aloof figures; the later age at marriage that often made them ten to fifteen years older than their wives may have contributed to their emotional distance from their children. By many accounts their wrath was greatly feared and respected. Some of the older Nisei men felt that they had escaped much punishment in the early settlement years because their hard-working parents were simply too busy to keep a constant eye on them. However, Takashi Date expressed the more common sentiment: "We certainly didn't want to get caught doing anything wrong—you'd never live through it!"[22] Other Nisei mentioned their parents' use of *yaito*, the Japanese practice of treating certain ailments by burning fibrous wads of a dried herb directly on the skin. However, for children, *yaito* was intended to cure misbehavior. One Nisei man explained that his parents would place the burning wad on the crack between the index and middle fingers; this left a blister which, until it healed, served as a painful reminder of disobedience. This punishment was meted out to boys and rarely, if ever, to their more constrained sisters.

The values the Issei instilled in their children served to channel their energies into work and education. The Cortez Nisei—like Nisei everywhere—were exhorted to study hard and to do their best in whatever they attempted. As Kitano has asserted, the Issei viewed these ideals as the key components to survival and success. "I don't know what other parents told their kids," said George Yuge, "but my mother— she was the dominant force in our family—always felt that no matter what kind of work you were going to do, you should excel at it." She said, he added, " 'As long as you try hard and you're honest, you'll never bring shame on yourself or your family.' "[23] The Issei placed great importance on effort and diligence as the means of betterment, but as May Kuwahara Sakaguchi pointed out, "Things like honesty and kindness—those things were stressed, too, because what is life without love for each other? It wasn't just getting ahead, and money."[24]

22. Takashi Date interview, Cortez, Calif., February 7, 1982.
23. George Yuge interview, Cortez, Calif., February 8, 1982.
24. May Sakaguchi interview, Cortez, Calif., March 10, 1982.

The Nisei were admonished to think not only of their family—
"family *ni haji ga aru"*—but also to remember that their actions would
reflect upon their community and Japanese people in general.[25] In
very immediate ways, the Nisei served as representatives and inter-
mediaries between their parents and the surrounding white society.
The Nisei often translated for their parents, and more frequently
interacted with non-Japanese Americans than did their parents, especially in the public schools. And by virtue of their American citizenship, they held the precious titles to the family farms.

Typical of most farm families, the Cortez family schedule revolved
around work. Children had farm chores before and after school. As
Brown observed in the early 1940s, "almost without exception, all
children *do* work."[26] In the first two decades of the community, work
sometimes took precedence over education. Some of the older Nisei
stayed home to provide the necessary labor, delaying, and in at least
one case preventing, their graduation from high school. In the early
1920s, the demands of fledgling farms resulted in shifting patterns of
classroom attendance in the grammar schools. On rainy days, parents
kept the small children at home while their older siblings attended
classes; on fair days, the older students worked in the fields while the
younger ones trudged off to school.

The nature of agriculture in Cortez demanded the labor of all family
members. In the prewar years, row crops—primarily strawberries,
eggplants, squash, onions, and carrots—constituted the mainstay of
Cortez's economy. Grapes were a major enterprise, but during the
Great Depression, row crops proved more valuable in meeting people's day-to-day needs. Vegetables and strawberries could be planted
and harvested annually, unlike grapes which took three or four years
to mature and produce a crop. The row crops, also known as "truck
crops," provided some income in the lean years, but they also served
as a main food source for the Cortez families, who often raised a few
chickens for private use.

The cultivation, picking, and packing of the vegetables and grapes
required a never-ending round of work. Strawberries were one of the
most labor-intensive crops. The Yamamoto family raised strawberry
plants, which meant "a lot of chores to do, all on our hands and knees.
We had to weed them, cut and set the 'runners,' irrigate them, and

25. Miyamoto, p. 30.
26. Brown, p. 73.

Ada and Leona Narita with grapes from the Narita farm, Cortez, October 1940.
Photo courtesy of Saburo Narita.

help pick them."[27] May and June were the months of strawberry harvest, followed by the eggplant harvest, as well as peaches and apricots, so the Nisei were kept busy making stacks of produce crates. Furthermore, all summer long, they nailed fifty-pound lug boxes in preparation for the grape harvest in the fall. May Sakaguchi recalled that there were always boxes to nail: "During the summer when I was home . . . I could nail them every day, but when school started in the fall, on weekends she [my mother] always wanted me to have a big

27. Kiyoshi Yamamoto interview, Cortez, Calif., February 6, 1982.

pile made! We used to be pretty fast. And then competition was quite a thing in those days. We would hear about so-and-so who could nail so many boxes in an hour," May laughed, "so we would all try."[28] Nailing boxes also offered a means of earning extra money; fast workers could make five dollars in a day for making four hundred crates. Besides making boxes and picking crops, in August they planted carrots, and later weeded and thinned them for harvest in December. In January the Japanese planted onions, to be harvested in June. During peak harvest times, the Nisei stayed home from school to help, as would their own children, a generation later. In addition to farmwork, there were also chores to do around the house. Water was pumped to fill the *ofuro* (Japanese bath) every day, and for the horses to drink.

Like other rural women, the Issei and Nisei women were engaged in farmwork in the Livingston–Cortez area. During the planting, pruning, and harvesting seasons women labored in the fields and orchards. During the packing and canning seasons, Brown found, they worked in the local packing sheds or went to nearby towns to do cannery work. She added, "The Japanese and Mexican women and girls work much harder and for longer hours in the family vineyards, fields, and orchards than do the women of any other racial groups."[29]

Within the Japanese household, there was a definite sexual division of labor in the area of domestic chores. Boys and girls alike grew up doing farmwork, but housework remained the private domain of women and girls. Many daughters of Cortez found dirty dishes waiting for them after school, and many were expected to help with cooking at an early age in order to give their mothers more time to work in the fields. There was always laundry to do, and ironing, for which irons had to be heated on top of the stove until electricity came to Cortez in the 1930s.

For the entire family, work began early in the morning and, during crucial harvest times, stretched long into the night. When the winery trucks came to pick up their grapes in the evening, Hiroshi Asai and his brothers might be loading the fifty-pound boxes of grapes into the grape tanks until ten o'clock at night. Like several Cortez families, the Taniguchi family filled orders for vegetables for a neighbor, Mr. Baba, who was a produce peddler. For the Taniguchis, this meant kneeling

28. May Sakaguchi interview, Cortez, Calif., March 10, 1982.
29. Brown, p. 36.

Yukihiro Yotsuya, Asaji Yotsuya, Frank Goi, and an unidentified man in the Yotsuya peach dry yard, 1941. Photo courtesy of Yukihiro Yotsuya.

on the frosty ground, their legs wrapped in burlap sacks for protection, pulling carrots or peeling green onions, often until midnight, so that the orders would be ready by morning.

In general, Issei parents held high standards for their oldest child. They expected him or her to set a good example, to keep an eye on younger siblings, and to shoulder a good deal of responsibility. Mae, the middle of the seven Taniguchi children, felt that her parents expected most of her oldest sister; she had the most work and responsibility. Of all the children, she stayed up to nail the last of the strawberry boxes. Similarly, Haruko Narita was often reminded by her parents that, as the *onesan*, or "oldest sister"—the male counterpart of which was *oniisan*—she must be reliable and steady. According to

Japanese custom, the oldest son, or *chonan*, would also inherit the family farm—the "home place"—or business and in return he and his family would care for his parents in their old age. In Cortez, this traditional passing of the mantle from one generation to the next occurred with increasing frequency after World War II as the Issei reached retirement age.

When not in the fields, the Cortez Nisei were usually in school. The first Cortez children attended the Madison School on the corner of Cortez and Bradbury avenues. When George Yuge and four other Nisei entered the Madison School in 1920, they swelled the number of students to a total of thirteen. Their first teacher, Nellie Armstrong, rode to school on horseback from her home in Ballico. On rainy days when her husband would bring her in a Model T Ford, her pupils would wait in front of the school for the thrill of seeing him give her a farewell kiss. The majority of the Cortez children attended the Ballico Grammar School, though some who lived closer to Vincent Road attended the Vincent School.

A number of the Cortez children drove to school. Many of them learned to drive at an early age, which enabled them to do tractor work in the fields and also meant that they could return home from school faster to help their parents. The older Nisei men recalled learning to drive by the age of seven or eight by steering tractors through fields. One Nisei was so small that he had to stand up and peer through the steering wheel in order to drive the family car, and he disappeared momentarily from sight when he stepped on the clutch with both feet. Some Nisei learned how to drive from their peers. May Sakaguchi was in the third grade when her friend Frances Yuge Kirihara gave her lessons on the Santa Fe highway and then along the canal bank by the Yuge home.

It was in grammar school that the Cortez Nisei, like most Japanese American children, first grappled with the English language. "We didn't know a word of English when we went to the first grade," said Kiyoshi Yamamoto, "and surprisingly, we learned, by hook or by crook."[30] Some of the Nisei were held back a grade or two until they had mastered English. In the struggle with language, the majority of their parents could not assist them. Issei like Kamiya Shizuko and Yuge Yei were rare in Cortez: the former may have studied English in

30. Kiyoshi Yamamoto interview, Cortez, Calif., February 6, 1982.

Japan; the latter learned to speak and read it while doing domestic work for a white family in Watsonville. Kamiya Shizuko's knowledge of plane geometry—probably gained in normal school in Japan—greatly impressed her son Mark, who remembered, "I thought she was pretty smart because some problems I couldn't figure, she'd work it out for me."[31] In general, the older children helped the younger. One Nisei recalled, "Some of the older kids were really after us, saying that we shouldn't speak Japanese. That's why I think we tried to Americanize . . ."[32] Like most Japanese Americans, the Cortez Nisei mainly spoke English with their siblings and friends and Japanese with their parents.

Like most Nisei on the West Coast, Cortez youth were sent by their parents to *nihongakko*—Japanese school—after public school hours, to receive a grounding in the language and culture of the Issei. Although they learned to write *hiragana* and *katakana* (the Japanese syllabaries) and a few *kanji* (Chinese characters), most report regretfully that they were not attentive pupils at the *nihongakko*. Their skill in English quickly outstripped their knowledge of Japanese. The language they spoke with their parents was an elementary form of Japanese, mixed liberally with English words. Because of the patterns and exigencies of everyday life, they seldom developed a deeper understanding. Today, as Bill Hosokawa, Robert A. Wilson, and Darrel Montero have suggested, many Nisei feel that they did not—and do not—have the close relationship with their parents that they have with their own children primarily because of this language barrier.[33]

Although a few Nisei became acquainted with the children of white neighbors, for the majority, grammar school provided the first experience of interaction with non-Japanese American peers.[34] Comprising from 30 to 45 percent of the student body in the prewar years, the Nisei

31. Mark Kamiya interview, Cortez, Calif., February 8, 1982.
32. Haruko Narita interview, Cortez, Calif., January 26, 1982.
33. Darrel Montero, *Japanese Americans: Changing Patterns of Ethnic Affiliation over Three Generations* (Boulder, Colo.: Westview Press, 1980), p. 21; Robert A. Wilson and Bill Hosokawa, *East to America: A History of the Japanese in the United States* (New York: Quill, 1982), p. 162.
34. Not all Japanese American children attended such racially mixed schools. A small number were relegated to legally, or de facto, segregated schools, the latter arising, as Hosokawa and Wilson have noted, from segregated housing patterns (p. 162). Legal segregation occurred, for instance, in Sacramento County in the 1920s; an example of de facto segregation is the Bailey Gatzert grade school in the Asian section of Seattle.

who attended the Ballico School report that they got along well with their classmates and teachers. They particularly remembered Frank Postill, the principal who took them to baseball games, and Florence Greenough, a teacher who was one of their staunchest and most outspoken advocates when wartime evacuation was imminent.

As numerous scholars have reported, the Japanese Americans were diligent, well-mannered students, regarded favorably by their teachers.[35] Yet even where they composed a large percentage of the school, they did not wholly escape interracial tensions or prejudice. "We were second-class citizens and second-class students," one Nisei remarked quietly. Another Nisei who attended the Vincent School related his bewilderment one Valentine's Day during the early 1920s. On the day that the children were exchanging one-cent valentines, the teacher came to his desk and picked up one of his cards. She angrily exclaimed, "Made in Germany!" threw his valentine on the floor and stepped on it. He observed that "I didn't know what the meaning was. So, you know, we [Nisei] had a lot to think around." This included initial friction between the Nisei and the other students, predominantly of Portuguese and Swedish descent. However, "In three or four years' time, the Portuguese families respected us. . . . In three or four years, we were bringing *onigiri* [rice balls] with *tsukemono* [Japanese pickles] inside, and trading with these Portuguese for their *linguizas* [sausages]."

Beneath the Nisei's diligence and manners ran a fierce competitive streak that found outlets in sports and scholarship. For instance, the games played during recess time at Ballico sometimes split into racially determined teams, according to one Nisei, "the whites against the Japs." He laughed and added, "We used to beat them all the time, so they decided, 'Better have a different set-up to choose sides—mixed teams.' We excelled in sports, we excelled scholastically." By the end of Cortez's second decade, a Nisei girl or boy was almost always the Ballico School valedictorian or salutatorian.

This competitiveness, according to John Connor, stemmed from a system of ranking that itself arose from the Japanese emphasis on hierarchy. Kitano, who described competitiveness as a characteristic

---

35. Brown, p. 106; Kitano, p. 25; John W. Connor, *Tradition and Change in Three Generations of Japanese Americans* (Chicago: Nelson-Hall, 1977), p. 301; Thomas James, *Exile Within, The Schooling of Japanese Americans, 1942–1945* (Cambridge: Harvard University Press, 1987), pp. 13–14.

value of the Japanese Americans, linked it with the ideal of personal excellence, fostered by family and community. When combined with the expectation of "eventual upward mobility,"[36] the drive to achieve, instilled by the Issei, became part of the impetus to overcome the status of "second-class student" and "second-class citizen." It was a tool to win respect in school. As one Nisei explained, "We were walked on so much that we *had* to be competitive, we *had* to be tough. If we got socked, we couldn't do anything about it. We'd just have to beat them in another way."[37]

This drive to achieve was firmly intertwined with a deep-rooted belief in the importance of education—a belief reinforced by family, community, and the Japanese associations. Most of the Cortez Nisei reported parental stress on academic achievement, although not all excelled in school. Hosokawa and Wilson have attributed the Issei's emphasis on education to the Confucian traditions. Influential in Japan since the seventeenth century, these teachings stressed loyalty over self, national goals before individual ones, and personal improvement through learning.[38] In addition, scholars have contended that the Issei, feeling economically limited by their own lack of formal training, viewed education "as the key to breaking through American discrimination," to gaining economic success and social status.[39] On the eve of World War II, after several years of teaching at the Livingston High School, Betty Brown remarked on the Issei's pride and ambition for their children, and that counsellors' "recommendations that a youngster change to shop, agricultural, homemaking, and non-academic courses were coldly received by Japanese parents."[40] She further observed that more Nisei went on to institutions of higher learning after high school than did white students. It must be noted that higher education, even for the minority who attained it, seldom

36. Kitano, p. 39, 136; Connor, *Tradition and Change*, p. 302. Chicana teacher and supervisor of an acclaimed folklorico dance group, Rosa Guerrero, born in 1934, described similar motivations behind her multifaceted high school achievements in El Paso, Texas. Her determination to surmount racial barriers and to excel in creative expression is vividly chronicled in an article by Vicki L. Ruiz, "Oral History and La Mujer: The Rosa Guerrero Story," in *Women on the U.S.–Mexico Border: Responses to Change*, ed. Vicki L. Ruiz and Susan Tiano (Boston: Allen & Unwin, 1987), pp. 219–31.

37. Takashi Date interview, Cortez, Calif., February 7, 1982.

38. Minako K. Maykovich, *Japanese American Identity Dilemma* (Tokyo: Waseda University Press, 1972), pp. 27–34.

39. Wilson and Hosokawa, p. 165; Montero, p. 64; Kitano, pp. 98–99.

40. Brown, p. 106.

guaranteed access to careers in white society. College graduates with degrees in engineering, business, and education might well end up working at fruit-stands or in fields, their aspirations blocked by racial barriers.

Their dreams still undimmed, the Cortez Nisei boarded the school bus for the thirteen-mile ride to the Livingston High School where they encountered new social situations. There they interacted not only with non-Japanese American peers and teachers, but also with the Nisei of the Livingston Yamato Colony. Most remembered the high school years as being laden with more tension and uncertainty than their grammar school days. The earlier challenges of wrestling with English and coming to terms with non-Japanese American classmates were replaced by adolescent change, concern for the future, and inevitable comparison with the more affluent and socially sophisticated Livingston Nisei.

Like most people, the Cortez Nisei have ambivalent feelings about their high school years (especially since about half of them spent those years in the Amache Relocation Camp during World War II). The older Nisei who came of age in the 1920s and early 1930s, when their parents most needed their labor, had little time for extracurricular activities. For them, high school was a space of time between work and work. They could not participate to the extent of their younger siblings. The majority of the Nisei interviewed for this study had entered or just graduated from high school by the outbreak of World War II; in 1942 the median age of the West Coast Nisei was eighteen and a half.[41]

When asked about their treatment in high school, the Nisei reported that the teachers liked them because they were well behaved and hard working. As in grammar school, one Nisei explained, this was their way of trying to become equal with others. In high school, they competed not only with the white students but with the Livingston Nisei.

The rivalry between the Japanese Americans of Cortez and Livingston had taken root before the Nisei met in high school—a rivalry stemming from the uncertain relations between the two communities during the intense anti-Japanese agitation of the 1920s. The Livingston Yamato Colony had had a thirteen-year lead on the Cortez Colony and

41. U.S. Department of the Interior, War Relocation Authority, *The Evacuated People, A Quantitative Description* (ca. 1946), p. 90.

had prospered during the post–World War I boom while the younger community struggled to establish farms and gain an economic toehold. The all-Methodist Yamato Colony had early developed ties with the white community in Livingston and enjoyed a degree of social acceptance rare among Japanese Americans. The situation in Livingston, for instance, contrasted sharply with the ethnic isolation of the prewar Japanese American community in San Francisco.[42] These differences, combined with a sense that the Yamato Colony settlers had a more highly educated background than the Cortez colonists, created a socioeconomic gap that resulted in tension, if not overt friction.

The Issei were particularly sensitive to class difference, a sense that filtered to their children in terms of education. Several Cortez Nisei perceived the unspoken Livingston-Cortez rivalry as stemming from the Yamato Issei's greater level of education, which provided more advantages for their children and made them "more cultured or more refined." One Cortez Nisei said: "It didn't really bother me because I felt as if I were just as intelligent as the Livingston Nisei were. But I've heard it said that we [Cortez Nisei] were known to be roughnecks— we didn't have much manners, or were crude and boorish." He added, "I think we *were* on the rough side," and chuckled when recalling two of his peers who were known to be handy with their fists.

Class differences among the Nisei manifested themselves in the formation of high school cliques. "In the schools," Brown reported, "the Japanese children had definite cliques which did not speak or mingle with any Japanese whom they felt to be of an inferior caste." As further evidence of class lines, Brown added that "at no time did any of the Livingston colony Japanese intermarry with any of the Cortez group." This observation suggests that the Livingston Issei preferred to arrange marital alliances elsewhere for their children.[43]

There were constant reminders of the economic differences between these two communities. According to one Cortez woman:

> Socially we couldn't keep up because there were some that were really much better off financially than we were. We were very poor in those days—this was the Depression. I remember one [Livingston] girl saying to me, "How come you keep wearing the same dress over and over?" I

42. Kiefer, p. 12; Kitano, pp. 25, 69, 71; Miyamoto, p. x.

43. Brown, p. 87. Several Cortez-Livingston marriages have occurred in the postwar period among the third generation.

just didn't have anything else to wear. I would wear one dress on Monday and Tuesday, and then it would go into the laundry. I'd have maybe another dress to wear Wednesday and Thursday, and on Friday maybe I'd be wearing the dress I wore Monday. That's just how it was.[44]

Despite the friendships among Cortez and Livingston Nisei, and ties of postwar intermarriage, a sense of disparity and competition has lingered to the present day.

The older Nisei, because they had little time for school activities and limited transportation, rarely socialized with the Livingston Nisei or non-Japanese Americans beyond class hours. By the end of the 1930s, however, the younger Nisei had more opportunities for participation in extracurricular activities, especially athletics. The boys played basketball and baseball, and went out for track, although their relatively smaller size prevented them from playing first-string football. The girls played volleyball and basketball. Edna Maeda Yamaguchi and May Sakaguchi reminisced warmly about the camaraderie among their Cortez basketball teammates Tomiye Baba, Rose and Mary Narita, Peggy Taniguchi, and two Atagi sisters. Their involvement in school athletics also provided an opportunity to transcend some community norms. "Actually we were what you call the *otembasans*, the tomboys," said May. "Lots of the other parents didn't feel that girls should be doing such things like that. But it was fun! We really got along well. . . . We had such great teamwork."[45]

In high school as in grammar school, the Cortez Nisei generally got along well with their peers and teachers, but they could not ignore discrimination. "There was quite a bit of prejudice all through school," said one man. "The trustees of the schools were all *hakujins* [whites] and so, somehow or other, we knew we weren't getting a fair shake. But we just kept quiet, and we tried to study as hard as we could."

The discrimination they faced took the form of omission—the "invisibility" that poet Mitsuye Yamada has termed an "unnatural disaster."[46] One Nisei said, "The teachers liked us because we were well

44. To protect the anonymity of the source of this interview and others hereafter, I have not revealed their identities. Hereafter I do not footnote their anonymous remarks.

45. May Sakaguchi interview, Cortez, Calif., March 10, 1982.

46. Mitsuye Yamada, "Invisibility Is an Unnatural Disaster: Reflections of an Asian American Woman," *This Bridge Called My Back, Writings by Radical Women of Color,* ed. Cherríe Moraga and Gloria Anzaldua (Watertown, Mass.: Persephone Press, 1981), pp. 35–40.

behaved and there were never any problems in class. But when it came to recognition, I think the non-Japanese got the recognition for honors." He remarked that in the year he graduated, shortly before the United States entered World War II, the high school principal decided to have the class presidents speak at graduation rather than a valedictorian, who would have been a Nisei. This interviewee himself, who had earned letters in track for all four years of high school, was not surprised when the senior honor in track was awarded to a Euro-American who had a letter for only one year.

The Japanese Americans were also keenly aware of the boundaries of permissible interracial socializing. Although many Cortez and Livingston Nisei developed close same-gender friendships with their non-Asian classmates, there existed clear limits to the extent to which cross-gender interracial friendships were socially acceptable. Few Cortez Nisei dated at all in the prewar years, and interracial dating was unthinkable for most. As Brown noted of high school dances: "Although several Japanese girls were quite popular with the white boys and danced often with them (they never dated one another, however), the Japanese boys never asked the white girls to dance. These boys did dance with white teachers but seemed to lack the courage to ask white girls to dance." Brown, oblivious to interracial sexual taboos, attributed this to the fear of refusal, shyness, or lack of self-confidence on the part of Nisei boys. She noticed, however, that no such hesitance hindered the white girls: "When girls' tag dances were called, these white girls often tagged some of the more popular and Americanized Japanese boys."[47] Serious liaisons were never even considered by either the Japanese Americans or the mainstream society, both of which, as Kitano has pointed out, held negative feelings about intermarriage.[48] Anti-miscegenation sentiment was so deeply entrenched in the dominant white culture that marriage between Asians and whites was illegal in California until after World War II.[49]

Given the constraints of work and school, in addition to economic limitations and racial barriers, the youths of Cortez most often sought recreation within their own community. When they could snatch the time, they invented diversions. Children carved samurai swords out

47. Brown, p. 87.
48. Kitano, pp. 106–7.
49. For a discussion of the antimiscegenation laws and their application to Asian Americans, see Osumi, pp. 1–37.

of broken grape stakes and made toys out of wood scraps. They also swam in the irrigation canals on their way home from school in the spring and in the blistering San Joaquin Valley summers; occasionally they were joined by overheated parents. To this day, the third generation still likes to cool off in the canals, and there have only been two swimming pools built in Cortez homes. The Nisei also played games like mumbletypeg and kick-the-can. Baseball was a community favorite, and many Issei and Nisei would turn out to watch their team play on the diamond by the Education Society (the Gakuen).

Electricity did not arrive in Cortez until the 1930s, but once it did, families wasted little time in buying radios. Like their neighbors, the Nisei listened to popular programs of the day: Amos 'n Andy, Fibber Magee and Molly, Jack Benny, and Jack Armstrong, the All-American Boy. Their movie heroes were mostly cowboys like Tom Mix, Gene Autry, and Roy Rogers. Shirley Temple, Fred Astaire, and Ginger Rogers were also favorites whom they enjoyed watching on rare jaunts to the Fox Theater in Turlock, the nearest town. Telephones were less common than radios in Cortez; only three families had telephones until after World War II. Kiyoshi Yamamoto still chuckles to think of the neighbor who used to come to his house to telephone his girl friends.

Except for a few of the men who came of age just prior to the Great Depression and who held jobs that gave them mobility beyond the community (e.g., truck driving), the Cortez Nisei dated only other Japanese Americans. In fact, the majority did very little dating at all in the prewar years, since rural Issei parents—Christian and Buddhist alike—viewed this activity with suspicion and disapproval. Haruko Narita and her sisters were not allowed to "go out," except for club or group activities, which were also limited by the demands of farmwork. Others found the prospect of one-on-one socializing unnerving; as one Nisei man remembered, laughing, "I was scared to date! I was afraid of girls."

During the 1920s, as Miyamoto found in the Seattle Japanese American community, the major arena for socializing was the church. This seemed particularly true for the Presbyterians, who held religious services every week and offered special programs. The Buddhists, who did not have a church building until just before the war, held services once a month in a private home, presided over by a visiting minister from Stockton. The Buddhist and Christian Nisei got along more amiably than the Issei, although they tended to be closest to friends from their own churches. This trend was influenced in large part by geographic distribution: the majority of Christian families lived on the south side of the Santa Fe railroad tracks; most of the Buddhists lived on the north side.

The seasons of work were punctuated by holidays, which brought both families and the community together. The major holiday in Cortez—as for most Japanese Americans—was New Year's. In preparation, families gathered with their closest friends or relatives for *mochitsuki*—to pound rice in a large mortar with pestles and then to shape the sticky dough into small cakes. New Year's, or *Oshogatsu*, was sometimes celebrated for three days, during which the menfolk would visit other households and everyone would partake of the painstakingly prepared traditional dishes, like chicken *teriyaki, ozoni* (a soup containing the pounded rice cakes, symbolizing prosperity), *mame* (beans, symbolic of good health), and *sushi* (flavored rice rolled in sheets of toasted seaweed or stuffed into soybean wrappers). In the prewar years, the whole community of Cortez would get together on one day to celebrate New Year's, potluck style, at the Gakuen.

Religious holidays were observed as regularly as possible in Cortez. The Christians gave a special church program on Christmas day and, when they could afford it, a "Santa" would distribute small gifts to the Sunday School children. The Cortez Christians also gathered on Thanksgiving for a big turkey dinner at the church. In the late 1930s, when they began to hold services at the Gakuen, the Buddhists had a special service for *Hana Matsuri*, to commemorate the birth of Buddha, and celebrated the *Obon* festival with traditional folk dancing. Some of the Presbyterians came to watch and join.

Community celebrations were more frequent than individual family occasions. Cortez residents rarely celebrated birthdays during the 1920s, as this custom was unknown in Japan. Birthday cakes were also not part of most Issei's culinary repertoire. One Issei woman recounted how she would stack pancakes and write the birthday child's name on the top with food coloring, to create a birthday "keiki." By contrast, everyone attended the annual community picnic in April or May, adults to chat with friends and children to participate in games and races. At an annual outing, the community gathered to honor recent graduates from grammar school and high school.

The Cortez Nisei created their own social outlet in November 1934 with the formation of the Cortez Young People's Club (CYPC), open to all Nisei of high school age or older. The first meeting of the CYPC took place at the Cortez Gakuen, under the sponsorship of the Japanese language school teacher Mr. Kobayashi and under the temporary chairmanship of George Morofuji, a Cortez Nisei.[50] The CYPC, as Kitano observed generally of such groups, did indeed provide valuable opportunities for the second generation to gain leadership experience, to set their own goals, to retain ethnic identity, and to build a sphere of social participation from which they were barred in the white community.[51] The development of the CYPC illustrates the joint cultivation of ethnic solidarity and the adoption of certain elements of mainstream culture.

The formation of the CYPC also evidenced the growing number and maturation of the second generation. By 1940, Brown stated, Nisei constituted two-thirds of the Japanese American population in the Livingston area. By the time war broke out, 65 Nisei had signed the CYPC membership roster.[52] The CYPC minutes, faithfully recorded by a series of male and female secretaries from November 10, 1934, to January 20, 1942, reveal not only a dogged adherence to parliamentary procedure but also the development of the Nisei's role in community affairs and the changes that occurred in their relationship with the Issei. The minutes also provide a glimpse, between the lines, of some of the Nisei who later assumed leadership positions in the CGA, the churches, and in two postwar organizations, the social Young Married Group and the more political Japanese American Citizens League (JACL).

The CYPC planned Japanese cultural events as well as American sports and community service projects. The primary activities of the CYPC were athletic. It sponsored boys' baseball and basketball teams known as the Cortez Wildcats and a girls' basketball team, the Cherry

50. The first officers elected on December 8, 1934, were Takashi Date, president; Chizuko Narita, vice-president; Kenso Miyamoto, recording secretary; Keiji Date, corresponding secretary; George Morofuji, treasurer; Seio Masuda, assistant treasurer; and Nobuhiro Kajioka, sergeant-at-arms. The initial membership fee was 25 cents, and the monthly dues were ten cents. CYPC Minutes, p. 3.

51. Kitano, pp. 67–68.

52. The CYPC's constitution reflected a strong sense of community ties and obligations, declaring that its purpose was to "activate sponsor and promote the welfare of the young peoples in this community and to initiate such other projects as may be of service to the local community." This description served as an umbrella for a wide range of activities and functions, from the CYPC's inception until the World War II internment.

The Cortez Nisei in costume for the Turlock Melon Carnival parade, August 1931, posing in front of the Cortez Educational Society Hall. Front row, seated left to right: Mrs. Yuge, Kiyoko Ogata, June Morimoto, Peggy Taniguchi, Masae Kubo, Miyoko Sakaguchi, Rose Narita, Buichi Kajiwara, Ernest Yoshida, Ray Yuge, Fred Miyamoto, Tsutomu Sugiura, Jim Yamaguchi, Susumu Yenokida, and Hiro Asai. Middle row, standing, left to right: Mrs. Shimizu, Sachiko Kimura, Grace Narita, Matsuye Miyamoto, Frances Yuge, Jean Morimoto, Shizuma Kubo, Dorothy Kajioka, Y. Sugiura, Naoko Kajioka, Bob Morimoto, Yeichi Sakaguchi, Eddie Nakagawa, Tom Inano, Kaoru Masuda, and Henry Kajioka. Back row, left to right: Aiko Ogata, Mari Shimizu, Tomiye Baba, Edna Maeda, Yaeko Yotsuya, Clara Yamaguchi, Mr. Yotsuya, Frank Date, Key Kobayashi, Jack Nakagawa, Yoshio Asai, and Ben Yenokida. Photo courtesy of Pat Sugiura.

Blossoms.[53] The CYPC was also linked through the Gakuen with the Kendo Club, which practiced the martial art of Japanese fencing. Each

53. The only recorded complaint of the Issei regarding the CYPC was that the Nisei were not coming home early enough from baseball and basketball games. CYPC Minutes, p. 113.

In May 1939 the Cortez baseball team beat Lodi, 6–0. The Cortez Wildcats were the only team in a league of six Japanese American teams to own their own ballpark. Posing after the Cortez-Lodi game are, front row, from left: George Tashiro, George (Cobby) Kajioka, Ernest Yoshida (manager), Nobuhiro (Nogi) Kajioka, Henry (Hank) Kajioka, and Yukihiro (Yuk) Yotsuya. Back row, from left: Keichi (Deacon) Yamaguchi, Yeichi Sakaguchi, Fred (Pinto) Kajioka, Shizuma (Shiz) Kubo, Kaoru Masuda, Kaname (Ben) Miyamoto, Bill Noda, and Minoru (Min) Yenokida. Photo courtesy of Yukihiro Yotsuya.

year the CYPC usually staged a Japanese play and also planned a skating party, or, by the end of the 1930s, a snow outing at Yosemite. The members also handled tasks like watering walnut trees and chopping wood for the Gakuen.

The structure of the CYPC exemplified the patterns of action that have proved crucial to the survival and growth of the Cortez Colony. All of their activities, from baseball to wood chopping, were organized through committees delegated to clean the baseball diamond, to prepare refreshments, to sell tickets, to plan entertainment for meetings, or to carry out whatever tasks should arise. These rotating committees have remained the basis of efficient activity within the Cortez community organizations today; they give every member the opportunity—and the responsibility—to participate.

The minutes of the CYPC rarely mention conflict, although two instances suggest how it was handled when it did occur. In January 1937, Mr. Kubota, a teacher and advisor in the Japanese School, gave a speech, after which the club's secretary noted: "In this club there shall be no relegion [sic] matter to be brought up by anyone."[54] As the club composition remained a mixture of Christians and Buddhists, a "live and let live" philosophy seems to have prevailed over any religious differences.

In March of the same year, a gender-defined rift proved more difficult to reconcile when "the girls moved out from the club." The recording secretary did not specify their reasons, but observed that they were "pretty good." This matter was less easily handled, for women's names did not appear in the lists of officers or committees again until 1939. In 1942, its last year, the CYPC elected not only President Albert Morimoto but also a Girls' Vice-President, May Kuwahara, and a Boys' Vice-President, Yeichi Sakaguchi.[55]

Through the CYPC, the Nisei developed skill in cross-generational relations. From its beginning, the group maintained close ties with the first generation, choosing Issei advisors shortly after electing its first officers. In 1937 it was decided not to have official advisors, unless the Issei organization, the Colony-kai,[56] sent a representative; however, cooperation with the Issei continued in joint activities. Teachers from the Japanese School in particular remained involved with the CYPC, and Mr. Kobayashi and Mr. Yoshida regularly supervised the CYPC's Japanese theatrical productions.

Indicative of change and continuity in community needs, some of the Issei's and Nisei's joint activities persisted beyond the war years, and others did not. One of the latter was the *zadan-kai*. In 1935, the CYPC held its first *zadan-kai* (a symposium or roundtable gathering) to

54. CYPC Minutes, p. 54.
55. The other CYPC officers in the last year were Chidori Shiotani, recording secretary; Rose Narita, corresponding secretary; Yukihiro Yotsuya, treasurer; Frank Yoshida, assistant treasurer; Mac Yamaguchi, social chairman; Merry Atagi, assistant social chairman; George Kajioka, sergeant-at-arms; Asaji Yotsuya, assistant sergeant-at-arms.
56. None of the Issei or Nisei I interviewed provided any substantive information about the Colony-kai. Unfortunately, the Issei men who had played an active part in the organization had died long before my project began.

which all "the old folks of 60 years or over" were invited as "honorable guests." The diversion of the evening was an open discussion of the relationship between "the old and the younger generations." The topic of another *zadan-kai* in 1936 was "The Present and Future Problems of the Young People." These prewar *zadan-kai* mirrored urban Japanese American discussions of intergenerational dynamics and the future of the Nisei. Other social events have become Cortez traditions, including the annual community picnic and the June celebration to honor Cortez graduates from grammar school, high school, and college.

As the Nisei grew older and the approach of war made the position of the Japanese Americans increasingly uncertain, the relationship between the CYPC and the Issei's Colony-kai shifted. In 1941, the CYPC began to send representatives to the Issei's meetings. And in the last two recorded meetings of the CYPC in January 1942, the CYPC prepared to take over the Colony-kai's work, since the Issei were not permitted to hold meetings or to travel. The Nisei also decided to form an additional group—the Cortez Citizens League, open to Nisei of eighteen years or older—to handle the wartime affairs of the community. In the faded ink of these matter-of-fact entries is recorded the passage of authority in Cortez—a passage prematurely precipitated by the external forces of American history. Through the CYPC the Nisei began to exercise the decision-making skills necessary for community building. At this time, they also began to make decisions about their personal lives.

Like the majority of Nisei, the young men and women of Cortez anticipated a future of work and marriage. Oldest sons were expected to continue farming with their parents, and most did. Many Nisei—women as well as men—left Cortez to seek jobs. Most of the men pursued work related to agriculture; the majority of the women did domestic work, as other positions proved hard to come by. Here the work patterns of the Cortez women correlate with the sociological research of Evelyn Nakano Glenn, who found that, in the prewar period, the most common form of nonagricultural labor for both Issei and Nisei women was domestic service.[57] In Cortez, the Narita sisters exemplified this pattern, although they were unusual in that their employers were Japanese government and business executives: of

57. Glenn, "The Dialectics of Wage Work," pp. 432–71.

four who went to San Francisco, one worked in the home of a Mitsu-
bishi manager, one worked for a Mitsui official, another found a position in the home of a Sumitomo bank officer, and the fourth worked for
the Japanese consul general. A few Nisei women acquired training for
other jobs: Yuri Yuge became a nurse, and Yuki Kuwahara, after
attending a Methodist school in San Francisco, worked as a youth
director at various churches on the West Coast.

Despite the economic limitations and social barriers, a number of
Cortez Nisei began to attend college. In 1941, the honorees of the
annual graduation party included five college students from the Modesto Junior College, the California Polytechnic Institute at San Luis
Obispo, and the University of California at Berkeley. In the fall of the
same year, two Nisei guest speakers offered CYPC members advice
about schools.

Like most Japanese Americans, the Cortez Nisei also expected their
future to include marriage. Nisei and Issei alike expected that they
would marry other Japanese Americans. Some of the older Nisei entered arranged, or semi-arranged, marriages. In the instance of Takeo
Yotsuya and Edith Goi, the Cortez Yotsuya family and the Goi family
of Sacramento knew each other because both were from Fukui-ken in
Japan. Mrs. Yotsuya passed away at an early age, leaving seven children, of whom the youngest was twelve years old. Someone was
needed to take care of the family, so "they asked for me," Edith
explained. She and Takeo were married in 1938 at the Cortez Presbyterian Church, and, despite the ice-cream-melting heat of July, the
whole community attended.

In another example of traditional marriage arrangements, Haruko
Narita and Tachiki Saburo were introduced to each other by a *baisha-
kunin*, or go-between, Mr. Yoneyama, a neighbor of the Naritas who
had helped the family a great deal after Mr. Narita's death in 1931. Mr.
Yoneyama and Saburo were both from Odawara-machi in Kanagawa-
ken, Japan, and Saburo had worked for a nephew of Mr. Yoneyama in
Newark, California. Because there were seven daughters in the Narita
family and no sons, Saburo became a *yoshi*, taking the Narita name so
that the family line would not disappear.[58]

The majority of the Cortez Nisei—like their non-Japanese contem-

58. In Japan, a family lacking sons might resort to the practice of adopting one, or
securing a son-in-law who would agree to take the family name to ensure its continuation. An adopted son or man thus marrying into a family was termed a *yoshi*.

poraries—chose their own marriage partners, in accordance with mainstream American notions of romance and personal preference. The Nisei version of companionate marriage, as Sylvia Yanagisako has suggested, synthesized American and Japanese ideals: The desire for romantic affection was combined with expectations of duty and commitment.[59] Of the fifty-six Nisei interviewed—all of them married—only ten had had arranged marriages, and of the ten, six were married before World War II.[60] All of their marriages, arranged or not, have endured—a source of community pride. To my knowledge, only one Nisei living in Cortez has been divorced.[61]

The Cortez Issei expected their children to marry other Japanese Americans, and almost all did, like the vast majority of Nisei. George Yuge recalled his mother telling him, " 'We're in America now,' so . . . it didn't matter what kind of girl I married, what nationality or anything. She said that to me, but she didn't mean it." In high school, when George became friends with a young woman of half-Japanese, half-Mexican parentage, he found that "what she [my mother] said and what she meant were two different things entirely."[62] Eventually George pleased his parents by marrying Helen Matsuda, a Nisei from Watsonville. Most of the Cortez Nisei discerned no such parental ambivalence: the message was clear. The dominant society transmitted an equally unmistakable message: California law prohibited interracial marriage until 1948. Only a handful of Cortez Nisei have married interracially—primarily Euro-Americans—and they did so after the war; they are also among the youngest in their generation, being closer in age to the Sansei. Even in the postwar period, the Issei strongly opposed the first interracial marriages.

Creating a niche in the world required a great deal of cultural synthesis by the Nisei, who grew up integrating the values of their par-

---

59. Yanagisako, pp. 107–8.
60. Only nine of the fifty-six interviewees married before World War II.
61. A number of scholars, including Stephen Fugita and David O'Brien, have noted the low divorce rates among Japanese Americans historically. They and others have posited that these rates will rise as the incidence of interracial marriage increases among the third and fourth generations. For statistical data, see Fugita and O'Brien, chap. 8, "Intermarriage," pp. 130–40. Also helpful is an article by Harry H. L. Kitano, Wai-Tsang Yeung, Lynn Chai, and Herbert Hatanaka, "Asian American Interracial Marriage," *Journal of Marriage and the Family* 46(1984):179–90.
62. George Yuge interview, Cortez, Calif., February 8, 1982.

ents with the ways of the country's mainstream society. They worked and studied hard, believing these to be the primary tools of betterment. Public education introduced them into the larger local community and, especially as they entered adolescence, honed their awareness of social boundaries of race and class. Class differences colored intraethnic as well as interracial relations. While the Nisei might live and work within a Japanese American enclave, they were also attuned to the rhythms of popular culture. Like other teenagers they hummed favorite songs heard on the radio and found fodder for their dreams in the silver-screen adventures and romances purveyed by Hollywood. Prewar marriage practices reflected the growing influence of American ideals of love and individualism; although some Nisei entered arranged marriages as had their parents, a number of their peers insisted on choosing their own mates. The Nisei youth observed both American and Japanese celebrations, and participated in the formation of their own community's holidays and organizations. The Cortez Young People's Club illustrates their synthesis that encompassed baseball, kendo, girls' basketball, skate fests, and wiener roasts as well as Japanese dramas and the *zadan-kai* evenings. The structure of the CYPC also mirrored the patterns of community organization that have persisted to this day. Rotating committees and offices—whether delegated to plan a picnic, to investigate the building of a meeting hall, or to handle the arrangements for a funeral—have remained the flexible bases of activity in the CGA, the churches, the Japanese American Citizens League, and the Shinwakai (senior citizens' group). The strength of these community and family bonds, developed in the colony's first two decades, enabled them to endure the hardships of their pioneering days and the lean depression years. The crucial test would come, however, during World War II.

CHAPTER 3

Merced
Assembly Center

December 7, 1941, was the day that Sam and Florice Kuwahara had chosen to hold their wedding reception. Married in May at the start of the busy summer-produce season, they had decided to postpone the reception until a more convenient time after the fall harvest. Because Sam was the manager of the Cortez Growers Association and Florice a member of the large Morimoto family, nearly the entire Cortez community of 262 had been invited to enjoy catered Chinese food at the American Legion Hall in Merced. Their preparations were interrupted by a phone call from the sheriff's department, notifying them that such a celebration would be inappropriate on the day of the Japanese bombing of Pearl Harbor. In the midst of their shock over the bombing and the entry of the United States into World War II, the Kuwaharas canceled the reception in Merced and made hasty plans to hold it at the Gakuen in Cortez, since all the food had been cooked and delivered. By five o'clock that afternoon, however, the local authorities forbade them to gather at the Educational Society Building.

Helen and George Yuge had driven down from Watsonville with their daughter Lynn and Helen's sister to attend the wedding reception. It was an unusually warm day for December, and they decided to stop in Turlock first for refreshment. Four-year-old Lynn, one of the first Sansei—third-generation Japanese Americans—put money in the jukebox to hear a record she liked. The Yuges were puzzled by the angry stares directed at them by other customers, until they heard the radio announce that Japan had bombed Pearl Harbor. They froze.

On December 7, Hiroshi Asai and his brothers had loaded up a truck with their extra carrots—the culls that were not good enough for the produce market—to be sold to local farmers for cow feed. They usually went to Turlock, going from dairy to dairy to see if anyone would buy the culls. At one dairy they were asked, "Are you Japanese or Chinese?" When they informed the dairy owner of their ancestry, they suddenly found he didn't want any of their carrots. This struck them as a strange reaction; then they returned home and "found out there was a war on."

In 1941, Mark Kamiya was in San Luis Obispo. He had completed one year of agriculture courses at the California Polytechnic Institute and was financing his own education by working part time. Enjoying college and being away from home for the first time, he felt accepted by his fellow students. Mark had spent the early morning working at the university farm on that fateful day. When he came back to the cafeteria for breakfast, another student told him that Pearl Harbor had been bombed. "I wondered what was going to happen to me. . . . I knew I'd be deeply involved because I was Japanese."

By the end of the day, the shock waves had rippled through Cortez as they had through many Japanese American communities in the West. In an atmosphere of growing confusion and alarm, Sam and Florice's relatives gathered at their Issei parents' homes to eat together, and the rest of their Cortez friends and neighbors brought pots and pans so that the vast quantities of Chinese food could be distributed. Then people went home quietly to reflect on how deeply they might be involved in the war. Soon, because of the way the government chose to view Japanese immigrants and their families, they would be more profoundly affected than they imagined.

In the aftermath of Pearl Harbor, the Cortez community endured the ordeal experienced by almost all of the Japanese in the western United States: curfews, travel restrictions, searches and arrests by the Federal Bureau of Investigation (FBI), hostility and harassment from neighboring Euro-Americans, confiscation of firearms and radios, and the agonizing preparation for an "evacuation" of unpredictable duration. The Japanese Americans of the Livingston–Cortez area first went to the temporary Merced Assembly Center in May of 1942 and then in August and September to the Granada Relocation Camp (Amache) in

Colorado—one of ten concentration camps set up by the War Relocation Authority (WRA).[1]

Because of the chaos of the evacuation period, the brief time allowed
for preparations, and the uncertainty of their return, the vast majority
of Japanese Americans in the West lost the leases for rented farmlands
and were forced to dispose of homes and businesses. Others fearfully
liquidated property into ready cash for emergency needs. Of the approximately 6,000 established Japanese farm operators removed by
evacuation, 30 percent were landowners.[2] In the judgment of Leonard
Broom and John L. Kitsuse, this uprooting of urban and rural Japanese
Americans "virtually eliminated the prewar community."[3]

In contrast, because of their cooperative origins and strong community institutions, Abiko Kyutaro's three colonies—Cortez, Cressey,
and Livingston—avoided this fate. The people of these colonies negotiated a unique economic arrangement that provided for the supervision of all their farms during their absence. The combined efforts of the
three Japanese American cooperative associations—the Cortez Growers Association (CGA), the Livingston Fruit Growers Exchange, and
the Livingston Fruit Growers—enabled the Issei and Nisei to maintain
not only economic stability but also a remarkable degree of social
cohesion during the evacuation. The growers' associations ensured
that the Cortez Japanese Americans would have homes to return to at
the end of the war.

Powerful forces influenced internment and shaped the experiences
of the Cortez people from the chaotic days after Pearl Harbor to their
departure from California. The impact of their interim stay in the
Merced Assembly Center prefigured the crude communal living conditions and hardship they would encounter in the Colorado relocation
camp. Amid these trials, shared with the majority of Japanese Ameri-

---

1. These camps were located in: Manzanar and Tule Lake, California; Poston and
Gila, Arizona; Minidoka, Idaho; Heart Mountain, Wyoming; Granada, Colorado;
Topaz, Utah; Rohwer and Jerome, Arkansas. Roger Daniels, *Concentration Camps: North
America, Japanese in the United States and Canada During World War II* (Malabar, Fla.: Robert
E. Krieger, 1981); Wilson and Hosokawa, p. 212; Michi Weglyn, *Years of Infamy: The
Untold Story of America's Concentration Camps* (New York: William Morrow, 1976), pp. 86,
176–77.

2. Adon Poli and Warren M. Engstrand, "Japanese Agriculture on the Pacific Coast,"
The Journal of Land & Public Utility Economics 21(November 1945):359–60.

3. Leonard Broom and John Kitsuse, *The Managed Casualty: The Japanese-American
Family in World War II* (Berkeley: University of California Press, 1956), p. 46.

cans, the actions of individuals and cooperative associations pre-
served both community networks and the idea of community.

December 7 was followed by a swift series of jolts to Japanese
Americans on the West Coast. On December 8, a government order
froze the Issei's bank assets. Unchecked rumors spread through Hawaii and the mainland that Japanese Americans had somehow collabo-
rated in the bombing of Pearl Harbor. The FBI began to arrest Issei
community leaders suspected of being pro-Japan. Politicians and journalists in the western states warned against possible fifth-column
activity by Japanese Americans and called for stringent measures to
prevent it.

The American public, Robert A. Wilson and Bill Hosokawa have
maintained, was not initially antagonistic toward the Japanese Americans.[4] Many factors contributed to the growing atmosphere of suspicion and fear, including "guilt by association," fueled by resurfacing
anti-Asian sentiments on the West Coast. At the same time, business
competitors scented the "opportunity for a quick takeover from the
Japanese Americans."[5] Although the flag-waving "campaign of hate
and vilification" by the press and politicians did not arouse great
public outcry for the removal of the Japanese Americans, it influenced
the decisions of military leaders and other government officials.

In the Cortez area there also existed a history of anti-Asian sentiment, but over two decades the Japanese American community had
taken root. By 1940, there were 715 native and foreign-born Japanese
among the 46,988 residents of Merced County. Of these, approximately 600 lived in the three Abiko colonies, comprising 6 percent of
the population in the Livingston area of Merced County.[6]

At first, the people of Cortez hoped to stay and weather this uneasy
period in the familiar surroundings where they had established their
families. The local newspaper evidenced their inclusion in local war-

4. Wilson and Hosokawa, p. 189.
5. Ibid., p. 190.
6. U.S. Census, 1940. These figures come from the Merced County Township 5
statistics. Livingston, Cortez, and Cressey are all located within the boundaries of
Township 5, which in 1940 had 8,466 inhabitants. Betty Frances Brown, the Livingston
High School teacher who studied the local Japanese Americans for her Master's thesis,
indicated that approximately 600 people lived in the Abiko colonies and constituted
about 6 percent of the Livingston area population. Some of her detailed data on the local
racial-ethnic composition does not appear in the 1940 census; Brown may have received
this information from census takers in Livingston.

time defense activities as well as the governmental restrictions to which they were subject. Early in 1941, for example, a Civilian Defense Unit, composed of both Nisei and non-Japanese, was formed to cover the Delhi-Ballico-Cortez area. Home-front activities increased when the United States entered the war. In January and February of 1942, the Cortez community took part in a Red Cross membership drive, and ethnically mixed groups met for classes in first aid and home nursing.[7]

Meanwhile, a gulf began to develop between the Japanese Americans and their neighbors. In January, the "Japanese and Italian people" of the Livingston and Cressey area, in compliance with a federal order, went to the office of the Livingston chief of police, Horace Gilbert, and turned over their cameras, radios, and firearms. The police removed the shortwave connections from thirty-six radios and returned them to their owners.[8] This order was followed at the end of February by the registration of 361 "enemy aliens" at the Livingston justice court. In March, by order of the head of the Western Defense Command, Lieutenant General John L. DeWitt, curfew hours were set for "all enemy aliens and American born Japanese." They were required to remain home between eight P.M. and six A.M. every day; failure to comply meant a penalty of $5,000 or one year's imprisonment, or both.

As happened in many Japanese American communities, the FBI questioned some of the Issei men of Cortez; the agents also searched a number of homes, apparently looking for weapons. Even those who were not searched or interrogated recalled the FBI agents cruising past their homes or parking in their driveways. At this time, the FBI began to seize Issei leaders suspected of pro-Japan loyalties; many were sent to internment centers run by the U.S. Department of Justice. Because the existence of these camps fell under wartime censorship, little information could be obtained about them. These camps, most of which were considered temporary, were located in Arizona, California, Idaho, Massachusetts, Montana, New Mexico, North Dakota, Texas, and Wisconsin.[9]

Cortez did not escape the arrests that seized from the Japanese

7. *Livingston Chronicle*, January 22, 1942 and February 12, 1942.
8. *Turlock Journal*, January 2, 1942.
9. Weglyn, pp. 176–77. It is very difficult to locate information about the Justice Department detention camps and the camps run by the Immigration and Naturalization Service; much is still classified information. *Personal Justice Denied*, the most recent official account, makes only passing mention of these camps; no details are given in this report from the Commission on Wartime Relocation and Internment of Civilians (Washington, D.C.: U.S. Government Printing Office, 1982).

American communities their established leaders. Kajiwara Hajime and his family had lived in Pismo Beach, California, where he operated a trucking company until 1936, when the family moved to Cortez to farm. In 1942, suddenly and without explanation, the FBI seized quiet, well-respected Hajime; his family did not see him again until the end of the war. He spent the next three years in a series of Justice Department internment camps designated for male Issei leaders. He was sent first to Santa Fe, New Mexico, then to Fort Bliss, Texas, and finally to Lordsburg, New Mexico. In Lordsburg there were sixty Issei, a sizable number of them Buddhist and Christian ministers. Hajime, one of the youngest, tried to salvage what he could from this painful experience by availing himself of the opportunity to learn from these experienced community leaders.[10]

Issei and Nisei in the United States were not the only ones to suffer seizure and incarceration. One hundred and fifty-one Alaskan Japanese—many half-Eskimo—were also interned under Executive Order 9066. Canada removed its 23,000 Japanese to work camps in the mountainous interior; Japanese in Mexico, Haiti, and the Dominican Republic met a similar fate.[11] The virtual kidnapping of Japanese immigrants in Central and parts of South America, chronicled by C. Harvey Gardiner and by Michi Weglyn, was particularly tragic. Due to the U.S. State Department's initial fears concerning hemispheric security, and then because leaders like Secretary of State Cordell Hull wanted to have ready hostages to exchange for Americans in Japanese-occupied territories, these Latin American Japanese were also rounded up and shipped to the United States. Here they were incarcerated in secret detention centers run by the Immigration and Naturalization Service, separate from those of the Japanese Americans.[12]

10. In *Years of Infamy*, Michi Weglyn includes an examination of several of the primarily male internment camps as well as two "Citizen Isolation Camps" to which feared "dissidents" were sent. Both Weglyn and C. Harvey Gardiner, in *Pawns in a Triangle of Hate: The Peruvian Japanese and the United States* (Seattle: University of Washington Press, 1981), discuss the tragic fate of Japanese immigrants in South America, who were also interned in "special" camps in the United States.

11. Weglyn, pp. 54–56. For an examination of the experiences of the Japanese Americans in Alaska, see Claus-M. Naske, "The Relocation of Alaska's Japanese Residents," *Pacific Northwest Quarterly* 74(July 1983):124–32.

12. At the end of the war, many of these kidnapped Japanese were barred from returning to the Central and South American countries where they had established families and businesses. The United States also refused to allow them to stay, and deported a number to Japan, regardless of whether they wished to go there. Weglyn has

In the uncertainty of the times, while they tried to demonstrate American loyalties by participating in the war effort and complying with restrictions, the people of Cortez also sought to cut off the ties to Japan that might damn them in the eyes of hostile whites. Fear and anxiety drove them, like so many Issei and Nisei, to destroy Japanese magazines and books, pictures of the Japanese emperor, family photographs, and other prized possessions. They painfully burned or buried in outhouses their ties to the past—an ominous sign of what the war would take from them.

The federal machinery that would uproot the Cortez Japanese Americans from their homes and community was already in motion early in 1942. A number of governmental officials and military heads had expressed doubts regarding the necessity of removing the Japanese Americans from the West Coast. Nevertheless, on February 19, 1942, with political expediency in mind and under the influence of civilian leaders and men like Secretary of War Henry L. Stimson and Assistant Secretary of War John J. McCloy, President Franklin Delano Roosevelt signed Executive Order 9066. This order arbitrarily suspended the civil rights of American citizens—in absence of martial law—by authorizing the "evacuation" of 110,000 Japanese and their American-born children from the western half of the Pacific coastal states and the southern third of Arizona. Approximately 70,000 of these evacuees were Nisei and American citizens by birth. Eventually 120,313 persons of Japanese ancestry were incarcerated, including 1,275 individuals sent from institutions, 1,118 people from Hawaii, 219 voluntary residents, 1,735 from Justice Department camps, and 5,981 who were born in the relocation camps.[13]

In recent years, scholars and political leaders have called into question the causes of, and rationale for, the internment of the Japanese Americans. This critique reflects an epochal shift in the social climate of the United States. The civil rights movement, accompanied by the efforts of ethnic minority and feminist groups to reclaim their pasts, launched a serious challenge to the inequities in American society and opened new forums for change. In the 1970s and 1980s, Japanese

---

briefly chronicled the efforts of San Francisco attorney Wayne Collins and the ACLU on behalf of 365 stranded Peruvian Japanese. C. Harvey Gardiner's more recent work, *Pawns in a Triangle of Hate*, is a thorough study of the trials of the Peruvian Japanese.

13. U.S. Department of the Interior, War Relocation Authority, *The Evacuated People: A Quantitative Description* (1946), p. 8.

Americans forged a national movement, spearheaded by organizations such as the National Coalition for Redress and Reparations (NCRR), to seek redress for their wartime incarceration and losses. At the same time, a team of Sansei lawyers reopened the three crucial cases of Gordon Hirabayashi, Fred Korematsu, and Minoru Yasui, disputing on procedural and constitutional grounds the legality of the evacuation orders.[14] The redress movement and the three major legal battles spurred a reexamination of events that have long been omitted from the pages of most U.S. history texts.

In the nearly fifty years since the wartime incarceration of the Japanese Americans, the official verdict has shifted from a justification by military necessity to the damning indictment of a grave injustice. Under pressure by the redress movement, Congress in 1980 established a Commission on Wartime Relocation and Internment of Civilians. After hearing the testimony of more than 750 witnesses and analyzing extensive archival materials, the commission issued a 467-page report, tellingly titled *Personal Justice Denied*. The detention and exclusion of the Japanese Americans had no basis, the report concluded, in military justification but instead had arisen from "race prejudice, war hysteria and a failure of political leadership."[15] In 1988, following the commission's recommendations, President Ronald Reagan authorized the Civil Liberties Act, offering a national apology and redress payments of $20,000 each to 60,000 survivors of the camps. The first payments reached the most senior Issei in 1990. Such vindication has spurred the redress movement's efforts to foster greater public awareness of the social conditions that can threaten the civil liberties of both minority groups and the larger citizenry.

The wartime internment of the Japanese Americans has stimulated a rich body of historical literature. Scholars such as Roger Daniels, Michi Weglyn, Richard Drinnon, Eugene Rostow, Gwynne Nettler, C. Har-

---

14. The Supreme Court chose to uphold the criminal convictions of Hirabayashi, Yasui, and Korematsu for curfew and exclusion violations, privileging "military interests" over "the presumption against invidious racial discrimination which requires that racial classifications be given strict scrutiny." *Personal Justice Denied*, p. 238; see also pp. 114–16, 236–39. Peter Irons in *Justice at War: The Story of the Japanese American Internment Cases* (New York: Oxford University Press, 1983) and *Justice Delayed: The Record of the Japanese American Internment Cases* (Middletown, Conn.: Wesleyan University Press, 1989) provides a detailed narrative history and a documentary record of the cases. See also Weglyn, pp. 215, 228; Hosokawa and Wilson, pp. 207, 250–55.

15. *Personal Justice Denied*, p. 18.

vey Gardiner, and Peter Irons have explored the combination of factors that underlay the incarceration of a vulnerable racial minority group. The long legacy of anti-Asian sentiment in the West contributed to this resurgence of nativism. Additional factors included the strength of anti-Asian organizations that clamored for restrictions, and the politicians and journalists who jumped on the bandwagon in order to garner votes during an election year or to boost newspaper sales.

The course of events in the Livingston-Cortez area and the not-so-subtle shift in local attitudes toward the Japanese Americans support these analyses. The lingering, if attenuated, anti-Asian sentiment and the economic motivations for the removal of the Issei and Nisei appear particularly striking in the light of Cortez's agricultural base. As late as 1937, white residents of nearby Ballico and Delhi opposed the sale of local land to Japanese Americans. One farmer explained, "We get along fine with our Japanese neighbors at Cortez. They are good farmers and good neighbors, but we believe that colonization of any race in a restricted or limited zone is unwise. Racial predominance is not good for a community."[16] Perceived encroachments by American-born Nisei obviously were still regarded as a threat by the dominant white society, which echoed, in less blatantly hostile tones, the anti-Japanese pronouncements of the 1920s. In their reminiscences, the economic reasons for their removal loomed large in the minds of the Cortez farmers. By the 1940s, they had begun to prosper and to reap the benefits of their hard labor through the pioneering years and the period of the Great Depression. A number of them still bitterly recall the harvest they were forced to leave to be gathered by others and the wealth of those who farmed their land during the war years.

The development of local attitudes toward the Japanese Americans followed the general pattern identified by Wilson and Hosokawa. Immediately after the attack on Pearl Harbor, the atmosphere was one of tension and ambivalence. Betty Frances Brown, a Livingston High School teacher, noted that although the local white residents were outraged by the bombing attack, "they distinguished between the warring Japan and their neighbors of Japanese descent. On all sides were heard expressions of sympathy for the local Japanese."[17] On December 8, in Livingston area schools, while the Nisei students

16. *Livingston Chronicle*, April 27, 1937.
17. Brown, p. 110.

tended to avoid the white pupils and sat to one side of the classrooms, there occurred instances of white students deliberately attempting to sit and mingle with them. The prevailing attitude among the children, according to Brown, was one of "concerned sympathy" for their Nisei classmates.

Soon, however, disturbing rumors began to spread through Livingston, fueling fears regarding Japanese Americans. Stories proliferated that "such and such a person had been arrested by the FBI; Black Dragon emblems were found at so and so's house; this person and that were caught sneaking about after 8 o'clock."[18] The Japanese Americans found themselves increasingly regarded with suspicion and hostility by whites, many of whom had previously been their friends. One Cortez Nisei recalled that a Euro-American who had served on a county board with him and who had liked to hobnob with the Cortez people, started carrying pistols. "He'd show me—'See this? I want you guys to observe curfew. If you ever get out of line, you know what's going to happen.'"[19]

Those friends and neighbors sympathetic to the Japanese Americans feared incurring the wrath of the surrounding majority and, in general, kept a low profile. An exception was Florence Greenough, a teacher at the Ballico Grammar School. She persisted in her strong public advocacy of the Japanese Americans and her denunciation of the evacuation, despite the personal cost. At a 1943 State Senate Fact Finding Committee Hearing concerning the possible return of the Japanese Americans to the Merced and Stanislaus counties during or after the war, Greenough was the only witness who spoke in favor of their return. Consequently, she very nearly lost her job.[20]

In the weeks before the evacuation, the attitude of their neighbors toward the Issei and Nisei changed from a reluctance to stereotype, to xenophobic hostility. The local newspapers reflected deepening racial antagonism. In 1942 the *Turlock Journal* included reports of the Cortez Presbyterian Church activities—a New Year banquet, Christian Endeavor youth groups, a memorial service for a white missionary—as well as an editorial titled "Hatred vs. Love." This column warned readers that "no matter how much we admire certain Japanese quali-

18. Ibid., p. 114.
19. Ernest Yoshida interview, Cortez, Calif., January 24, 1982.
20. *Livingston Chronicle*, June 24, 1943; Noda, p. 153.

ties or certain Japanese as individuals . . . these traits of respect on our part will not stop the Japanese from bombing our cities and killing our citizens, and, if they can, making actual slaves out of us." The editor declared the need, therefore, to develop bitter hatred and nationalism as "the most effective means of preservation."[21] Although the editorial included Germans and Italians in the first part of the article, it was only the Japanese who were singled out as the enemy. In addition, the editorial made no recognition of difference between the Japanese in Japan, and the Issei or American-born Nisei—all were lumped together. Such an editorial documented the growth of racial fears and the fragility of the esteem they subsumed.

The Western Defense Command, under the leadership of Lieutenant General John L. DeWitt, fueled public anxieties, sounding alarm at every panicky rumor of a Japanese threat. Unfortunately for the Japanese Americans, hysteria and indecision characterized DeWitt's headquarters, and he proved alarmingly malleable to bureaucratic pressure; as Roger Daniels observed in tracing DeWitt's wartime vacillation, he "often seemed to be the creature of the last strong personality with whom he had contact."[22] On December 26, 1941, DeWitt expressed doubts regarding the feasibility of interning the Japanese Americans, adding that "An American citizen, after all, is an American citizen."[23] Two months later, influenced by determined advocates of evacuation like Provost Marshall General Allen W. Gullion, Colonel Karl Bendetsen, and Assistant Secretary of War John J. McCloy, DeWitt wrote to likeminded Secretary of War Henry L. Stimson on February 14, 1942, urging that they be excluded from the West Coast. He based his argument on the assumption that patriotism was racially determined, at least in the case of the Japanese Americans. "The Japanese race," he asserted, "is an enemy race and while many second and third generation Japanese born on United States soil, possessed of United States citizenship, have become 'Americanized,' the racial strains are undiluted. . . . It, therefore, follows that along the vital Pacific Coast over 112,000 potential enemies of Japanese extraction, are at large today."[24] Or, as DeWitt later said to reporters, "A Jap is a Jap."[25]

21. *Turlock Journal*, January 7, 1942.
22. Daniels, *Concentration Camps*, p. 44. (See also Major General Joseph W. Stilwell's diary excerpts given on p. 37.)
23. Ibid., p. 40.
24. U.S. Department of War, *Final Report, Japanese Evacuation from the West Coast, 1942,*

Scholars like Daniels have asserted that the hardening of such sentiments reflected not only regional prejudice but a deeper strain of racism in United States society at large. Certainly the tide of public suspicion and animosity steadily effaced shared histories and gave growing impetus to the juggernaut of internment.

The *Livingston Chronicle* also evidenced the shift in feeling regarding the Issei and Nisei, although it occurred over a longer period of time, since the paper was based in a community with closely woven ties to Japanese Americans. The *Chronicle* only mentioned Pearl Harbor in an editorial column that stated: "Sabateurs, spys [*sic*], fifth columnists or enemy aliens of any kind will be just as quickly ferreted out and locked up here as anywhere. But because of our Japanese population we anticipate no more than our share of such troubles." "In fact," the editor concluded, "in spite of it, we have no more alarm here than have the people of Kalamazoo, Michigan, or . . . Troy, New York."[26]

Favorable front-page attention later showcased a statement of loyalty from the Yamato Colony proclaiming that when the time came, they would leave for camp uncomplainingly, and until the last would "do our part to help the United States."[27] At the end of April, as evacuation plans crystallized, E. G. Adams, once a foe of Japanese American settlement, noted in an editorial, "War does queer things to laws. For instance, it reverses the traditional American principle that a man is innocent until proven guilty (witness the concentration of American citizens of Japanese parentage just on the suspicion that some among them may be saboteurs)."[28] By the end of the war, however, Adams would change his tune and oppose the return of the Japanese Americans to California. As Gwynne Nettler has observed, "the very act of evacuation and enforced segregation served as an instrument of propaganda to crystallize heretofore marginal attitudes against this people." The early malleability of attitudes toward Japanese Americans began to harden as the government prepared to execute the plans for their removal.[29]

---

reprint of the 1943 ed. published by the U.S. Government Printing Office, Washington, D.C. (New York: Arno Press, 1978), pp. 33–34.

25. *Personal Justice Denied*, p. 23.

26. *Livingston Chronicle*, December 11, 1941.

27. Ibid., March 12, 1942.

28. Ibid., April 30, 1942.

29. Gwynne Nettler, "The Relationship between Attitude and Information Concerning the Japanese in America," Ph.D. diss., Department of Sociology, Stanford University, 1945, p. 42.

Past differences among the Abiko colonies dissolved in this acid concentration of racism, greed, and political expediency. Under the threat of impending internment, colony leaders began to make joint plans for the survival of their farms and communities. On March 9, 1942, some of the CGA members met with a Livingston-Cressey group headed by Nisei Masao Hoshino to consider a combined venture.[30] On March 18, the day that Executive Order 9102 established the War Relocation Authority intended to carry out the removal of the Issei and Nisei from the West Coast, the CGA members met and appointed a committee of eight of their members to outline a custodial program for their farms. At this time, the holdings of the thirty CGA members represented 1,100 acres in permanent ground and 800 acres of open ground.[31]

Plans for operating the farms took shape in CGA discussions with local white advisors. The committee consulted Hugh Griswold, a Merced lawyer who had previously assisted local Japanese Americans with legal matters. Griswold, who grew up in nearby Modesto, was then the deputy and partner of Claude Adams, the district attorney for Merced County. Together they discussed the problem of running the farms after evacuation and the question of appointing an operator. The members of the two Livingston cooperative associations also consulted advisors: The Livingston Fruit Growers Exchange contacted Dave Ritchie—head of the California Fruit Exchange, to which they belonged—in Lodi. The Livingston Fruit Growers consulted Peter McLaughlin of the Pacific Fruit Exchange, with which they were affiliated, also in Lodi. Representatives of the three cooperative associations and their advisors met at the Nishihara home in Cressey, the only possible meeting place, given the imposition of a five-mile travel restriction.[32]

Together, the colony representatives and their advisors established a unique custodial program to supervise and run their farms. Although some individuals in the larger Japanese American population took steps to leave their farms and businesses in the care of trusted friends, it does not appear that any other communities made collective arrangements as did the Abiko colonies. The operation they set up in

30. Noda, p. 132.

31. The committee members were Nobuhiro Kajioka (CGA president), Sam Kuwahara (CGA manager), Takashi Date, Yoshio Kubo, S. Maeda, Seio Masuda, George Morofuji, and Kumekichi Taniguchi.

32. Noda, p. 133.

the uncertain days before evacuation had three major components: a board of trustees, an advisory board, and an operations manager. The trustees, who were granted power of attorney to act for the Japanese Americans, consisted of Hugh Griswold as chairman, plus Peter McLaughlin and Dave Ritchie. The advisory board was composed of five members: Claude Adams; Dallas Bache, a Delhi farmer and insecticide businessman; C.L. Stringer, head of the local Farm Credit Administration; Gordon H. Winton, a Livingston insurance agent; and Joe A. Wolf, a director of the Merced Irrigation District.

It was the operator, however, who would have direct management of the 105 combined ranches of the Cortez, Cressey, and Livingston farmers, and who would arrange for the sale of their produce. For this crucial position, Hugh Griswold recommended Gus A. Momberg, the Fresno district manager for the California Lands Corporation, Bank of America's liquidating organization for farms foreclosed during the Great Depression.[33] With both practical experience and agricultural school training, he seemed a strong choice, especially since the Bank of America was beginning to close its liquidating organization. Momberg accepted the offer on April 12 and secured a leave of absence from California Lands. The terms of the agreement gave him a monthly salary, 1 percent of the gross, and 3 percent of the net income from all of the farms.[34] On April 20, 1942, he opened his business office in the Livingston Fruit Exchange Building, with Wilma Arnold as head bookkeeper and Bessie Austin as office worker. Additional employees were hired to assist with the farmwork.

The Cortez farmers remembered Gus Momberg as an efficient, energetic man who chainsmoked cigarettes in a holder. He was a bit "on the gruff side," said one Nisei, but then, "It was a tough deal to run." Considering that the people he worked for were in disfavor, and his transactions with both tenant farmers and produce buyers cannot have been easy, it was fortunate that he was a tough individual who "took no garbage from anybody." He certainly had to deal with a wide range of tenants, some of them local people, and others, mostly migrants from Oklahoma and Arkansas. There was wide variation in their amount of agricultural expertise and a high turnover rate among the less skilled.[35]

33. Ibid.
34. Ibid.
35. The following account draws on: CGA Minutes and records; the Hugh Griswold

At the outset, the new operation required considerable capital to implement a system adequate to handle the supervision of 105 ranches. Although other banks refused to finance them, the Bank of America lent them as much as two million dollars at one time. Momberg's workers farmed one-fifth of the land; the rest was leased to individual tenants. These share leases were drawn up as strictly as possible in order to protect the farms and their absentee owners. If, for instance, a tenant failed to spray his crops at the necessary time, Momberg's employees would do it for him and then would deduct the costs from his share of the end-of-season profit.

Each year after the harvest, Hugh Griswold, as chairman of the trustees, and another trustee—alternating by years—would journey to the Granada Relocation Center in Amache, Colorado, for ten to fourteen days to go over the farm records with each owner involved in the operation. Some of the farmers instructed the trustees to send them their share of the ranch earnings, but the majority preferred to let it accumulate in Merced County, until their return.[36]

The Japanese Americans' remaining days of freedom in their home communities dwindled inexorably. On March 27, 1942, Lieutenant General DeWitt issued Public Proclamation Number 4, prohibiting the Issei and Nisei from leaving Military Area Number 1, "in order to provide for the welfare and to insure the orderly evacuation and resettlement of the Japanese voluntarily migrating" from the area. By this time, DeWitt had issued the first of 108 Civilian Exclusion Orders, beginning the process of evacuation. The Army had divided California, Oregon, Washington, and part of Arizona into 108 "exclusion areas," each containing roughly 1,000 Issei and Nisei. Exclusion orders were issued about a week before the date set for evacuating a particular area; these orders defined the boundaries of the area and provided a list of instructions for evacuees.[37]

The dreaded exodus—which still seemed unreal to many—loomed closer. The people of Cortez began to make plans to pack and store their belongings with friends, or on their farms, or in Sam Kuwahara's shed. Those, like the Yamamoto family, who could leave their posses-

---

interview, by J. Carlyle Parker, January 25, 1975; Sam Kuwahara interview, Cortez, Calif., January 25, 1982; Noda, pp. 133–35, 161.

36. Hugh Griswold interview, by J. Carlyle Parker, January 25, 1975.

37. The last of the exclusion orders was issued on July 22, 1942.

sions in the care of non-Japanese friends, regained their belongings after the war. However, household appliances and items stored in tank houses often departed with the tenants. A visiting Euro-American minister informed an unhappy farmer in the Merced Assembly Center that his family's stove had been seen on the road to Oklahoma.

The imposition of the curfew and travel limitations, the hectic preparations for evacuation (and the uncertainty of its timing) made it impossible to follow the routines of normal life, yet the community struggled to do so. For example, after several postponements, the Ballico Grammar School succeeded in presenting in mid-April an operetta, "The Adventures of Goldilocks." The spirit of the teachers, reported the *Livingston Chronicle*, was, "Come war, or pestilence, or flood, we will still give our play." War came swiftly. In April, the Japanese American people of Cortez and Livingston stood in the first of many long lines at their churches, waiting to be vaccinated before going to an assembly center.

On May 7, 1942, DeWitt issued Civilian Exclusion Order Number 51, ordering the evacuation on May 13 of Merced County and a portion of Mariposa County. A responsible member of each family was required to report to the Civil Control Station at the Veteran's Memorial Hall in Merced on May 8 to receive further instructions and the numbered tags that would be attached to all family baggage. The Japanese could take with them only what they could carry; they were told to bring with them on departure for the assembly center bedding and linens, toilet articles, clothing, eating utensils, and essential personal effects.[38]

After taking care of final arrangements and making wrenching farewells, the people of Cortez left behind their ripening fields of strawberries and tomatoes, and departed for the Merced Assembly Center—bewildered, sad, excited, and anxious. Mary Noda wrote to one of her high school classmates the next day, describing the journey to the center. Her family had packed until the last minute and then drove to the CGA shed. "Around eight o'clock," as she recalled, "three Greyhound buses came for us. On the way to Merced, everyone was quiet. The only noise was the constant drone of the motor. I didn't feel exactly sad or happy. It still does not seem a reality. I gazed about the

38. Brown, pp. 121–22; *Livingston Chronicle*, May 7, 1942. For the complete instructions issued by DeWitt to the evacuees, see *Final Report: Japanese Evacuation*, p. 100.

fields and thought—'How silly it is to think we will never see these familiar fields, houses and people when we will be but twenty miles away.' "[39]

The Merced Assembly Center was one of fourteen crude temporary centers set up at race tracks, fairgrounds, and Civilian Conservation Corps camps: twelve in California, one in Oregon, and one in Washington. Located at the Merced County Fairgrounds, between May 6 to September 15, 1942, it held a total of 4,669 people from the northern California coast, the West Sacramento Valley, and the North San Joaquin Valley. Six hundred and fifteen Japanese Americans came from the area encompassing Ballico, Cortez, Cressey, Delhi, Livingston, and Winton.[40]

The assembly centers mirrored the relocation camps' ironic organizational structure as "model cities." The Merced Assembly Center was run by a center manager through a series of departments headed by Euro-American administrators, with the exception of the Health and Hospital Department, under the supervision of Doctors Iriki and Yamada. The first center manager was Dean Miller, who left in June to take a Work Projects Administration (WPA) position in Idaho. He was replaced by Harry L. Black, a WPA administrator and personnel trainer in Washington, D. C., who had also served as a military school superintendent and army officer. Before coming to the Merced Assembly Center, he had helped to organize the Manzanar Assembly Center, also in California. Like Black, a number of the administrators who worked at the assembly centers were men with WPA experience.[41]

39. Letter from Mary Noda to Barbara Carpenter, May 14, 1942, cited by Brown, p. 123.

40. For more information regarding the assembly centers, see *Personal Justice Denied*, esp. chap. 5, "Assembly Centers," pp. 135–48; John L. DeWitt, *Final Report: Japanese Evacuation from the West Coast, 1942*, U.S. Department of War (Washington, D.C.: Government Printing Office, 1943; reissued by Arno Press, 1978), Part V, "Assembly Center Operations," pp. 149–233; and "A Pilgrimage Guide to the Temporary Detention Camps," *Pacific Citizen* Holiday Issue, December 19–26, 1980, pp. 56–59.

41. The Merced Assembly Center administrators and departments were: Harry L. Black, Manager; A. P. Stronk, Supply; Steve R. Schramm, Mess & Lodging; R. M. Herlitz, Warehouse; Bert Mankins, Works & Maintenance; Vern S. Stockholm, Fire Protection; W. H. Bachman, Police; Leroy Stroder, Finance & Accounting; Dwight Darrow, Timekeeping & Personnel; Roy V. Jamison, Center Cashier; E. A. Woodside, Service; Doctors Iriki and Yamada, Health & Hospital; R. G. Mitchell, Recreation, Education & Welfare; Roy F. Hamilton, Center Exchange; Harvey D. McDowell, Chief Steward. *The Mercedian*, June 19, 1942.

Upon arrival at the Merced Assembly Center, the Japanese Americans and their baggage were searched for contraband items. Families were then assigned to quarters in hastily constructed tar-papered barracks. The Merced Assembly Center was divided into ten alphabetically designated wards, or blocks—"A" through "J"—each of which housed approximately 500 people in eighteen to twenty barracks. Each ward contained a recreation building, mess hall, latrines, shower rooms, and laundry building. Most of the Cortez people lived in Ward C, though some stayed in Ward D. The hospital, canteen, police department, and post office occupied the middle of the assembly center. On the western side of the assembly center lay the fairground race track, grandstands, and playing field, administration buildings, fire department, and supply houses.[42]

Life in the Merced Assembly Center, as in all of the assembly centers, was crowded, noisy, and uncomfortable.[43] The barracks were 100 feet long and 20 feet wide, divided into five or six rooms or "apartments" furnished with army cots. Only very large families were assigned two rooms; most were crammed into one. Privacy became a privilege of the past. The room partitions did not extend to the ceiling, thereby leaving an open space through which hollered greetings, babies' cries, and family quarrels carried from one end of a barrack to the other. One Nisei recalled the amusement of her siblings at hearing the splashing noises of their next door neighbor who, before ironing her clothes, would dampen them by spraying water from her mouth.

The trials experienced by the Merced Assembly Center residents were common to all evacuees. Confinement in the assembly center meant waiting in many long lines—for the latrines, the showers, the laundry facilities, the mess halls. The latrines and showers—divided into separate facilities for men and women—were humiliatingly crude, with no partitions in the showers nor in the latrines. The toilets consisted of a bench designed for eight people. Not only was privacy

42. The following account of life in the Merced Assembly Center draws on *The Mercedian*, the Merced Assembly Center newspaper; letters from evacuees, collected by Betty Brown; and the recollections of women and men interviewed in Cortez from 1982 to 1988.

43. See also Audrie Girdner and Anne Loftis, *The Great Betrayal: The Evacuation of the Japanese-Americans during World War II* (New York: Macmillan, 1969); for personal accounts, see Jeanne Wakatsuki Houston and James D. Houston, *Farewell to Manzanar* (Boston: Houghton Mifflin, 1973), and Yoshiko Uchida, *Desert Exile: The Uprooting of a Japanese American Family* (Seattle: University of Washington Press, 1982).

lacking but there was also a certain amount of risk involved in sitting on the toilets: Whenever the lever was tripped to flush the toilet—a long galvanized trough—water would surge from a tank and down the trough, and anyone sitting near the end of the bench would get splashed. This unpleasant arrangement had physiological as well as psychological effects. "It's not very sanitary," wrote one woman at the Merced Center to a white friend, "and has caused a great deal of constipation in camp for both men and women. The toilets are one big row of seats, that is, one straight board with holes out about a foot apart with no partitions at all and all the toilets flush together. . . . The younger girls couldn't go to them at first until they couldn't stand it any longer, which is really bad for them."[44]

The mess halls presented another trial. There the Issei and Nisei encountered foods they had never seen before: beef tongue, tripe, liver, and heart—"a lot of things that normally wouldn't sell in the grocery store." The Japanese American cooks were unaccustomed to preparing these kinds of meat, and many people refused to eat them. Evacuees also remembered an abundance of cabbage stew. In general, the food was plain but substantial; the quality of the meals also varied somewhat according to the ingenuity of the cooks in each block. The insanitary conditions and change of diet caused bouts of diarrhea, and the primitive unpartitioned latrines compounded the misery.[45]

During the first days in the assembly center, people felt numb and disoriented. "It was hot and depressing," said Takashi Date, who also noted the hardship placed on children unable to comprehend these trying circumstances. "I remember one youngster crying . . . 'Mommy, Mommy, I'm tired of vacation. Let's go home now.'"[46] The crowded communal living conditions, inactivity, and sense of helplessness created a strained atmosphere. Soon after arrival, a recent graduate of Livingston High School wrote to a classmate detailing the difficulties of adjustment to the lack of privacy, the idle gossip, and the injustice:

> I cried myself to sleep every night until last night. . . . My first four days were so miserable, I will never be able to forget it. I still shrink from the

44. Letter, [unknown] to Grace Nichols, June 1942, Conrad-Duveneck Collection, Hoover Institution Archives; cited at greater length by Daniels, *Concentration Camps,* p. 89.

45. Daniels, *Concentration Camps,* p. 89.

46. Takashi Date interview, Cortez, Calif., February 7, 1982.

thought of being in a camp for something I was not nor anyone else in this camp that I know of was to blame for.

Her thoughts of home contrasted sharply with the reality of incarceration:

Gee, what I would give to see Livingston and feel free from this awful sight of houses, people, and the sight of several measley barbed wires keeping us banded here together like a bunch of sheep or cattle.[47]

As soon as their shock abated, the Japanese Americans set to work to improve their bleak surroundings, and, within the parameters of WRA restrictions, to create some semblance of normal life. Apartments were partitioned with blankets; victory gardens began to appear around the barracks. Morning Glory Lane in Ward G gained particular fame as a scenic showcase, thanks to its chief gardener, formerly boss of the Paramutual Nursery. The Merced Assembly Center newspaper, *The Mercedian*, put out by a Japanese American staff under the direction of managing editor Oski Taniwaki, recorded the bustle of activity as recreation and education programs were established, and Issei and Nisei scrambled for jobs. In addition, talent shows, athletic events, and dances drew large crowds.

Men and women took jobs in all divisions of the assembly center, from supervisorial positions to mess-hall busing. They found work in the motor pool, in the administration offices, in the hospital and fire departments; they taught classes, organized recreational programs, and served as an internal security police force known as the "Green Peas" because of their green armbands bearing the letter "P." The hasty construction of the assembly center left a great deal of work to be done on the barracks, latrines, and other buildings. Carpenters were much in demand, Ernest Yoshida found as soon as he arrived. He was paid sixteen dollars a month to supervise two crews, one making screen doors and the other putting together "duck boards"—gratelike devices designed to enable people to walk over patches of soggy ground at the Merced fairground. Because of public pressure to keep evacuee wages no higher than the monthly $21 received by GIs (who

47. Letter from June Suzuki to Barbara Carpenter, May 19, 1942, cited by Brown, pp. 125–26.

enjoyed fringe benefits unavailable to the evacuees), the Japanese Americans in the assembly centers and later relocation camps received little recompense for their labor. The pathetically low wage scale in the assembly centers ranged from eight dollars a month for unskilled workers, to twelve dollars for skilled labor, and sixteen for professionals and technicians. This situation contrasted sharply with the rising wages in defense industries and the high profits realized by farmers during the wartime economic boom.

The evacuated people did gain a small measure of influence in the running of the center. In June 1942, Harry Black appointed Japanese American commissioners to supervise the public services, including Cortez Nisei Sam Kuwahara, who was in charge of safety—"police, fire, military, surveillance, signals, camp hazard, curfew, etc." Dr. M. Higaki, head of welfare, was also elected chief of the commissioners and acted as representative of the general community and ward representatives.[48]

The election of ward representatives, however, illustrated the ambivalence of the WRA regarding self-government within the camps. On June 23, *The Mercedian* announced that election fever would run high the next evening as each ward elected representatives—one woman and one man—to constitute the assembly center's governing body. Voters and candidates for office had to be eighteen years of age or older, and those running for office were also required to read, write, and speak English. The representatives would then choose a president and formulate a constitution. Ironically, the newspaper further remarked, "For Issei and most Nisei, this will be the first time they will have the opportunity to express their opinion." The Issei had been previously barred from voting in the United States by virtue of their alien status, and they were also ineligible to apply for citizenship. The majority of their American-born children were coming of age at this time. However, the next issue of *The Mercedian* declared that the election results had been annulled because of revised instructions received from the Wartime Civil Control Administration (WCCA) office in San Francisco. On the night of June 29, "with all the color and trimmings of a grand country election," a second and revised election was held in the mess halls. Twenty Nisei were elected to distribute center information, to promote the welfare of residents, and to serve as an advisory

48. *The Mercedian*, June 23, 1942.

assembly to Manager Harry Black. This advisory assembly organized a Relocation Committee and five standing committees—Works and Planning, Mess and Lodging, Service and Education, Health and Welfare, and Safety—which occasionally met with the center administrative staff to discuss specific issues.

The advisory assembly met with Harry Black and his departmental staff each morning to present requests and suggestions, and to receive orders to be disseminated. At least one staff member thought the Japanese Americans enjoyed some success in making demands and suggestions. Addison Kilgore, the disgruntled superintendent of guards at the Merced Assembly Center, felt that the evacuees "hollered for what they wanted and they always got it, too!" Kilgore considered the ward representatives—many of them professionals—"the worst of all the Japanese; they kept the others stirred up and were sure-enough leaders of discontent."[49] His dissatisfaction with the Green Peas further illustrates the strength of ethnic and community ties among the Japanese Americans, and, despite their differences, the preservation of solidarity. When infractions took place, Kilgore claimed, "the Green Peas and Supervisors were more of a hindrance than a help; they protected the offenders and covered up for them. . . . Not one of them informed on the wrong or illegal things they saw going on."[50] This may also reflect Kilgore's inability to perceive the Japanese Americans as individuals, instead lumping them together in a conspiratorial stew.

In an attempt to provide a worthwhile occupation for the evacuees' time, an informal educational program was started in the assembly center under Dr. Terami. The program, which ran from June 10 to August 21, 1942, served 980 individuals: 330 elementary school pupils, 450 junior and senior high school students, and 200 adults. Of these 200 adults, over half were Issei and Kibei (Nisei sent to Japan for education and then repatriated) men and women attending English classes. The majority of the rest were women taking courses in crafts like knitting and sewing.

Held in two recreation halls and in nine apartments in three different wards, the makeshift classes for the children and teenagers were beset with difficulties. They had no desks, blackboards, or books for weeks, although the Merced County Library eventually donated

49. Interview with Addison Kilgore, October 30, 1942, cited by Brown, p. 126.
50. Ibid.

more than 3,000 volumes. The pupils studied while sitting or lying on the floors. Youths already reluctant to spend the summer months in school delighted in tormenting their teachers, many of whom were only a little older than their senior students. A Nisei teenager who attended classes in bookkeeping, shorthand, landscape design, U.S. history, and American government reported, "The boys have a swell time teasing the young college girls who are our teachers. . . . Everyone kind of giggles and poor teachers just blush."[51]

In the assembly center all of the teachers were Japanese Americans. More than twenty individuals taught full time in the Merced Assembly Center. Only three had degrees in education, but over half had earned university degrees and none had less than two years of college. Young women also taught games and poems to groups of preschool and kindergarten children. Having Japanese American teachers proved an unusual experience for the children; it challenged their sense of established reality. The observations recorded in the final issue of *The Mercedian* at the close of the Merced Assembly Center School reveal the notions ingrained in the Nisei children by the time of evacuation, as well as a sense of the racial and cultural barriers that regulated their relations with their former teachers: "Because the teachers were Japanese, the children took this advantage to become very attached to them." In the assembly center they found teachers, however prepared or unprepared, who looked like themselves and who had the same ethnic background—teachers to whom they could relate on a personal level. This caused some confusion, however, for children who had learned to identify teachers as Euro-Americans: "the younger pupils 'just felt' that a Japanese teacher couldn't be a 'real teacher,' " a feeling illustrated by a student who asked, "Teacher, may I call you Miss Stanley, 'cause that was the name of my teacher back home? I feel funny to call you by your Japanese name."[52]

The Japanese American educators worried about the effects of camp life on the "young boys and girls—the group from which the leaders of tomorrow will emerge." They feared that "a long stay in the center, away from the normal outside world, will, more or less, kill the ambitions of many of these young people."[53] It would be a major task, they

51. Letter from June Suzuki to Barbara Carpenter, cited by Brown, p. 148.
52. *The Mercedian*, Souvenir Edition, August 29, 1942.
53. Ibid.

felt, to maintain a sense of faith, ambition, and pride within these young people.

For those finishing high school, it proved an equally uncertain time. As part of their attempt to sustain familiar life routines, the evacuees held commencement exercises on July 2, soon after the opening of the Merced Assembly Center School. The honorees included 275 students who would have graduated from 96 different schools in California. Few could have guessed that the long-awaited day would find them separated from their classmates, behind barbed wire fences. There were 21 university and junior college graduates, 135 high school graduates, and 119 from the elementary schools.[54] The graduates listened to an address, "An Accident of History," by Professor Hubert Phillips from nearby Fresno State College, and then celebrated at two socials, one for the high school students and one for the elementary. A graduation prom dance was held on July 4. The Nisei chair who was in charge of the high school social entertainment committee wrote to a friend in anticipation, "I sure hope the social goes over big to make up for all the things every graduate missed. We all dreamed of this day for so long."[55] Although their dreams for the future stood on shaky ground, high school graduates and college students turned out on July 10 to hear two speakers—Professor Henry Tyler and Dr. Walter Bolderston—from the National Japanese American Student Relocation Council. On July 14, 150 of these Nisei filled out questionnaires in the hope of continuing their education.[56]

In addition to work and classes, the Japanese Americans filled their time and sustained morale with social and cultural events. These group activities established patterns that continued in the relocation camps. Buddhist and Christian services were held in the mess halls, and there were Young Buddhist Association and Christian Endeavor activities for the Nisei. Dances drew large crowds of Nisei, and almost everyone turned out for the talent shows. These featured performers like Pat Suzuki, Professor Paul "Waldo" Higaki and the Stardusters (a Nisei band), as well as traditional folk dancing and music. As in the

54. *The Mercedian*, June 30, 1942.
55. Letter from June Suzuki to Barbara Carpenter, cited by Brown, p. 149.
56. For further information about the National Japanese American Student Relocation Council, see Robert W. O'Brien's *The College Nisei* (Palo Alto, Calif.: Pacific Books, 1949), which examines the experiences of the students and traces the development of the council. Education and public policy scholar Thomas James provides insights about the council in "Educating 'Projectiles of Democracy,'" chap. 4 of *Exile Within*.

prewar years, baseball games were especially popular, and the competition became fierce among several men's and women's leagues. The Livingston-Cortez teams made an impressive showing, and Peggy Taniguchi, an athletic Nisei from Cortez, maintained a reputation for "heavy circuit smashing" on the diamond.[57] The evacuees also played volleyball, basketball, and table tennis. There were six Boy Scout troops and three Girl Scout patrols, as well as contests that ranged from kite-making to *shogi* (strategy board game) tournaments.

Two major events, the summer *Obon* festival and Fourth of July celebrations, reflected both the evacuees' wish to retain their Japanese cultural heritage and their identification with the country in which they lived. The former occasion was a Buddhist celebration, commemorated with special dancing and services; the latter centered around an elaborate parade that ironically mirrored the patriotic sentiment that sent brass bands and floats down the main streets of many American small towns. In the Merced Assembly Center, the preschool nursery rhythm band marched, and the various departments and wards competed for prizes in creating floats decked in red, white, and blue.[58]

For most Japanese Americans, the assembly center environment— and the relocation camp that followed—meant a significant change from previous patterns of social life. Within the Merced Assembly Center, as in the Colorado camp later, all age groups began to spend more time than ever before in the company of their peers. Given leisure time and proximity, there were more opportunities to socialize, and in an almost entirely Japanese American environment. Rural teenagers who had lived on isolated farms found the prohibitions of distance and agricultural chores lifted. And, as in Amache (Colorado), the rural Nisei encountered increasing numbers of urban peers, whose differences in style of dress and interaction caused wonder. One local Nisei remarked, "The girls seem to be going sort of wild. I guess it is the camp atmosphere. Just like a holiday. They all get pretty nutty over the boys."[59]

Some of the teenagers found it exciting to see so many other Japanese Americans. Not all had grown up in concentrated ethnic communities like Cortez. One woman who came from a small coastal community reported that she had never before been among so many Nisei her

57. *The Mercedian,* July 14, 1942.
58. *The Mercedian,* July 7, 1942.
59. Letter from Mary Suzuki to Barbara Carpenter, cited by Brown, p. 125.

own age. She signed up to work in the mess hall, and in that way "got to meet everybody." Others, however, found the experience overwhelming, as did one Nisei woman, who wrote: "I never have seen and been sick of so many black heads in all my life." But she added immediately, "I should yell, because I guess I am one of those—too."[60] Every glance served to remind the evacuees that it was not individual foibles or misdeeds that herded them together in the thousands, but the fact of their ethnic background—the collective assessment of their black hair and eyes.

Thoughts of home lingered in the evacuees' minds. The Cortez Japanese Americans, still geographically close to their farms, eagerly awaited reports about their crops. The condition of the farms varied with the tenants. A few of the more fortunate Cortez families had old friends who took conscientious care of their ranches. However, there was turnover among the other tenants, who varied in their level of agricultural experience, and the properties in their hands fared accordingly.

Several of the Cortez Nisei were able to make quick visits to see their farms during the sojourn at the Merced Assembly Center. Grant Noda and perhaps six others were allowed to travel to Cortez to retrieve an organ; during this trip, he was able to check the family ranch and reported that it looked very good.[61] Ernest Yoshida was not so pleased when he saw the state of his farm. As foreman of a carpentry group, Ernest made regular trips out of the assembly center with a white supervisor to buy hardware equipment in Merced. In mid-May, the supervisor invited him along on an errand to Turlock and stopped by Cortez so that Ernest could see his farm. Ernest was particularly eager to view his five acres of ripe strawberries. "I saw this one big old lady sitting right in the middle of the five-acre patch picking berries. I guess she didn't know which way to start so she started in the middle." When he inquired about this, the farm managers told him they couldn't find anybody to do the picking.

I was so disgusted and discouraged that I didn't bother to bring any strawberries to the camp. . . . Then the next time I dropped by, they were irrigating and the water was running all over the place, nobody watching it. . . . it was sort of a lake. So I came back and told my Dad, "By the time

60. Letter from June Suzuki to Barbara Carpenter, cited by Brown, p. 125.
61. Letter from Pat Noda to Barbara Carpenter, August 1942, cited by Brown, p. 128.

we get back, we're not going to have anything left." And he said, "Well, *shikata ga nai.*" That's how the Japanese phrased this war and their misfortune—*shikata ga nai*, you have to take it, because you're the minority here. I think most of the Japanese parents told their kids, "*shikata ga nai.*" What else could they tell them?[62]

Shikata ga nai—meaning "it can't be helped," with the implication that hardship must be borne—lingered on many lips as the evacuees anxiously waited to find out their next destination. Beneath the bustle of activity in the Merced Assembly Center the atmosphere was one of uncertainty and speculation. People wondered where they would go, both during and after the war. The talk of where the relocation camp might be, the reception of the Japanese Americans in "outside" communities, and the question of postwar resettlement became intertwined, as the Issei and Nisei thought about the future.

The internees' uncertainty intensified their sense of urgency about the transitional nature of life in the assembly center—a feeling that things could and might change rapidly at any time. The fear of separation during removal to a relocation camp hastened a number of Nisei weddings during the evacuation. There were four marriages in the Merced Assembly Center. The third was the wedding on August 5 of two Cortez Nisei, May Kuwahara and Yeichi Sakaguchi. They made two trips to Merced, under the supervision of a security guard, to apply for a marriage license, find a suitable dress, and have a wedding photograph taken. Two hundred guests attended the wedding, held in the Merced Fairground Exhibit Hall. Afterward, Yeichi's co-workers in the assembly center fire department brought the fire truck, siren blaring, to escort the couple to their barrack.

In mid-July, the Army announced tentative plans to move the Merced Assembly Center residents to a War Relocation Project being built in Granada, Colorado, in the Arkansas River Valley. There they would be joined by approximately 3,000 evacuees from other assembly centers. Manager Harry Black explained that the announcement was made to "allay the confusion and unrest created by all sorts of unfounded reports and rumors concerning the relocation date and destination."[63]

Soon thereafter, the evacuees were alarmed by rumors, "spreading

62. Ernest Yoshida interview, Cortez, Calif., January 24, 1982.
63. *The Mercedian*, July 7, 1942.

like a forest fire in July" that a train bearing Turlock Assembly Center evacuees to Arizona had been derailed by dynamite, killing thirty passengers.[64] Manager Harry Black issued a denial that any of the evacuees had perished. The source of the rumor, it was later learned, grew out of the delay of a Turlock contingent due to traffic congestion. While the train was sidetracked, several evacuees fainted from the heat.[65] Given the hostility directed at the Japanese Americans from the outside, and the simmering anxieties and frustration on the inside of the assembly center, it is easy to understand the basis—and power— of such rumors.

As people prepared for another move, *The Mercedian* carried articles on Colorado and "Our Promising Home," and Town Hall Forums were held regarding evacuation and the future. On July 27, 1,000 attended the first of the forums to hear administrators Harry Black, J. M. Kidwell, and Richard Mitchell speak on the topic, "What Should Be Our Attitude Toward Evacuation?" Black commended the Japanese Americans for their loyalty and the sacrifices they had made, declaring that "there is more real Americanism [here] than there is to be found in many minority groups in this country." Richard Mitchell also compared the Japanese Americans to other minority groups in discussing the future aspects of evacuation. He cited America's failure to solve its racial problems in relation to the blacks, Jews, and Chinese, and warned with dismal accuracy that after the war, "given a victory by the allied nations, the Nisei are apt to still be classified as Japanese rather than as Americans." He advised the evacuees to counteract this problem by participating in the war effort, volunteering for military service, salvaging defense materials, and demonstrating their "desire to continue to live the American ideal of living."[66]

On August 12, a second panel composed of Nisei speakers addressed the topic of "Nisei in Post-War Resettlement." The "lively" audience participation and the opposing positions of the panelists— Takashi Moriuchi, James Nakamura, Mas Miyashita, and Fred Hashimoto—indicate the uncertainty and concern of Japanese Americans regarding their future. The speakers concentrated on the issue of postwar strategies: should the Japanese Americans disperse through-

64. *The Mercedian*, July 28, 1942.
65. *The Mercedian*, Souvenir Edition, August 29, 1942.
66. *The Mercedian*, July 31, 1942.

out the country or return to California and stay together? Although Miyashita mentioned two other possibilities—to remain in the relocation center or to leave the United States—none of the speakers, including himself, appeared to consider these as real choices. This underlines both the Nisei's view of themselves as Americans, despite what others might think, and their desire to live as citizens in the communities of their homeland.

Miyashita "straddled the issue," according to *The Mercedian*, but leaned toward dispersal, which was heartily endorsed by James Nakamura; he felt that the Japanese Americans were in the assembly centers because of misunderstandings by the American public. Dissemination of Japanese Americans across the country would prevent repetition of "past mistakes." On the other hand, Fred Hashimoto stressed that the largest field open to the Nisei would be agriculture, and he advocated that they return to their property and "stick together." Moriuchi, in accordance with this assessment, predicted future discrimination and maintained they would need to stay together for economic reasons.[67]

At the end of July, the Merced Assembly Center administrators and evacuees began to prepare for the move to the Amache Camp. By this time, Sears, Roebuck and Company had won the government contract to handle the Japanese Americans' clothing orders. The evacuees were advised to use their clothing allotment carefully, bearing in mind the kind of garments suitable to Colorado weather, as well as their families' immediate needs. A cartoon in the July 31 issue of *The Mercedian* illustrated the limitation in choice of clothes: A male evacuee, swivelling his head in surprise, finds himself surrounded by women in identical outfits, all coming from the direction pointed by a sign reading, "Free Clothing."

Final parties and games took place as the evacuees prepared for the move to the Amache Camp in Colorado. August articles in *The Mercedian* described Granada, the site of the Amache Camp for which the Merced Assembly Center residents were bound. Evacuees first read about the many recreational activities that would be available there because of the erroneous belief that the Arkansas River flowed through the center. On August 24, the advance party of 212 workers left for Colorado to make preparations for the arrival of all other contin-

67. *The Mercedian*, August 18, 1942.

gents, scheduled daily from August 31 to September 3, 1942. Each train load, consisting of approximately 500 individuals, would travel on the Santa Fe Railway through Arizona and New Mexico to southeastern Colorado.

In this atmosphere of change and leave-taking, the last Souvenir Edition of *The Mercedian* appeared, filled with reflections upon the months spent in the assembly center. A laudatory page by Harry Black headed the issue, praising the Japanese Americans for their "splendid spirit of cooperation" and exhorting them to work to build an ideal community in Colorado. Black professed his satisfaction with the clean record of the Merced Assembly Center, unmarred by arrests and no more than two critical violations of regulations. He looked forward to happy days after the war, when the Japanese Americans might be able to review the evacuation as an "unreal interlude."[68]

The "unreal interlude" whose duration none could foretell received a different assessment from some of the evacuees. For them, after all, the evacuation represented more than a temporary job assignment, as the white administrators might view it. The turmoil of the uprooting and the months in the assembly center had already affected the Japanese Americans deeply. Their articles in the final issue of *The Mercedian* presented a mixed bag of farewells, predictions for the future, an inventory, and an accounting.

Dr. H. O'Konogi, medical officer-in-charge of the Merced Hospital, and Reverend Harry Hashimoto both expressed concern over the effect of life within the center. Dr. O'Konogi observed, "It seems to be a general rule that all people, regardless of race when assembled together restricted in their movements and without work to do, become ill mentally."[69] This was evidenced by the many unnecessary hospital calls, he stated, which diminished over time as people adapted to the change in their lives.

Reverend Hashimoto similarly noted "greater tendencies to retrogress in habits, conduct, and morals within the confines of an assembly center." To illustrate this point, he described an ex-draftee who declared, "I prefer life in the army than to rot in a place like this." This outburst, more indicative of a decline in morale than in morals, serves

68. *The Mercedian,* Souvenir Edition, August 29, 1942.
69. Ibid.

as a reminder of the presence of conflict and frustration, even in a camp with a "record to be proud of."[70]

Reverend Hashimoto, like Charles Kamayatsu—a Nisei in charge of the Recreation Department—felt that leadership responsibilities in this critical time would fall squarely upon the shoulders of the older Nisei. "Our parents faced hardships to raise us," said Kamayatsu, "and we, who are taking their places, MUST CARRY ON!"[71] Both Hashimoto and Kamayatsu also stressed the significance of the Nisei's contributions and sacrifices in generational terms, and their admonitions reflect the importance of family and community in the thinking of the Japanese Americans, even as both underwent change in the crucible of war.

Reverend Hashimoto extended this concern beyond the Japanese American ethnic group: "Our attitude toward present conditions, the way in which we tackle each problem within these centers will determine the fate of other minority groups." As Richard Mitchell and Harry Black had compared the Japanese Americans with other ethnic groups, so did Reverend Hashimoto, investing the Issei and Nisei's experience with historical significance. His final summary of the situation presented a positive vision: "Though the past has been bitter, the present a severe shock, and the future unknown, we must contribute our best and all in order to create and maintain an ideal, vigorous community no matter where we are placed."[72] As a politically powerless minority, the evacuees' most meaningful actions were those that strengthened their sense of self-esteem and cohesiveness. The image of a vigorous community housed their hopes for a future in which they would assume as active a role as possible in the determination of their lives.

The evacuees had worked as hard as possible to maintain cohesion and normalcy during their trying stay in the assembly center, and they succeeded to a remarkable degree. Yet by the time they boarded the trains that would carry them to the relocation camp in Colorado, their lives had undergone enormous change. The drastic uprooting superimposed a common experience that transcended the differences

70. Ibid.
71. Ibid.
72. Ibid.

among them of age, gender, class, region of origin, work, and community. Regardless of their previous circumstances, in town or country, all faced the same limited allotment of space and resources, and the same suspect status. In the close confines of the barracks, mess halls, latrines, and shower rooms, they coped with crowded communal living; for rural families this was a far cry from life on isolated farms, and meant new exposure to the ways of the urban Japanese Americans. Severed from the regular demands of field chores and business, and set within an almost entirely Japanese American environment, the Issei and Nisei developed new patterns of socializing. They began to spend a great deal of time with their peers, away from the cramped family quarters. Because of the alien status of the Issei and their approaching retirement age, the responsibilities of community leadership increasingly passed to the American-born second generation. As short as their residence in the assembly center was, it had significant impact on the dynamics of family and community life. The patterns established in the assembly center would persist and develop broader ramifications in the environment of the relocation camp.

CHAPTER 4

Amache

At the end of August 1942, the Merced Assembly Center evacuees reached Amache, Colorado. Their last stop on the train from California was the town of Granada, Colorado, population 342, established as an Indian trading post in 1844. The evacuees were taken by truck from the railroad station to the nearby Granada Relocation Center, named Amache after the daughter of a Cheyenne Indian chief whose tribe had lived along the Arkansas River.[1]

The Amache Camp in southeastern Colorado, roughly one mile southwest of the Arkansas Valley, was one of ten "permanent" relocation centers constructed in desolate regions under the auspices of the War Relocation Authority (WRA) to house Japanese Americans. The Merced evacuees arrived five months after the first Japanese Americans had been moved from the temporary assembly centers to WRA camps. Amache was the smallest of the camps, with a capacity of 8,000 residents. Most of the camps held 10,000 and the largest, the Poston Camp in Arizona, contained 20,000 people in three units.[2] By November of 1942, all the relocation centers were filled.

Four months later—a year after President Roosevelt had signed Executive Order 9066—Dillon S. Myer, head of the War Relocation Authority, issued a statement censuring the "unnatural" and "un-

1. Henry Kusaba, James C. Lindley, and Joe McClelland, *Amache,* a report (Amache, Colo.: Documentation Section, Reports Office, ca. 1944).
2. Wilson and Hosokawa, pp. 212–13. The Poston and Manzanar camps were begun as assembly centers by the U.S. Army.

American" environment of the relocation centers. Myer particularly cited the disruption of the Japanese American family by the lack of privacy and by the absence of normal family economy and home routines, which led to a corresponding decline in parental authority. He concluded that the camps were "undesirable institutions and should be removed from the American scene as soon as possible."[3]

The relocation camps subjected families and individuals to severe stress. In accordance with many earlier scholars and observers, the congressional Commission on Wartime Relocation and Internment of Civilians reported in 1982: "The human toll the camps were taking was enormous—physical hardship, growing anger toward the United States and deteriorating morale."[4] Previous patterns of life—and the most fundamental relationships—underwent great change. As Audrie Girdner and Anne Loftis have pointed out, "the economic and social basis of the Issei's authority had been abolished by the welfare system under which all residents lived."[5] The cramped barracks, mess-hall dining, and increased peer-group interaction meant that family members spent less and less time together. In addition to the strain on family relationships, evacuees coped with internal rivalries arising between groups from different regions of the West Coast, as well as more general concerns regarding low-paying camp jobs, isolation, and negative public sentiment on the "outside."[6]

Amache was considered to be one of the more peaceful relocation centers, located in an inland area described by Michi Weglyn as "less unnerved by racially slanted media bombardment" and farther from the hostile racial climate of Arizona and California.[7] Even at best, however, as Robert Wilson and Bill Hosokawa have stated, "camp life was abnormal—subject to uncertainty, fear, frustration, anger, emotional pressures, great physical discomfort, resentment, and beset by an abundance of rumors that fed on boredom and bitterness."[8] While pondering an uncertain future, the internees strove to meet the phys-

3. Dillon S. Myer, *Uprooted Americans, The Japanese Americans and the War Relocation Authority during World War II* (Tucson: University of Arizona Press, 1971), p. 158. For a critical view of Myer's role in the internment, see Richard Drinnon, *Keeper of the Concentration Camps: Dillon S. Myer and American Racism* (Berkeley: University of California Press, 1987).

4. *Personal Justice Denied*, p. 185.

5. Girdner and Loftis, pp. 313–14.

6. Ibid., p. 247.

7. Weglyn, p. 145.

8. Wilson and Hosokawa, p. 220.

ically and psychologically exhausting demands of daily life in a concentration camp.

How did camp life affect the Japanese Americans? The first half of this chapter explores conditions within the Amache Camp, particularly focusing on the factors that made many evacuees eager to leave and rejoin life on the "outside." Even before the last evacuees had moved into the relocation centers, Myer and the WRA had decided to focus on resettlement out of the camps. Although the WRA's leave-clearance process proved initially cumbersome and slow, the first Japanese Americans began to trek out of the camps to the Midwest and East in 1942. The wartime demand for labor and the changes in WRA policy increased this trickle to a steady stream in 1943. The ranks of the hopeful men and women who left the camps for army duty, education, and work included a number of Cortez Nisei, whose lives beyond barbed wire illustrate the paths taken by the Nisei as well as the establishment of friend and kin networks upon which the relocating evacuees depended for emotional support and assistance.

Ernest Yoshida, a Nisei from the Cortez Colony, recalled the arduous trip to Amache. Despite the suffocating heat on the crowded train, armed guards would not allow the Japanese Americans to open windows. "We got to Bakersfield, and it got hotter and hotter. Then the train started pulling toward Tehachapi Mountain, and it got hotter, and the kids started crying." In the evening, when the Japanese Americans wanted to pull down the Pullman beds for the children to sleep on, the guards ordered them to "leave those things alone." The adults stood in the aisles so that the children could stretch out and sleep in the seats.

In the course of the two-day trip, the evacuees were permitted two twenty-minute rest breaks during which they could get off the train and stretch but were warned not to go beyond four feet from the train. "I think when we got to Arizona, they finally stopped. By that time the kids were sick and the old folks were half-dead. Then, when we got off, here are all the guards standing guard with machine guns, so that we couldn't run away. Crazy, I tell you."

Yoshida continued:

The kids started hollering for water, and we didn't have any water. It was hot and dry. And finally we reached Granada Station . . . two days, no bath and no water. It was four o'clock [in the afternoon], so we thought we had plenty of time to get off the train and go to the camp. "No," they said, "the camp isn't ready until tomorrow morning. . . . You have to stay overnight on the train." And we said, "Where are we going to sleep? You guys won't let us take the bunks down." "Well, that's the orders—we don't know what to do about it."

The following morning, the advance group of Japanese Americans who had arrived at the Amache Camp days earlier came to pick up the new arrivals in trucks. The weary Issei and Nisei set about moving into their new barracks, looking for straw to stuff mattresses, and locating the shower rooms, latrines, and mess halls. "That night we all slept like a log. The next morning we got up, and then the same old routine—nothing to do. Maybe go to a neighbor's, play cards. And those that wanted to . . . went to the scrap pile and picked up wood, and made shelves and desks. . . . That's the way we passed the time away."[9] Ernest Yoshida, like many of the evacuated Nisei, chafed at the confines of the camp and made plans to leave as soon as possible to seek opportunities on the "outside."

The Amache Camp was located within the southern boundary of a mile-square enclosure overlooking the Arkansas River. On the west lay a cemetery, dump pile, and sewer farm, and on the east, a prairie extending into Kansas. Along the northern boundary were a hospital, warehouses, housing for the appointed staff, administration buildings, and a military police compound.[10]

Life at Amache paralleled life in the assembly center with regard to organization, although the camp population was larger and the Colorado weather more extreme—many Californians saw their first snow in Amache. As in the Merced Assembly Center, the "evacuee residential section" was divided into blocks. Each of the twenty-nine blocks had its own mess hall, laundry, latrine, shower room, and recreation hall. The center also housed several churches—Buddhist and Christian—an elementary school, and a high school, for which a special building was constructed a year after the camp opened.

Each block was comprised of twelve barracks, 20 × 120 feet, each divided into six one-room "apartments." A family of seven members or less was assigned to a room and "allowed to make it as homelike as possible."[11] The barracks eventually had brick floors, although some

9. Ernest Yoshida interview, Cortez, Calif., January 24, 1982.
10. Kusaba, Lindley, and McClelland, p. 5.
11. Ibid., p. 6.

of the first arrivals found only dirt beneath their feet. The government sparsely furnished each apartment with steel army cots, a broom, a pot-bellied stove, and a coal bucket. Making a room "homelike" generally consisted of scavenging the lumber piles for scraps to make furniture, and partitioning spaces with blankets to provide a semblance of privacy.

Like the assembly center, the relocation camp contained a mixture of rural and urban residents. Approximately half of the Amache Camp inhabitants hailed from the Los Angeles area and had been funneled through the Santa Anita Assembly Center. These included urban merchants, doctors, lawyers, scientists, gardeners, and hotel and restaurant operators. The other half, sent from the Merced Assembly Center, were predominantly rural people from the agricultural sections of the central California valleys and the San Francisco Bay Area. Forty percent of the evacuees had been engaged in agriculture; 15 percent did domestic work; 10 percent held professional and managerial positions; 13 percent had done clerical and sales work. Sixteen percent did semi-skilled labor, and 6 percent unskilled.[12] At its population peak in 1943, Amache had 7,318 residents.[13]

About 260 Cortez people entered the Amache Camp, and the majority lived in Blocks 9E and 10E. Even among old friends and relatives, living so close together necessitated a certain amount of rearranging, as Sam Kuwahara learned. "I remember helping arrange the people moving into different barracks. I was all wrong. . . . They shifted around quite a bit. We thought relatives would want to stay together—naw, they didn't want to do that [Laughs]."[14]

The residents of the city that rose so quickly and completely from the prairie continued to follow the patterns of life established at the Merced Assembly Center, filling time with work, social and religious activities, classes, athletic and cultural events, and visiting. Amache, too, was run like a model city, through a series of departments headed by Euro-American administrators, with James Lindley, formerly of the Soil Conservation Corps as project director. As in the assembly cen-

---

12. Ibid., p. 7.

13. U.S. Department of the Interior, War Relocation Authority, *The Evacuated People: A Quantitative Description* (Washington, D.C.: Government Printing Office, 1946), p. 17. As Table 8 on p. 21 makes clear, the camp population fluctuated a great deal, as people transferred between camps, left for and returned from seasonal work, departed for military service, and left to seek education and work in the East and Midwest.

14. Sam Kuwahara interview, Cortez, Calif., January 25, 1982.

ter, there existed an internal fire department and police department, staffed by Japanese Americans.

In Amache, a community council of elected representatives became an established body. This contrasted with the situation at the Merced Assembly Center, where the vacillations of the Wartime Civil Control Administration (WCCA)—and the short period of duration—had hindered such attempts. In the relocation camp, members of each block who were eighteen years and older voted for a representative to the council, which was charged with "the prescription of ordinances, regulations, and laws governing community life within the center." In addition, a judicial commission of three administrative personnel and five Japanese Americans heard and tried cases regarding the violation of rules.[15] However, scholars have questioned the efficacy of such attempts at "community self-government," contending that elected representatives had little authority to effect change, and that the policy itself—by making only citizens eligible for election—widened the divisions between Issei and Nisei, vying for leadership.[16] As the Commission on Wartime Relocation and Internment of Civilians concluded, "many evacuees regarded the system as a sham, further evidence that they were not trusted, and an example of bad faith by the WRA."[17]

Each block also had a block manager, usually Issei, to oversee administrative matters. The duties of the manager, nominated by the residents but appointed by the project director, included handling requests for housing, heating, and household supplies, and relaying announcements and instructions from the administration. The other block staff person was the personnel director, in charge of the population and occupational records files. It was his job to facilitate labor recruitment, to ensure adequate distribution of food, to keep track of migration in and out of the camp, and to record vital statistics.[18]

Amache had a large educational program, similar to the other relocation camps.[19] In January 1944, the enrollment included 199 nursery school children, 802 kindergartners and elementary school pupils, 433 junior high school students, 549 high school students, and 1,043

15. Kusaba, Lindley, and McClelland, p. 10.
16. Wilson and Hosokawa, p. 219.
17. *Personal Justice Denied*, p. 174.
18. Kusaba, Lindley, and McClelland, p. 11.
19. For an examination of education in the camps, see James, *Exile Within*.

enrollees in the adult school. The school staff consisted of three principals, a superintendent, fifty-one WRA teachers, and forty-four Japanese American assistant teachers. Except for the high school, classes were held in remodeled barracks, and adult classes—ranging from sewing to English—met in the high school building or in special rooms of the 8H school block.

Envisioned as a longer-term project than the assembly centers, the Amache Camp had several internal enterprises: a silk-screen printing shop, cooperative stores, and a large agricultural section. Because of the WRA's early decision to encourage relocation outside of the camps and its desire not to compete with the industrial production of private business on the outside, most of the enterprises established within the relocation centers were geared to internal consumption. A notable exception was the Amache Silk Screen Shop, organized in June of 1943 at the request of the United States Navy. It was the only such project in all of the relocation centers. The forty-five evacuees who worked in the shop under the supervision of a WRA administrator contracted with the Navy to print thousands of training-aid posters. They also produced a calendar that prominently featured an Amache guard tower, as well as covers for in-camp publications.

In Amache, as in the nine other relocation camps, a cooperative handled most consumer services. The Amache Consumer's Cooperative, owned and operated by the evacuees, was established in 1943. WRA policy not only authorized such associations but prohibited the establishment of any other kind of consumer services, causing *Fortune* magazine to comment that the WRA was forbidding individual enterprise within the camps.[20] This policy appears to have been linked not only to the WRA's emphasis on relocation outside the camp, but also to anxieties regarding the maintenance of uniform wages in the camps,[21] a source of controversy among anti-Japanese forces. Barbers, clerks, and other cooperative workers all received a standard stipend according to the low WRA wage scale under which professionals received $19 a month, skilled workers were paid $16, and the unskilled $12. The Amache cooperative was supervised by a board of directors and several committees elected from among the 2,650 members. The cooperative stores and shops, housed in a U-shaped building composed of

20. "Issei, Nisei, Kibei," *Fortune* (April 1944), p. 7; Myer, p. 46.
21. Myer, pp. 40–43.

three barracks, offered clothing, shoes, and shoe repairs. In addition, there was a barber shop and beauty parlor, a canteen, a newspaper department, and a cleaning-and-pressing service.

Agriculture became the largest of the Amache enterprises. Early on, the WRA had determined that the evacuees should grow as much of their own food as possible and in that way assist in keeping camp menus to the ration cost of not more than 45 cents per person daily. Consequently, all of the camps grew vegetables and raised hogs. According to the report of a Euro-American staff officer, the Amache farm program had two main objectives: to produce as much of the crops and livestock needed to feed the evacuees and to "provide physical and mental employment acceptable to the residents."[22]

The federal government had acquired the sprawling 10,221.92 acres of the Granada project—another name for the Amache Relocation Center area—from private owners by direct purchase or condemnation. The camp center, the location of the administration buildings and barracks, occupied 640 of these acres. The two largest pieces of land were gained by condemnation: The biggest piece comprised 4,688 acres owned by Elbert S. Rule; the second largest piece—3,712 acres known as the Koen Ranch—was bought from the American Crystal Sugar Company.[23] Some of this land had been used for pasture but no one had ever before tried to grow vegetables on it.

In this agricultural endeavor, the camp supplied evacuee labor and supervisors; the government provided water, equipment, seed, and technical personnel. Initially, the technical staff consisted of four men and later, six: a chief of agriculture, a farm superintendent, two assistant superintendents, and two labor foremen. The farmland and various enterprises such as vegetable production, livestock, and food preserving were divided into a number of operating units, each headed by a Japanese American supervisor.[24] The agricultural section operated through 1943 and 1944. Although vegetable cultivation ceased in 1945,

22. Granada Relocation Center, Agricultural Section, Operations Division, *Historical Report* (Amache, Colo., ca. 1945), p. 1 (published by the Amache Historical Society, Torrance, Calif., in 1978).

23. The Amache Historical Society noted in their republication of the *Historical Report* that there was a great deal of inequity in payment for the Granada/Amache Project land—large companies and owners received generous reimbursement; small private owners received only a pittance.

24. Ibid., p. 1.

meat production continued until the closing of the center on October 15, 1945.

The evacuees grew a variety of crops that ranged from produce such as mung bean sprouts, daikon (Japanese radish), celery, lettuce, tomatoes and tea to feed crops like alfalfa, corn, sorghum, and milo. In all, the Amache farm yielded 6,051,661 pounds of vegetables grown on 1,044 acres, as well as 1,237,463 pounds of pork and beef, of which 285,230 pounds were sold to the highest bidder and to the Denver Livestock Commission companies. About one-fourth of the feed crops grown for Amache livestock was sold to the public as surplus. Despite the initial problems of inadequate machinery and facilities, and the internees' unfamiliarity with the Colorado terrain, the Amache farm produced enough of a surplus to ship some produce to other relocation centers.

As the Euro-American staff officer observed in his report, the farm project faced "numerous problems distinctly peculiar to the unusual circumstances under which it was conceived." One of these problems involved the lack of facilities: The poultry unit had 8,000 laying hens and housing for only 3,000; this resulted in feeding difficulties and low egg production, as hens laid eggs in an open twenty-acre field. Similarly, the hog project lacked enough pens for the segregation of new pigs and was also troubled by severe epidemics. Hundreds of acres of grain and corn were lost to drought because of irrigation problems.

Labor supply, however, proved to be the most crucial problem of the Amache farm program. Soon after the farm operations started, the WRA began issuing short-term leave permits to internees. Many, especially the Nisei, anxiously desired to escape the confines of camp and to seek higher wages than the standard $16 per month offered to relocation camp farm workers. Although both women and men left, most of those who did temporary agricultural work were male. Given the wartime labor shortage, many farmers were eager to have Japanese American workers, and as the staff officer ruefully noted, this placed the camp in competition with the labor demand on the outside. "It was not unusual for the [Amache] farm to lose all of its tractor drivers over night or to have 25–50 % of its trained supervisors leave within a period of two weeks. . . . When, in the spring of 1944, 29 of the 42 farm supervisors left, it created a problem little short of tragic."[25]

25. Ibid., p. 2.

The staff officer's report reveals not only the patronizing attitude of government administrators but also the evacuees' resistance to low-paid camp labor and their determination to act in their own interest. Not all could be described as willing docile workers in the relocation camp. Anger and frustration led some to say, "The government brot me here. They will have to feed me. I no work."[26] The most "loyal and willing workers," the officer found, were the Issei men and women—coincidentally those least likely to be able to leave the camps in search of temporary work elsewhere. The staff officer's approval of their willingness suggested mixed motives. He lauded the effort of hundreds of Japanese American volunteers who took time from their regular nonagricultural jobs to help with the harvest, but qualified his praise: "Too many wanted to work in the melon patch and some of the crops such as sweet potatoes, pop corn, daikon and beans made poor recorded yields because the volunteers carried home a large percentage of the crop they harvested."[27]

In addition, workers sought to exert come control over the pace of their labor. For instance, workers on the Koen Ranch section ate lunch at a mess hall established in the old Koen Hotel at the center of the farm. From the administrators' point of view, this practice "discouraged the tendency for workers to remain home in the afternoons," but it also allowed some workers to "sit under the shade for two hours each day."[28]

Despite the talk of common effort and self-sustenance, the hard fact remained that the evacuees performed arduous labor for poor wages, and the crops they produced did not mean individual bonuses or improvements. Little wonder, then, that many seized the opportunity to leave in search of better "physical and mental employment." And in light of the working and living conditions in the camp, the personal reaping of melons and daikon can be seen as a small means of resistance, individual and peer sanctioned. Securing a few hours of rest in the shade meant exercising a fraction of control and choice, which in turn provided a minimal basis of self-esteem.

The conditions of work and life in the relocation center necessitated flexibility. Like the Merced Assembly Center, the Amache Camp

26. Ibid., p. 4.
27. Ibid.
28. Ibid.

brought together a diverse group of people, young and old, urban and rural. Although most Cortez interviewees recalled that everyone had gotten along "pretty well," it is useful to balance these memories with evidence from the past that can illuminate details ordinarily filtered out by time. The massing together of so many different people in a small camp sparked strong reactions from some of the youth, whose letters indicate that harmonious relations did not come easily or quickly. Many adjustments had to be made. For example, urban-rural tensions erupted often in the early months. One Livingston teenager wrote to a former teacher, describing the animosity between the "Livingstonians" and "Santa Anitans": "I wish we could get unity here but it seems an impossible situation. If one from L.A. gets a grudge against a certain country person, they get in a big gang of fifteen or so and just knock the dickens out of this *one* person." She went on to detail the differences in urban Nisei fashion, which astonished some of the rural onlookers: "They carry knives, too, and are proud of it. They also wear zoot suits (pleated at the cuffs of the pants legs) and long 3/4 length coat-jackets—really disgusting."[29]

Two other high school students, one from Cortez and the other from Livingston, also complained of the rowdy behavior of the Santa Anita and Tanforan Nisei who were "always fighting or making trouble for us" at camp dances. "We don't get along with them," one concluded, "because they're city slickers and we're mostly country hicks."[30] These conflicts at Amache also exemplify some of the internal dissension that arose from regional loyalties at the various camps, each of which, according to Girdner and Loftis, "had its own atmosphere, dependent on the previous experience of evacuees there."[31]

A concern common to all the centers in the eyes of administrators, scholars, and inmates was the effect of camp life on the family. Nisei sociologist Harry Kitano, interned at the Topaz Camp, has asserted that in general, "the evacuation tended toward the destruction of established family patterns of behavior."[32] Daisuke Kitagawa, a Christian Issei minister at Tule Lake, similarly reported the breakdown of

29. Letter from June Suzuki to Barbara Carpenter, from Amache, Colo., December 9, 1942; cited by Brown, p. 157.
30. Letter from Haruko Kubo to Pat Carpenter, from Amache, Colo., October 4, 1942; cited by Brown, p. 157.
31. Girdner and Loftis, p. 247.
32. Kitano, p. 77.

traditional functions and the sense of family unity in the artificial community.[33] Both agreed that this brought about significant change in individual roles and expectations.

Notable alterations occurred in gender dynamics, with corresponding changes in family relations. A number of Issei women, accustomed to long days of work inside and outside the home, found that communally prepared meals and limited living quarters provided them with spare time. Although some experienced disorientation, many availed themselves of the opportunity to enjoy the company of their female peers and to attend adult classes ranging from handicrafts and Japanese arts to English.[34]

While these women gained an increased measure of independence, Kitano and Kitagawa observed, Issei men faced the loss of the authority and responsibility to which they were accustomed. No longer the major breadwinners of the family, they might in some cases be earning the same wages as their wives and children. And no matter how hard the Issei man worked, Kitagawa stated, "he could not improve the living conditions of his family."[35] The Issei men also lost much of their control of community leadership, because their alien status barred them from political activity under WRA rulings. These blows, as Jeanne Wakatsuki Houston recorded in her autobiographical account, *Farewell to Manzanar*, contributed to the deterioration of morale suffered by a number of the first generation.

A major anxiety of Issei parents and the older Nisei concerned the effect of the camp environment on the younger Nisei. In the relocation centers, the federal government assumed the family's function of providing food, clothing, and shelter, which in conjunction with the physical conditions loosened the reins of family social control.[36] In 1944, Leonard Bloom reported that the peer group had replaced the family as the organizing principle, and that the arrangement of community activities along age lines reinforced this tendency. Consequently, he asserted, each family member had become a "free agent," and "children detached themselves from parental supervision, return-

33. Daisuke Kitagawa, *Issei and Nisei, The Internment Years* (New York: Seabury Press, 1967), p. 86.

34. Ibid., pp. 89–90.

35. Ibid., p. 90.

36. Kitano, pp. 75–76.

ing to the home barracks perhaps only to sleep."[37] One worried parent at Tule Lake, Professor Yamato Ishihashi, lamented the "stealing out of stores and homes, smart alec thievery which we never had among Japanese children," and declared, "We no longer control our own families."[38]

A Nisei who voiced similar concerns was Eddie Shimano, editor first of the Santa Anita center newsletter and then of the *Communique* of the relocation camp at Jerome, Arkansas. He later served with the all-Nisei 442nd Regimental Combat Team. In an article published in the liberal journal *Common Ground* in 1943, Shimano indicted the camp's work system and its education courses, but he leveled his harshest critique at the effect of camp conditions on the Japanese American youth, who, "somewhere in the evacuation . . . had lost their pride." Genevieve Carter, a psychologist at Manzanar, echoed this concern over the fear and insecurity of adolescent Nisei regarding their place in a hostile society that denied their rights as citizens.[39] Shimano particularly noted how, as a substitute for lost pride and sense of belonging, many young men from their late teens to mid-twenties had formed "pachuco gangs" in the camps. These youths were emulated by the younger boys, who formed "junior gangs." Shimano observed, in accordance with the Cortez and Livingston teenagers, that "The pachuco gangs, easily spotted . . . by their 'uniforms' and long haircuts and zoot suits, crash social affairs, settle all personal grudges with physical assault, and follow pretty closely the pattern set by the Dead End gangs."[40] There are certainly parallels between the second-generation Mexican American youth of Los Angeles who, facing an "iron curtain" of discrimination, turned to close-knit peer groups for security and status, and those Nisei teenagers who, branded as enemy aliens by fellow Americans and conscious of their parents' vulnerability, banded together in the camps.[41] Journalist Carey McWilliams's interpretation

---

37. Leonard Bloom, "Familial Adjustments of Japanese-Americans to Relocation: First Phase," *American Sociological Review* 8(October 1943):559.

38. Girdner and Loftis, p. 317.

39. Genevieve W. Carter, "Child Care and Youth Problems in a Relocation Center," *Journal of Consulting Psychology* 8(July–August 1944):223–24.

40. Eddie Shimano, "Blueprint for a Slum," *Common Ground* 3(Summer 1943):81.

41. Carey McWilliams, *North from Mexico, The Spanish-Speaking People of the United States* (New York: Greenwood Press, 1968), pp. 240–41.

of the pachucos' zoot suits as "at once a sign of rebellion and a mark of belonging" can be extended to the Nisei's style of dress.[42]

At Amache, a number of Cortez Issei parents had cause to lament the influence of gangs and the wild behavior of their sons. (They hardly imagined their children's eventual respectability within the community.) One group of boys organized to counter the forays of the Los Angeles gangs, under the leadership of a very young Cortez teenager, Takeshi Sugiura, still known today as "General."

In the camps, where individuals spent most of their time with companions of their own age and gender, peer pressure could exert enormous force. For some, groups did provide a sense of camaraderie, but for others, gangs and peer pressure left lingering scars. One Cortez Nisei still remembers with pain the humiliation of being forced to shoplift items from the canteen for the older boys.

The majority of teenagers and children did not participate in gangs and violence. Many found outlets for their energies in sports, cultural events, and religious groups. Some, like Howard Taniguchi, took part in dramatic productions. Others, like Yuri Yamamoto and her siblings, were very much involved in Christian Endeavor activities. Like the assembly center, the camp offered a variety of classes and activities. However, this was not "summer camp." The dark side of internment shadowed the lives of the Nisei and provided yet another impetus for those who wished to leave.

Regardless of age and activities, the Nisei were highly conscious of their separation from "life on the outside," and their banishment to somewhere that wasn't quite America to them. This awareness— whether angry, wistful or bewildered—permeated their wartime writings. In this vein the 1944 Amache High School yearbook was dedicated to the Japanese American soldiers: "our brothers, our friends, our schoolmates, and our heroes—who will be 'over there' fighting for those ideals that they believe in and wish to establish and maintain for us." The yearbook was titled the 1944 *Onlooker*, implying that "we are onlookers—of necessity" but also looking to the future with the hope of "being once again within the orbit of world affairs."[43]

A Nisei woman soon to leave Amache expressed some of the evacuees' ambivalent feelings in a "love letter" to America, included at the

42. Ibid., p. 243.
43. *1944 Onlooker*, Foreword.

end of the yearbook. The letter was dated April 30, 1944, two years from the very day "I ceased to be a part of you [America]." She found:

> The new surroundings and experiences occupied all my attention at first, and my loneliness for you was crowded out. . . . I crammed my hours with continuous activity so that there would not be a chance for that loneliness to enter my being and begin its steady flow through my veins.

Like other evacuees, she discovered that "This plan worked wonderfully at first, but the activities soon became a drudgery to me." She also wrote obliquely of the injustice of evacuation:

> I worship you in spite of the errors you have made. Yes, you have made errors and you have roamed on many wrong roads; but everyone makes mistakes. . . . All I ask is that you do not make the same mistake twice; that is inexcusable even in the eyes of one who loves you so.

She concluded her letter with the anticipation of her approaching return to life on the outside. "I hope that your faith in me has grown since the last time I saw you," she wrote in quiet challenge, for "that faith must grow for my faith in you to grow."[44] Many Nisei carried such hopes with them to the Midwest and East when they left the isolated world of the camp, unsure of their reception but eager to return to America.

The machinery of their return moved slowly. The WRA's leave-clearance procedures and resettlement policy evolved cumbrously in the first two years of internment. The first to leave the camps in 1942 were workers with temporary leave permits. Because of the complicated screening process, few besides college students departed on "indefinite leave." In 1943 the WRA tried to expedite the clearance procedure by broadening an army registration program, aimed at Nisei males, to include all adults. With this policy change—and despite some tragic consequences, including postwar expatriation—an increasing stream of Japanese Americans, mostly Nisei, left the camps to seek work and education, or to go off to war.[45]

44. Betty Kanameishi, *1944 Onlooker.*
45. The disastrous consequences of this poorly thought out clearance procedure have been examined in depth by Weglyn, pp. 134–73; Wilson and Hosokawa, pp. 226–33; Girdner and Loftis, pp. 342–43; and Dorothy S. Thomas and Richard Nishimoto, *The*

In 1942 the WRA began to release temporarily Japanese Americans from assembly centers and relocation camps to do voluntary farmwork in neighboring areas hard hit by the wartime labor shortage. There was a particular demand for sugar-beet workers in Colorado. "During the harvest season a lot of farmers came into the camp to get the workers," recalled Kumekichi Taniguchi. "We went, too. We got stung."[46] After Kumekichi and a group of workers finished a backbreaking stint of beet-topping at one place, the farmer refused to pay them. Kumekichi's experience was not an unusual one. Vulnerable to exploitation, the evacuees had no real recourse to reimbursement when cheated. Their work conditions varied from situation to situation and from region to region, depending largely on the integrity of the individual farmer.

Despite their being credited with saving the sugar-beet crop of Utah, Idaho, Montana, and Wyoming, and having harvested much of Arizona's staple cotton crop, the Japanese Americans were not well received in all regions.[47] When the WRA began issuing "indefinite leave" permits, it directed the evacuees to the Midwest and East and also had to launch a public relations campaign, as Weglyn explained, "not only to mitigate evacuee fears but also to reeducate a paranoiac public to differentiate between the bitterly despised foes across the Pacific and fellow U.S. citizens."[48] A number of religious groups and service organizations—such as the American Friends Service Committee—provided invaluable aid in resettling internees.

By the fall of 1942, the likelihood of a Japanese attack on the United States had faded before Allied victories in the Pacific and, with it, the military justification for the internment of the Japanese Americans. How the WRA should proceed became the subject of complicated wrangling among civilian and army leaders.[49] The debate over whether the Nisei—then classified as enemy aliens—should be allowed to enlist in the armed forces soon meshed with the larger issue of the evacuees' return to normal life. The decision to probe their loyalty meant agonizing choices for many of the interned. As the Commission on Wartime Relocation and Internment of Civilians stated forty years

---

Spoilage, Japanese American Evacuation and Resettlement during World War II (Berkeley: University of California Press, 1969).

46. Kumekichi Taniguchi interview, Cortez, Calif., January 26, 1982.
47. Weglyn, p. 98.
48. Ibid., p. 101.
49. "Loyalty: Leave and Segregation," in *Personal Justice Denied*, pp. 185–212.

later, "It is a bitter irony that the loyalty review program, which the WRA and the War Department established as the predicate for release from the camps—the first major governmental decision in which the interests of the evacuees prevailed—was carried out without sufficient sensitivity or knowledge of the evacuees. Designed to hasten their release, the program instead became one of the most divisive, wrenching episodes of the captivity."[50]

In early 1943 army officers began to administer a questionnaire designed to determine the background and loyalties of the Nisei men; the WRA also prepared an "Application for Leave Clearance" geared to the Issei and the Nisei women. The distribution of these questionnaires to all evacuees over the age of seventeen resulted in a brutal streamlining of the clearance process. Elderly men and women, who were barred from naturalization, and American-born Nisei, who had been denied the rights of citizenship—all of whom had been recently torn from homes, businesses, and communities—were now expected to affirm their allegiance to the United States. This meant forswearing loyalty to any other country, as well as testifying to their willingness to serve in the armed forces of the country that had imprisoned them. This "colossal folly" became further compounded by the combining of the mass registration with an army recruitment drive which, as Weglyn pointed out, evidenced the restoration of one right: "the right to be shot at."[51]

The loyalty oath and army registration issue created painful dissension within many families, often between parents and sons, especially in the California and Arizona camps, which were surrounded by strong public hostility. Despite the internal conflicts, many Nisei men registered, eager to demonstrate their loyalty and willing to pay with their blood for acknowledgment as Americans. Just as registration required courage, so did the decision not to register. One Cortez Nisei who refused to go for an induction physical when called for duty by the Selective Service challenged the authorities: "If you were an able-bodied person in my situation, what would you do?" The answer was a six-month sentence in federal prison.[52]

50. Ibid., p. 186.
51. Weglyn, p. 136.
52. Some of the works dealing in depth with resistance within the camps are Daniels, *Concentration Camps*; Thomas and Nishimoto, *The Spoilage*; Kitagawa, *Issei and Nisei*; John Okada's novel, *No-No Boy* (Seattle: University of Washington Press, 1979); Gary Y. Okihiro, "Japanese Resistance in America's Concentration Camps: A Re-Evaluation,"

Other Cortez Nisei—including Hiroshi Asai, Key Kobayashi, Kaoru Masuda, Ken Miyamoto, Howard Taniguchi, and Kiyoshi Yamamoto—joined the approximately 33,000 Japanese Americans, half from Hawaii and half from the mainland, who fought in World War II.[53] Like many Nisei men, they served in the highly acclaimed 442nd Regimental Combat Team and with military intelligence after receiving training at the Military Intelligence Service Language School, which graduated nearly 6,000 Nisei by the end of the war. Nisei women served as well: more than 200 joined the U.S. Cadet Nursing Corps and some 100 entered the Women's Army Corps, including 51 linguists trained as translators by the Military Intelligence Service Language School at Fort Snelling.[54]

Of the Japanese American men and women who served in many capacities during World War II, the best known are the 100th Infantry Battalion and the 442nd Regimental Combat Team who together became known as "The Purple Heart Regiment" for the allegiance they proved in blood. Their motto, "Go for broke," was a Hawaiian gambler's expression, and their emblem—chosen in preference to the War Department's original design of a yellow arm grasping a red sword— was a silver hand bearing a torch, on a field of blue. By the end of the war, they had garnered 18,143 individual awards for valor, becoming "the most decorated unit for its size and length of service in the history of the United States."[55]

The 100th Battalion had its inception in a recommendation by Hawaiian Commander Lieutenant General Delos Emmons. In February 1942, upon learning that the Department of War intended to release the Nisei from active duty, Emmons—mindful of both the Hawaiian Japanese Americans' wish to participate in military service and their

---

Amerasia Journal 2(1973):20–34; Arthur A. Hansen and David A. Hacker, "The Manzanar Riot: An Ethnic Perspective," *Amerasia Journal* 2(Fall 1974):112–57; Douglas W. Nelson, *Heart Mountain: The History of an American Concentration Camp* (Madison: State Historical Society of Wisconsin for the Department of History, University of Wisconsin, 1976); Brian Masaru Hayashi, " 'For the Sake of Our Japanese Brethren': Assimilation, Nationalism, and Protestantism among the Japanese of Los Angeles, 1895–1942," Ph.D. diss., University of California at Los Angeles, 1990.

53. Wilson and Hosokawa, p. 243.

54. Masaharu Ano, "Loyal Linguists: Nisei of World War II Learned Japanese in Minnesota," *Minnesota History* 45(Fall 1977):283; Nakano, p. 170.

55. "Go for Broke" exhibition brochure, Presidio Army Museum, 1981, p. 21; Girdner and Loftis, p. 330.

role in the local workforce—suggested the formation of a Nisei unit. After more than a year of training on the mainland, the initial 1,432 men of the 100th Battalion arrived in North Africa in September 1943. They sustained heavy casualties and earned 900 Purple Hearts in the grueling Allied campaign through Italy.[56]

The 100th Battalion soon met with the 442nd Regimental Combat Team in the offensive from the Anzio beachhead in June 1944. Comprised principally of Hawaiian and mainland Nisei, the 442nd had trained primarily at Camp Shelby in Mississippi from October 1943 to February 1944. The 100th Battalion formally became part of the 442nd on June 15, 1944.[57] The officers of both the 100th and the 442nd were predominantly Euro-Americans, but all of the enlisted men were Nisei, classified by their draft boards as "4-C, Enemy Alien."

Hiro Asai, one of the Cortez Nisei who served in the 442nd, joined in 1943, went to a training camp in Florida and then to Fort Meade, Maryland. He reached France with the 442nd in the winter of 1944. They stayed at Brest, on the Atlantic Coast of Normandy, holding the line until more replacements arrived; then they received orders to ship out to Italy. They fought all the way up northern Italy, from Leghorn to near Genoa. The day before the war ended in Italy, Hiro was wounded by a hand grenade: "We were fighting from hill to hill . . . up in the mountains. . . . We were advancing so fast that they told us to hold the line until the rest of the Allied Forces could come up in line, because there would be too much of a gap." The commanding officer wanted to press on, but contented himself with sending a scouting force—Hiro's platoon—ahead to gauge enemy resistance. When they reached the "next hill" several miles away, "all hell broke loose. They started shooting us from all sides and from behind, too." Six of the platoon were wounded, but all escaped.[58]

The 100th and the 442nd fought in seven major campaigns in France and Italy, including the famed rescue of the "Lost Battalion." Ordered to reach at any cost the 211 survivors of the 141st Regiment, sur-

---

56. *Personal Justice Denied*, p. 256. For fuller accounts of the 100th and the 442nd, see Masayo Umezawa Duus, *Unlikely Liberators, The Men of the 100th and 442nd*, trans. Peter Duus (Honolulu: University of Hawaii Press, 1983, 1987), and Thomas D. Murphy, *Ambassadors in Arms* (Honolulu: University of Hawaii Press, 1954).

57. *Personal Justice Denied*, p. 256. As Gary Okihiro has helpfully pointed out, a Korean American and several part-Hawaiian men also served in the 100th Battalion.

58. Hiroshi Asai interview, Cortez, Calif., February 23, 1982.

rounded by Germans near Bruyères, the 442nd did so with a sacrifice of more than 200 dead and 600 wounded. By the end of the war, the 100th and the 442nd had suffered 9,486 casualties, "more than twice the assigned complement of men in the unit."[59] The exploits of the 442nd and the 100th attracted much public attention in the United States and, in the words of writer Noriko Sawada Bridges, made them "Our stepping stones to freedom."[60]

The Nisei who graduated from the Military Intelligence Service Language School (MISLS) and served in nonsegregated units in the Pacific have received less recognition, despite the critical role they played as translators, interpreters, interrogators, and cave-flushers. Major General Charles Willoughby, MacArthur's chief of intelligence, claimed that "the Nisei MIS shortened the Pacific war by two years."[61] Their activities long remained a military secret, partly for their own protection, partly to conceal from the enemy the existence of expert linguists who were translating intercepted materials and questioning prisoners.[62] Joseph D. Harrington has contended that "a grudging Pentagon" kept silent about the details of their service for three decades after the war.[63]

The MISLS, according to Masaharu Ano, was the only source of linguists for the U.S. military during World War II. The school opened in November 1941 at the Presidio in San Francisco; there the students immersed themselves in intensive study of spoken and written Japa-

59. "Go for Broke" exhibition brochure, p. 21. The usual regimental complement is 4,500. Given their distinguished record, Hosokawa and Wilson have pointed out that it is strange that only one Nisei received the Medal of Honor. Fifty-two Nisei were awarded the next highest decoration, the Distinguished Service Cross, indicating that a number were recommended for the Medal of Honor and that the recommendations were downgraded. At the end of the war, following a Military Affairs Committee investigation, Pfc. Sadao Munemori—one of 650 who gave their lives—became the only Nisei to win the Medal of Honor in World War II. "Had the men of the 442nd been of a different color," Wilson and Hosokawa ask, "would there have been more Medal of Honor winners?" (p. 240).

60. Noriko Sawada Bridges, "To Be or Not to Be: There's No Such Option," broadside, no date. The experiences of the 442nd find parallel in those of the also segregated Chicano "E" Company of World War II, chronicled in Raul Morin's *Among the Valiant: Mexican-Americans in World War II and Korea* (Alhambra, Calif.: Borden, 1966).

61. *Personal Justice Denied*, p. 256; for accounts of the Nisei MIS, see Joseph D. Harrington, *Yankee Samurai (The Secret Role of Nisei in America's Pacific Victory)* (Detroit, Mich.: Pettigrew, 1979), and Ano, pp. 273–87.

62. Wilson and Hosokawa, pp. 240–41.

63. Harrington, pp. 11–12.

nese, document analysis and interrogation, as well as Japanese geography, culture, and military structure. In June 1942 the program moved to Camp Savage in Minnesota, spurred both by the need for larger facilities and by public hostility toward the specially recruited Nisei students. Rapid growth prompted another move to Fort Snelling, Minnesota, where the program remained until it found a permanent base in 1946 at the Presidio in Monterey, California.[64] The first MISLS graduates met with suspicion by military officers who balked at accepting them. This changed, however, after they proved their loyalty and skill in the Aleutian Islands and at Guadalcanal.[65] More than 5,000 MISLS graduates, the large majority of them Nisei, served with 130 different units of the armed forces and on loan to Allied armies.[66] After the war, they became a "language bridge" between the Allied occupation forces and the Japanese, working as translators at war crimes trials, gathering statistics for an Atomic Bomb Survey, and acting as censors.[67]

Among the highly trained MISLS graduates was Kiyoshi Yamamoto, a Cortez Nisei. Kiyoshi had finished his last year of high school in Amache and then, after discovering resistance from some state universities toward Japanese American students, he attended, like many Nisei, a church-affiliated school. After a year of studying engineering in Iowa, he received his draft notice. "I thought, 'Well, there's an opportunity to go to the language school and go to the Pacific.' " Kiyoshi passed the qualifying exam and went to the MISLS—first at Camp Savage and then Fort Snelling—for nine months of rigorous training in Japanese. "We had intensive schooling from eight to four during the day, and compulsory studies from seven to nine. We were required to go from seven to nine, but most of us studied from six to ten, so we really studied hard."[68] The MISLS teachers were all Japanese Americans—some Kibei (Nisei sent to Japan for education and then repatriated) and some Nisei—as were all of the students.

Inequities persisted at the MISLS as in other branches of the army. Kiyoshi noted that at Fort Snelling there was also "an officers' candidate school . . . and it was all *hakujin* [white people] taking Japanese.

---

64. Ano, pp. 273–87.
65. Harrington, p. 89; Ano, pp. 277–79.
66. Ano, p. 283.
67. Ibid., p. 287.
68. Kiyoshi Yamamoto interview, Cortez, Calif., February 6, 1982.

But when they graduated, they were officers. When we graduated, we were just enlisted men. . . . All we got was a few stripes."[69] Harrington reached a similar verdict, stating, "Nisei got an unfair deal regarding advancement during the war although 100 or so were commissioned in 1945 as a public relations ploy. Very few got commissions before then. . . . Despite their colossal combined achievements, few Nisei ended the war higher than Staff Sergeant, and most finished at a lower grade."[70]

After Kiyoshi had completed nine months of language studies and two months of basic training, the war with Japan ended when atomic bombs were dropped on Hiroshima and Nagasaki. "So they rushed us—we went to the Philippines first and then from the Philippines some of the boys went to the war crimes trial in Manila; some went to the signing of the peace on the *Missouri;* and some went to the war crimes trial in Tokyo."[71] Kiyoshi was sent to Tokyo where he interrogated Japanese Air Force officers and translated the index of an air force manual. During his tour of duty, he traveled in Japan and met his parents' relatives in Yamaguchi-ken: "It was a strange feeling, because they felt strange, too. They knew I was their nephew, yet serving in the occupational forces. They couldn't quite understand. But it was nice. I went to visit them twice."[72]

While Nisei like Kiyoshi Yamamoto and Hiro Asai departed from the camps to serve in the armed forces, others left the barbed wire perimeters to face new challenges on the home front.

College students were the first to depart from the camps with indefinite leave permits. Between 1942 and 1946, 4,084 of them did so with the assistance of the National Japanese American Student Relocation Council, a nongovernmental agency largely composed of concerned educators.[73] The NJASRC proved instrumental in persuading schools outside the Western Defense Zone to accept Japanese American students and helping them to obtain leave clearances.

Some of the students had graduated from the makeshift high schools set up in the camps; others were trying to continue a college

---

69. Ibid.
70. Harrington, p. 87.
71. Kiyoshi Yamamoto interview, Cortez, Calif., February 6, 1982.
72. Ibid.
73. According to educator Robert O'Brien (p. 90), 4,300 Japanese American students were relocated altogether.

education abruptly terminated by the evacuation. In 1941, on the eve of the war, 3,530 Nisei were attending college.[74] Mark Kamiya had completed one year of agricultural studies when the war began. While doing temporary work outside the Amache camp—washing, sacking, and loading potatoes and working in fields of sugar beets and cantaloupes—he began to apply for college admission. The first to accept him was Brigham Young University, but he found the racial attitudes prevailing there incompatible with his own. After taking a required course in religion in which the professor expounded on the inferiority of African Americans, Mark could stand it no longer. Three quarters after his arrival, he left. He then went to Cornell University, known for its fine agricultural department, to see if the college would accept him. Cornell denied him admission, first on the grounds that they preferred not to take out-of-state students. Mark knew that the school was practically empty. He finally asked a university administrator, "Isn't it because I'm Japanese that you don't want to accept me?" The man admitted it was true, and then said, "Well, after talking to you, I think we can accept you for one semester."[75] In anticipation, Mark took a job in a local dairy, but discovered during his eight months there that he wanted to study Hegel and Marx rather than crop rotation. After the war and his completion of an eighteen-month tour of duty in the army, he enrolled in the University of California at Berkeley and graduated with a degree in philosophy.

Nisei women comprised an unprecedented 40 percent of the relocating college students.[76] According to the U.S. Census of 1940, women constituted 32 percent of the 1,132 Nisei over the age of twenty-five who had completed one to three years of college, and 29 percent of the 1,049 who had four or more years. Among them was Mary Noda, who finished high school in Amache and then attended Colorado State University at Greeley for two years. It was her "first time away from home," and like many other students, she worried about the transition to college. "I was worried about my ability to do the work. . . . I worried so much I couldn't study."[77] The strain of adjustment to the university and life away from her family was compounded by a taxing schedule of domestic work that helped pay for her education.

74. Ibid., p. 135.
75. Mark Kamiya interview, Cortez, Calif., February 8, 1982.
76. O'Brien, p. 74.
77. Mary Noda Kamiya interview, Ballico, Calif., February 13, 1982.

Despite their uncertainties about the reception awaiting them and several early incidents of hostility, the Nisei continued to leave for schools, many in areas where they became the first Asian Americans ever seen. The previous presence of Japanese Americans in an area, however, did not necessarily make the adjustment any easier. The Japanese Americans in Colorado were among the fortunate minority who lived outside the military defense zone on the West Coast, and so escaped internment. As one Cortez Nisei remembered painfully, some of the Colorado college instructors compared the evacuated California students unfavorably with the uninterned Nisei with whom they were familiar and demanded, "Why aren't you like the Colorado Japanese?" The differences in economic concerns, clothes, poise, and self-confidence were obvious, but any answer to that insensitive question would have been painful and unspeakable during the war years.

By 1943, as the WRA's resettlement program developed, increasing numbers of Japanese Americans streamed from the relocation camps to the Midwest and East. By August 1943, almost 11,000 evacuees had left the camps on indefinite leave and by the end of 1944, approximately 35,000—or a third of the original camp population—had gone.[78] These included predominantly single Nisei and young couples whose language skills, citizenship, and age gave them a better chance than the Issei in the labor market. Among them were a large number of women; as Leonard Bloom noted, "Japanese traditions of control over young women failed to materially affect their relocation rate."[79] Women's developing sense of independence in the camp environment and their growing awareness of their abilities as workers contributed to their self-confidence and hence their desire to leave. By the end of the war, 37 percent of the evacuees sixteen years or older had already relocated, including 63 percent of the Nisei women in that age group.[80]

Because job availability and general reception of the Japanese Americans were better in urban centers than in rural areas, most headed for the cities. Accordingly, the WRA established field offices in Chicago, Cleveland, Denver, Kansas City, Little Rock, New York, and Salt Lake City.[81] There, with the placement assistance of the WRA and various

78. Leonard Bloom, "Transitional Adjustments of Japanese-American Families to Relocation," *American Sociological Review* 12(April 1947):206.

79. Ibid., p. 208.

80. Leonard Bloom and Ruth Riemer, *Removal and Return: The Socio-Economic Effects of the War on Japanese Americans* (Berkeley: University of California Press, 1949), p. 36.

81. Wilson and Hosokawa, p. 218.

religious and service organizations, the Japanese Americans turned their energies to adjusting to life in new environments.

Although they found work in restaurants, factories, and businesses, the most numerous job requests for Japanese American women and men were in the field of domestic service. As the wartime labor shortage opened new doors for African American, Mexican American, and Euro-American women, many of them left domestic positions for better-paying work in factories and defense plants. Nisei like Yeichi and May Sakaguchi and Miye Kato filled the open positions.

Like many Japanese Americans who traveled with friends or kin, Miye Kato left Amache in September, 1943, with three other Nisei—June Taniguchi, Takako Hashimoto, and Sumi Nishihara. Miye found a domestic job in Medford, Connecticut, through a Methodist church. Two of the ministers had visited Amache and subsequently helped to relocate the Japanese Americans. "They looked after us and whenever we had free time, they would invite us over to their home. If we had any problem, we asked them."[82] June worked with Miye's sister in a girls' dormitory in Bridgeport, Connecticut, and soon Miye obtained a position with a lawyer's family there.

After a year in Bridgeport, Miye and her sister decided to go to Chicago. She recounted: "We tried hotel work, but we lasted only one day! We didn't like it at all. So we went again to find a domestic job." From Chicago they moved to Evanston, Illinois, to be closer to their brother who was stationed at Camp Savage in Minnesota. There they found work situations with families who treated them well; and there Miye stayed until her marriage to Nobuzo Baba at Amache in July 1945.[83]

While some Nisei found mutual support in journeying forth together, others ventured alone into regions where few, if any, Japanese Americans had ever traveled. After she spent two years at Greeley, Mary Noda's brother—then a teacher in Iowa—helped her find a position in North Dakota. There, at age nineteen, she taught strapping seventh- and eighth-graders in a town of 200. "It was a nice experience," she recalled. "They had never seen a Japanese American." The superintendent had been too afraid to tell anyone that the new teacher was Japanese American, but tried to mitigate the surprise by saying, "I don't know what's coming. She might be an Indian." In fact, Mary

82. Miye Kato Baba interview, Cortez, Calif., July 18, 1982.
83. Ibid.

said, "People thought I was an Indian on the train." During her year in North Dakota, Mary boarded with a Russian-German immigrant woman and grew accustomed to eating meat, white bread, and potatoes three times a day. The townspeople invited her to stay on, but she returned to California in 1946 to finish her education degree at San Francisco State University.[84]

Many men and a lesser number of women—like Florice Kuwahara and Ruth Nishi Yoshida—found jobs as factory workers. Florice and Sam Kuwahara left Amache in May 1943 to work on a farm in Adams City, Colorado. After one painful week—"Whatever I earned, I was spending on liniment," recalled Sam—they moved to Denver. There Sam worked in the produce business and Florice took a job doing piecework in a garment factory. "I don't know how much they paid us, I think it was about 25 cents an hour, but by the time they took my income tax, my Social Security, and war bonds, there wasn't much left." Florice laughed and added, "Of course, that was when I just started. . . . But everything was cheap in those days."[85] Florice worked there for three years, a long record among the Nisei during the war.

Because of the varying work conditions and wages, job turnover among the Nisei was high. Ernest Yoshida's wartime work history illustrates this trend. Admitted to the Milwaukee School of Engineering in the fall of 1942, he arrived on campus only to find that most of the instructors had been drafted, and no one could teach the courses he wanted to take. The school refused to refund his tuition payment and told him he could take classes in welding, a skill he already had. Ernest encountered another Nisei in the same situation, Tad Morishige (whose cousin knew Ernie), and together they went to Chicago to seek work. On their first night there, on a lead from their landlady, they began work as stockboys at a soda-water bottling plant, for $1.82 an hour. A short time later, they found work at the Cuneo Press which printed *Time* magazine and *Newsweek*. There for six months Ernest was assistant to a "trimmer" who trimmed the sides of the magazine. Then the two Nisei began making pup-tent valves at a factory where Ernie met his future wife, Ruth Nishi. For a short time he installed radios in army jeeps, but the cold, dark workplace motivated him to apply elsewhere. After three weeks as a bottler for Canadian Club, a blended whiskey, Ernest went to a house-trailer factory where he could use his

84. Mary Noda Kamiya interview, Ballico, Calif., February 13, 1982.
85. Florice Morimoto Kuwahara interview, Cortez, Calif., January 25, 1982.

skills as a carpenter. The piecework payment was excellent but the management's treatment deplorable. One day, a janitor's accidental push caused Ernest to lose part of a finger to a wood router from which the safety guard had been removed for the sake of speed. The boss said he was "too busy" to take him to a doctor, so, bleeding profusely, Ernest had to find a streetcar. When he quit the job, two other angry Nisei left with him.[86]

According to Hosokawa and Wilson, "The first evacuees to be hired by a firm were often the best argument for hiring additional evacuees."[87] They were not only the best argument, but also frequently the means of hiring the additional evacuees. After George Yuge found a job making ammunition boxes at a Denver defense plant, the boss, impressed by the crate-nailing skills that he developed in Cortez, asked, "Do you know any other Japanese who can do that?" "I know a few," George said, and soon Smile Kamiya and five other Nisei were hard at work hammering together boxes with him.[88]

In the midst of their travels and job hunting, like earlier groups of working-class rural migrants and foreign immigrants, the Japanese Americans relied upon a flexible support network of friends and relatives, otherwise known as chain migration. Many of them combined forces in the search for jobs and lodging, like Ernest and Tad. Their ties to associates from their former communities and the camps formed vital grapevines, passing news of work and hospitable neighborhoods as well as warnings of exploitative situations. News traveled quickly, as Ernest learned at his next job at the Fowler McCormick tractor assembly plant. After a week of sweeping the floor, he was put on the line for small tractors. Two days later, a manager promoted him to the position of line foreman and asked him to find some more Japanese Americans to work on the line. Ernest told Brush Arai, a Hawaiian friend, that he needed fifty people right away. In a week, fifty arrived from three camps: Amache, Rohwer Camp in Arkansas, and Heart Mountain Camp, Wyoming. To the delight of the management, tractor production increased from 74 to 86 on their first day of work, and within three months they had increased the production to 136 tractors a day.[89]

---

86. Ernest Yoshida interview, Cortez, Calif., January 24, 1982.
87. Wilson and Hosokawa, p. 219.
88. George Yuge interview, Cortez, Calif., February 8, 1982.
89. Ernest Yoshida interview, Cortez, Calif., January 24, 1982.

The Japanese Americans who resettled first not only passed along information but also provided way stations for the friends and relatives who followed. When George and Helen Yuge left the Poston Camp for Denver, they lived with Helen's father and mother-in-law, Helen's sister and brother, George's brother, Smile Kamiya, and another Nisei who later died in Italy serving with the 442nd. "It used to be like a boardinghouse." When Helen and George moved to their own home in a different part of town, one of Helen's nieces lived with them, as well as several other people. "And every Saturday night, never missed, there used to be great big poker parties," George recalled.

> I never played poker at home [before the war], but the fellows there would come, and she'd always have a big dinner for them. . . . All these Nisei GIs on furlough would congregate down at our place. Many of them we knew—they were all kids from Watsonville and Salinas and places like that. They didn't have any place to go, so they'd come over, or a friend would bring a friend. . . . Gosh, it was nothing Saturday night to have eighteen, twenty people sitting there.[90]

Although they often worked with *hakujin*, the Nisei generally socialized with other Nisei. It was their ties to Japanese American friends and family on which they drew for emotional support and understanding during the war years.

It is impossible to summarize neatly the wartime experiences and feelings of even one family or community, much less the entire Japanese American population. A small number, living beyond the Western Defense Zone, were not evacuated, but 120,000 in the zone were: some to prison camps, the majority to ten concentration camps or "relocation centers." Of these, Wilson and Hosokawa have stated, "It can be safely said that there were no happy Relocation Centers. All had their problems."[91] The Issei and Nisei did their best to make that life as bearable and regular as possible, and a large number of them— both women and men—left it as soon as they could.

Regardless of the length of their stay in the camps, all were affected

90. George Yuge interview, Cortez, Calif., February 8, 1982.
91. Wilson and Hosokawa, p. 220.

by the evacuation. In addition to economic and psychological losses, internment altered family roles and accelerated the trends that differentiated the second generation from their parents. Kitano has emphasized the impact of evacuation and relocation on the acculturation of the Japanese Americans: "New exposure, new opportunities, the dissolution of old institutions and structures, and life away from the ghetto hastened change."[92] While the structure of camp life loosened parental control of children, the WRA policies transferred community leadership from the Issei to the Nisei, resulting, as several scholars have contended, in competition between the two generations and the increasing independence of the Nisei.

In addition to generational roles, as Kitagawa and others have observed, gender roles also changed. As before the war, most family members worked, but men, women, boys, and girls all received the same low wage, which increased the independence of women. Furthermore, when the relocation program began, Nisei women as well as men traveled far from their families to seek opportunities in the Midwest and East.[93]

The experiences of the Cortez people reflect the stress and hardship of camp and relocation. However, the patterns of their lives also evidence the strength of support networks formed before and during the war, and the continuity of ties of affection and responsibility. Whether they departed for military service or to pursue jobs and education, all faced adjustment to unfamiliar environments and work. They were sustained through this period by deep-rooted networks of relatives and friends, and they maintained family bonds even though many journeyed farther from home than ever before. It was a time of independence, camaraderie, and experimentation as well as frustration, insecurity, and loneliness.

By 1945, 35,000 Japanese Americans had already resettled outside the Western Defense Zone. After the War Department ended the exclusion of the Japanese Americans from the West Coast, the majority chose to return. Many individuals and families journeyed back to the areas they called "home," but the available evidence indicates that Cortez, Cressey, and Livingston are the only communities that re-

92. Kitano, p. 75.
93. I have examined the wartime experiences of Nisei women—particularly those who left the camps to seek work and education—in greater detail in an article, "Japanese American Women during World War II," *Frontiers* 8, no. 1 (1984):6–14.

turned *as communities*, in an organized fashion. The hardship of re-building and the salvaging of dreams that awaited them would prove as demanding of their resources and stamina as the initial evacuation. The new Cortez would be a different one, the structure and contours of its relationships altered by the transfer of leadership to the Nisei, the influx of newcomers—mostly women marrying into the commu-nity—and the arrival of the Sansei, the third generation.

CHAPTER 5

Reweaving the Web
of Community

On January 2, 1945, eight months before the surrender of Japan, the U.S. Army ended the total exclusion of Japanese American civilians from the West Coast. By mid-1944, it became obvious that a Japanese attack on the West Coast would never materialize. Furthermore, the Endo and Korematsu cases had brought the constitutionality of exclusion before the Supreme Court. Anxious about the possible undermining of their authority by the court, the military—including the Western Defense Command, then headed by General Delos Emmons—began to approve relaxation of territorial restrictions.[1] However, to avoid losing votes for the Administration, no action was taken until after Roosevelt's reelection in November 1944. On December 17, the day before the Endo decision ruled continued detention of loyal citizens unconstitutional,[2] Emmons's successor, Major General Henry C. Pratt, proclaimed that exclusion would end on January 2, 1945. This news was followed the next day by a War Relocation Authority (WRA) statement of the closure of the relocation centers by the end of 1945 and the termination of the WRA relocation program by mid-1946.

The army's announcement sparked quick reactions on the West Coast. Emotions ran high in some sectors of California, as politicians and the Hearst Press decried the decision. Although some groups like

---

1. Daniels, *Concentration Camps*, p. 156.
2. Wilson and Hosokawa, p. 232 and chap. 16; Daniels, *Concentration Camps*, p. 157.

the Fair Play Committee and the American Friends Service Committee worked to ease the transition, there grew concerted opposition to the return of the Japanese Americans and violent outbursts of hostility in interior farming regions, from the Mexican border to Placer County.

The evacuated growers of the Cortez and Livingston colonies had anticipated the rescission several months earlier and had begun to contemplate their return. Because they had, before the evacuation, jointly arranged for the supervision of their farms and produce marketing by an experienced Euro-American manager, they were among the approximately one-fourth of prewar Japanese American farmers who had land to which they could return. The larger historical record of Japanese American resettlement also suggests the uniqueness of the Abiko colonies in their ability to return *as communities.* The Livingston, Cortez, and Cressey growers met on January 13, 1945, in Amache to discuss both the return to California and the liquidation of the G. A. Momberg organization that had operated their farms during their absence. Momberg, trustee Hugh Griswold, and advisory board members C. L. Stringer and Dallas Bache attended the meeting, as well as four Amache Camp administrators, including J. L. Lindley, the project director.

At this time, all evacuees in the relocation centers could return to the West Coast but needed to have an approved relocation plan in order to qualify for WRA assistance—a stipulation that the Cortez and Yamato colonies were in a good position to meet. Momberg and the three advisers spoke in favor of an early return to California, unlike other councillors who caused the WRA officials much frustration by suggesting that the evacuees wait until the end of the war and for an improvement in public opinion. Momberg advised that a few well-known growers return immediately to "break the ice for others to follow," and to become familiar with the new farm operations in field and office. Griswold cautioned that opposition to the return of the Japanese Americans was quite strong. He cited the feelings expressed in the newspapers, but Stringer added that "anti-Japanese sentiment derived from the talk of irresponsible and uninformed people," and that he anticipated no incidents of hostility. Amache Camp director Lindley agreed that the people of the Abiko colonies could return home.

These meetings set in motion the mechanics of their return to California and the rebuilding of the postwar community, the focus of this chapter. In the demanding years ahead, the community underwent

A meeting with Gus Momberg in 1945 at Amache. Front row, from left: Kumataro Matsumoto, Nobuhiro Kajioka, Saburo Minabe, Franklin Okuda, Chokichi Sakaguchi, Norman Kishi, Kenji Minabe, Gus A. Momberg (manager and agent), Yakichi Kajioka, Katsuchika Kashiwase, Frank Toyoji Konno, Tomoshiro Tanji, Hugh Griswold (attorney and trustee), and Dallas Bache (advisory board member). Middle row: Kenji Tsuchiya, Uhei Tanaka, Yonekichi Kuwahara, Nobuyoshi Baba, Cy L. Stringer (trustee), Saburo Narita, Jirokichi Kimoto, Jitsuo Handa (?), Masao Hoshino, Isaji Kirihara, Ichijiro Kinoshita, Ichiro Minabe, and Tatsuzo Hoshino. Back row: Buichi Kajiwara, Kiyoshi Asai, Zenshiro Yuge, Yukihiro Yotsuya, Genichi Kimura, Rokutaro Yamamoto, Joe Kamiya, Gennosuke Kimura, Kumekichi Taniguchi, William B. Yoshino, an unidentified woman, Mrs. Reiko Yoshino, Rinai Shoji, Ikuko Yamamoto, Roy Kishi, Sanmatsu Miyahara, Heigoro Yoshino, Takeo Yotsuya, Nobuzo Baba, George Morofuji, and Mack Yamaguchi. Photo courtesy of Nobuzo Baba.

considerable change and growth. Nisei marriages brought in an influx of newcomers, primarily Nisei women marrying the sons of Cortez, and thus also heralded the appearance of the Sansei, the third generation. Alterations in the social climate, personal expectations, and resources catalyzed change in the parent-child relationship, causing marked differences in the Sansei's experiences of childhood and adolescence, as compared with those of the Nisei. As the Issei retired, authority and responsibility increasingly passed to the second generation—a shift reflected in community organizations. While these institutions continued to provide support, they also evolved to meet changing needs and attitudes within the community.

As news spread of the Army's pending decision regarding the return of the Japanese Americans, many California politicians and journalists protested, including Elbert G. Adams, editor and owner of the *Livingston Chronicle*, as well as past president of the Merced County Anti-Japanese Association of the early 1920s. In a brief editorial on December 14, 1944, he pronounced the wartime return of the evacuees "a grave mistake in policy" and warned that resultant disorders "in any community could well get beyond the control of local peace officers."[3] A week later, with definite confirmation of the end of exclusion, Adams wrote a lengthier and more ambiguous column, perhaps reflective of the mixed sentiments in the Livingston–Cortez–Cressey area.

Adams's ambivalence regarding the interned people echoed the tone of his earlier editorials written at the height of the anti-Japanese movement of the early 1920s. While Adams reiterated his opposition to the army's decision, he also predicted that "no matter what the general picture may turn out to be, it is reasonably certain that it will be different from the one here in Livingston and vicinity. The picture here always was different." He added that the local results would "be different in that they will be less a cause of trouble."

Like many other Americans, Adams had taken an interest in the military service of the Japanese Americans and devoted one-third of this editorial to the exceptional record of the Livingston Japanese. "The highest per capita record of army enlistments among Japanese Americans of any community, including Hawaii," he noted, "come

3. *Livingston Chronicle*, December 14, 1944.

from Merced County. . . . The percentage of casualties among Livingston Japanese in the armed service is somewhere more than twice that of the Livingston men as a whole, and Livingston, be it remembered, has had the highest casualty rate of any community in California with the possible exceptions of Salinas and Watsonville."[4] Whether statistically accurate or not, this statement reflects the impact of the Nisei soldiers' impressive service record on the U.S. public.

In 1944, Dillon S. Myer, head of the WRA, estimated that three-quarters of the evacuees would return to the West Coast. Adams, however, speculated that 40 percent of the former local population would come back, and that of this number only half would remain permanently. In July 1945, he corrected his prediction with the announcement that most of the Livingston and Cortez evacuees still at Amache planned to return home.[5]

A month after the rescission, another journalist, Robert Sullivan, writing for the *New York Daily News,* observed that less than 300 Japanese Americans had left the camps for familiar territory; he assessed public sentiment on the West Coast as uncertain, "definitely antagonistic in places, indifferent in others."[6] The antagonism, he asserted, often had "an economic basis. Their farms and their shops were good ones. Those who are operating the Japanese properties do not want to see the owners come back." However, Sullivan, who mainly focused his article on the history of the Livingston Colony, the Amache Camp, and the Momberg operation, reported "no trouble in Merced County" and restated the ambivalence of local feeling: "Opinion is that when the Japanese do come back, they will be lawfully treated, but the general hope there seems to be that something will happen persuading the Japanese not to return." The difficulties met by the first returning evacuees began when their opponents stopped hoping and decided to make "something happen."

The people of Cortez and Livingston had considered the logistics of their return for months. In October of 1944, Griswold and Momberg wrote to the evacuees, telling them of the rumor that they would soon be released. Griswold suggested that, rather than all returning at once, it might be in the best interests of both communities if a few individuals arrived first to break the ice gradually. The discussion continued

4. *Livingston Chronicle,* December 21, 1944.
5. *Livingston Chronicle,* July 19, 1945.
6. *New York Daily News,* February 4, 1945, p. C6.

in this vein during the January meetings in Amache when Momberg presented his annual report to the growers and trustees, and all conferred about plans for return. One of the most pressing problems of returning Japanese Americans was that of housing. Griswold suggested that the evacuees stay temporarily on the church grounds between the time of their arrival and the termination of their tenants' farm leases. They also agreed that the Momberg operation would be liquidated on November 30, 1945, at the end of the fall harvest.

At the suggestion of Dallas Bache, each of the growers' associations decided to form two committees to handle resettlement, one in Amache and the other in California. Kumekichi Taniguchi and Kajiwara Hajime (finally released from a segregated camp for Issei leaders) were elected as the Amache committee members representing Cortez. After a brief preliminary visit to Cortez by George Morofuji, Nobuhiro Kajioka, Nobuzo Baba, and Sakaguchi Chokichi, it was decided that Morofuji and Kajioka would leave for Cortez to facilitate their homecoming. In preparation for their early return, they sent notices to the Merced County authorities and the headquarters of the Western Defense Command,[7] announcing their arrival around March 5 and requesting assistance "in whatever difficulties that may arise."

The difficulties began early, not only for the Cortez, Livingston, and Cressey people, but for many of the Japanese Americans returning to the West Coast from the camps and resettlement in other states. As the congressional Commission on Wartime Relocation and Internment of Civilians found, "For many, leaving the camps was as traumatic as entering them."[8] Terrorism surged in rural areas. It was so widespread that Dillon S. Myer believed it was "part of a planned campaign aimed at frightening away the Japanese American agriculturalists and thus making their lands available to Caucasian competitors."[9] By May 1945, fifty-seven evacuees had returned to eight homes in the Livingston-Cortez area, and fifteen out of seventeen California nightrider inci-

7. The WRA's relations with the Western Defense Command's Wartime Civilian Control Administration were described by WRA head Dillon Myer as "a long series of frustrations" due to the difference of opinion between WRA officials and WCCA heads Colonel Karl Bendetsen and General William Wilbur. Myer, p. 282. *Personal Justice Denied*, the report by the congressional Commission on Relocation and Internment of Civilians, also documents the conflicting opinions between the WRA and the military leaders; see "Ending the Exclusion," pp. 213–43.

8. *Personal Justice Denied*, p. 240.

9. Myer, p. 200.

dents had occurred in the San Joaquin Valley. By June, of seventy instances of terrorism and nineteen shootings, 90 percent took place in Merced, Madera, Fresno, and Tulare counties.[10] Nightriders had fired shots from high-powered rifles into the Cortez Presbyterian Church parsonage where George Morofuji and Nobuhiro Kajioka were staying. Six other shootings occurred in Livingston: The Masazo Kishi place was targeted once, the tankhouse where the Morimotos were staying, twice, and the Andow home three times. In desperation, the Amache Committee of the Livingston-Cortez District wrote to Dillon S. Myer, appealing for assistance. Although the State Department of Justice sent a special investigator, as did the Stockton WRA field office, and Myer himself traveled through the San Joaquin Valley to visit Japanese Americans—"especially those whose homes had been shot into"[11]—returned evacuees received no concrete protection or aid.

It is difficult to assess the efficacy of the WRA's assistance to the relocating Japanese Americans. In the Livingston-Cortez area, neither the WRA investigator nor local authorities ever found any suspects for the shootings, and the Board of Supervisors at a county hearing denied County Sheriff Cornell funds to hire deputies for night patrol.[12] Perhaps the WRA's most effective measure was keeping the public in the more sympathetic East and Midwest informed of West Coast hostility. The WRA's efforts included a public statement by Secretary of the Interior Harold L. Ickes on May 24, 1945, denouncing terrorism, in addition to subsequent national editorials calling for an end to such unlawful violence.

By the spring of 1945, only 1,500 evacuees had returned to the West, out of 55,000 cleared for relocation; 40,000 lived in other states. By August, 5,000 had come back, representing about 4 percent of the Japanese American population.[13] Despite the initial grim reception, the majority of the Cortez, Livingston, and Cressey families—approximately 600 people—stood fast in their determination to return in the fall. George Morofuji had stayed on in the area, in spite of the threat of violence, and he continued to make preparations for the

10. Girdner and Loftis, p. 402.
11. One of Dillon Myer's most vivid memories of the trip was a stop at the Kishi residence in Livingston, which he recounts in *Uprooted Americans*, p. 201.
12. Noda, pp. 155–57.
13. Girdner and Loftis, p. 424.

Cortez people. The first contingent arrived in September 1945, followed by another group in October. WRA statistics recorded that 153 people returned to Cortez from Amache.[14] Over the ensuing days, others gradually made their way back from jobs in the Midwest and East, and from military service.

In their first months back, the Cortez families lived communally as they had in camp. While they waited for their tenants' leases to expire in November, most camped in rented army tents around the Gakuen building which also housed the Buddhist Church. "We used to take Japanese baths in the tents over here," Mae Taniguchi Kajioka recalled, "but every so often we used to walk over the railroad track and go to the [Presbyterian] minister's house to take a shower."[15] The women did all the cooking outside in large pots, and everyone ate together. The men went out every day, according to a schedule, to help their tenants with the grape harvest. Gradually as the tenants left, the Japanese Americans moved back into their own homes.

The condition of their farms and houses varied according to the skill—and good will—of the tenants. The few who had had friends running their farms found their belongings intact and their lands well kept. Many, however, were less pleased about the conditions to which they returned. The Taniguchis, for example, had to fumigate their house before moving in, and the weeds outside had grown taller than the windows; in addition, the locks had been jimmied and many of the family's possessions taken. The Sugiuras' place was "run down," and their apricot trees had died for lack of care. The Narita farm appeared "not so bad" overall, but the upkeep had been uneven. Their first tenant, who came from a coastal area where cabbages flourished, discovered through trial and error that they did not grow well in Cortez. The second tenant focused his attention on the vineyard and did not attempt to cultivate the unsuccessful cabbage patch. By the time they returned, Haruko recalled, "We had nothing but puncture vine on the east side."[16]

With the end of the Momberg organization, the handling of farm operations returned to the Cortez Growers Association (CGA) and the Livingston cooperative organizations. Regardless of the conditions of

14. U.S. Department of the Interior, War Relocation Authority, *The Evacuated People: A Quantitative Description* (1946), p. 47.
15. Mae Taniguchi Kajioka interview, Cortez, Calif., January 16, 1982.
16. Haruko Narita interview, Cortez, Calif., January 26, 1982.

their farms, the families of Cortez were fortunate to be among the approximately one-fourth of prewar Japanese American farmers who had property to which they could return. Except for these, most of the evacuees had to start over from scratch. Many farmers who had leased lands before the war lost their leases and reverted to doing farm labor for other operators. Many landless farmers moved to the cities to do gardening work.[17]

In the postwar years, life was difficult for the Cortez people, as for most Japanese Americans. Although the Cortez, Livingston, and Cressey internees were fortunate in having been able to return to their own land and communities, they still faced the suspicion of the surrounding society and economic hardship. Much of the money earned from the leasing of the farms was funneled back into land and equipment, and the refurbishing of bare, run-down houses. Produce prices fell as the wartime boom ebbed, and the Cortez farmers relied on their row crops, like canning tomatoes and eggplants, for daily sustenance as well as market crops.

Row crops provided an interim livelihood while the Cortez farmers adapted to two major changes in farming practices: a shift to orchard cultivation, and an increase in the mechanization of farmwork. Gradually, peaches replaced the canning tomatoes. "Peaches were more profitable," explained Sam Kuwahara. "A lot of growers didn't like peaches because they took so much labor and were an exacting crop. Everything had to be on time, especially harvesting—you had two or three days leeway, and that was it." Almonds—now the predominant crop in Cortez—were also put into production. "Almonds are a much more relaxed type of farming," Sam continued. "At harvest time, you had a whole month's leeway, getting the crop off. The only thing was, if the frost came, then you were busy watering and trying to save the crop. But other than that, almonds are much more relaxing."[18] In addition to peaches and almonds, many Cortez farmers continued to cultivate grapes, primarily for raisins and wine filler.

The Cortez people found the postwar atmosphere an uneasy one; only gradually did the tension dissipate. One Nisei described the atmosphere as similar to the one that had prevailed when the Japanese Americans had left—"It was still sort of hostile." Not surprising,

---

17. Girdner and Loftis, p. 287; Myer, p. 255.
18. Sam Kuwahara interview, Cortez, Calif., January 25, 1982.

considering that a public opinion poll taken at the end of the war revealed that 40 percent of the American public favored denying the Nisei equal opportunities, and 89 percent approved of denying the Issei equal opportunities.[19] A number of the Livingston–Cortez tenants had profited greatly from the high wartime prices for farm produce, and they felt reluctant to relinquish a lucrative situation.

In this uncertain state, the Issei and Nisei acted cautiously. "I guess we tried to associate with the ones that we knew were happy to see us and we just shied away from where there was a question mark," said one woman. "We were a little careful. And there were a few *hakujin* [white people] who let us know they were happy to see us back." In general, well aware of their delicate position, as another Nisei stated, the people of Cortez "took care of our own business, minded our business, and stayed out of trouble."

The postwar adjustment was particularly difficult for the youngest Nisei and earliest Sansei children, who encountered not only the difficulties of transition to a new school but also the initial hostility of their peers. As Audrie Girdner and Anne Loftis have suggested, hoodlumism is sometimes "perpetrated by youngsters who absorb adult attitudes, but who carry them out in a direct manner which would not be countenanced by the prejudiced adults themselves."[20] "When they went back to school, it was really rough on them," a Nisei explained, "because they [the non-Japanese peers] would say, 'Japs, why did you come back?!'" Nisei Haruka Ishihara remembered one of the school teachers' daughters asking her this. Haruka had never before heard the term "Jap." "All I could say was, 'Well, I'd rather be Jap than *hakujin*.' And then she started crying; she didn't know what *hakujin* was. To me, a *hakujin* was a white person, that's all I knew. . . . She thought I said something just terrible."[21] Some of the Japanese American children solved their harassment problems in ways not possible for their elders. At least one parent recalled, with a certain satisfaction, that "our son and the kids around here, when anybody would say those kinds of words, why then, they'd all band together and beat that kid up. And they used to get heck from the teachers, but that's how it was then."

19. Girdner and Loftis, p. 404.
20. Ibid., p. 403.
21. Haruka Ishihara interview, Turlock, Calif., April 25, 1982.

Although the interracial tension decreased over time, it still had lasting effects. The wartime experience, one Nisei felt, caused the Japanese Americans to try "to stay away from Japanese things. There was a time . . . when you felt ashamed. It's too bad, because that's where I think a lot of the Niseis—especially the Christian people—shied away from Japanese culture. Missed out on a lot." A Sansei similarly observed, that "when we came back and we went to grammar school, I think my mother just went out of her way to become a 'good American.' . . . She was really active in the PTA. . . . always was really . . . community involved, to say, 'We're still good people.' " Loss of confidence, denial, and internalized anger, all compounded by the government's assimilationist policies of resettlement and by public suspicion, spurred many Japanese Americans to make strenuous efforts to prove themselves loyal, nonthreatening citizens. The wartime internment cast long shadows, not only on the Issei and Nisei, but also in their rearing of the third generation.[22]

By the end of 1945, the families of Cortez had moved back into their homes and begun the slow painstaking task of rebuilding their community. The following years witnessed significant change in the structure of Cortez households. The primary shift was from a home headed by a pair of Issei adults to a household containing two sets of adults, Issei and Nisei, with the latter assuming major responsibility for farm work and domestic chores. Other shifts occurred as the youngest Nisei entered elementary and high school, while older siblings departed for work or education elsewhere, and others returned from military service or relocation in the Midwest and East. An additional factor in household composition was the appearance of the third generation, the Sansei.

After World War II, the majority of Cortez farm operations passed into the hands of the Nisei. Some of the Issei had died and others suffered from poor health. Many felt ready for their sons to take over the running of the "home place." Generally, as in Japan, the Cortez Issei followed the practice of expecting the oldest son (*chonan*) to manage and inherit the family land. Not all of the *chonan* wanted to farm, but most—even those who had had other ambitions—acquiesced as dutiful sons. To the oldest son and his family also fell the re-

22. *Personal Justice Denied*, p. 300.

sponsibility of caring for the Issei parents. More of the Cortez Sansei, or third generation, grew up with the presence of grandparents than did the Nisei.

The Nisei, like their parents, expected to marry and establish families, and most did. Although some prewar Nisei weddings had taken place, many of the Nisei married during or shortly after the war, and their spouses often came from other communities. A number of couples met during the war, like Ernest Yoshida and Ruth Nishi, who met making pup-tent valves in a defense factory in Chicago, or Takashi Date and Lena Hananouchi who married in Reno, Nevada, where Takashi had become a gardener on the estate of a former gold prospector and Lena worked as a live-in housemaid for a doctor's family. Takashi, then aged thirty, had for several years staved off parental attempts to arrange *omiai* (meeting with a view to marriage) for him. Much to the Issei's consternation, "I was pretty firm with my 'No, I'm not ready yet,'" Takashi remembered, but after meeting Lena, "I just was glad I waited that long."[23]

The Nisei, and society at large, also expected that they would choose as partners other Japanese Americans. Until 1948, California's miscegenation law continued to prohibit marriage between Euro-Americans and persons of Asian and Mexican descent.[24] It was not until the late 1950s that the first Cortez Nisei married interracially—and was disowned for doing so. Many years passed before such unions became accepted. Thus, in the postwar years, endogamous marriages prevailed.

One major aspect of marriage, however, had changed between the Issei and Nisei generations: the choice of marriage partner had become a personal one, based on a concept of romantic affection accepted in popular mainstream culture. This represented a significant departure from the marriages of the Issei, arranged by families as a matter of alliance. It was not uncommon for an Issei bride and groom to meet for the first time at their wedding ceremony, as did Yonehichi and Suye Sugiura. Picture brides did not encounter their husbands until after the marriage, when they arrived in the United States. By contrast, the majority of the Nisei, who came of age during the war years, chose

23. Takashi Date interview, Cortez, Calif., February 7, 1982; Lena Hananouchi Date interview, Cortez, Calif., February 7, 1982.
24. Osumi, pp. 1–37.

their own marriage partners, as did May Kuwahara and Yeichi Sakaguchi, Mary Noda and Mark Kamiya. Few Issei would have come to
their wedding day with the same emotions and expectations as their
children. "We were married in the almond orchard by the house,"
Mark Kamiya remembered. "It was hot, but I had the ground all
wetted down and the trees were green. When you're young and in
love, everything's rosy!"[25] Few arranged marriages took place among
the Nisei after the war. However, as Sylvia Yanagisako has documented, Nisei unions represented a synthesis of Western and Japanese ideals, valorizing romantic love and companionate marriage in
tandem with commitment and family duty.[26]

According to the dictates of Japanese cultural expectations, most
of the postwar Cortez households consisted of two primary sets of
adults sharing responsibility and authority. One set was Issei—in
some cases, a single Issei parent—and the other, Nisei—the oldest son
and his wife. Gene N. Levine and Colbert Rhodes noted the presence
of this pattern among the larger Japanese American population in the
1960s. At that time, one-fourth of all Nisei included non-nuclear family
members, usually parents, in their households.[27] Despite the fact that
this pattern was common in Japan, many of the Issei actually had had
little experience of living with in-laws because of their immigration to
the United States. Although some of the Nisei, like George and Helen
Yuge, had established their own families before the war, few had lived
with their parents as they did after their return to California. In addition to these two generations, a third began to appear in the households of Cortez. These alterations in household structure led to
changes in family dynamics and necessitated a great deal of adjustment, primarily for the eldest son and his wife. A number of the Nisei
daughters-in-law were strangers to farm life and found the early postwar years especially taxing.

The position of a rural daughter-in-law was by tradition difficult. In
the Japan the Issei had left, rural *yomesan*, or daughters-in-law, occupied a vulnerable position in the family. Only after the birth of a
child—preferably male—was the *yomesan*'s place secure within the
family. In Japan, however, she did have the possibility of returning to

25. Mark Kamiya interview, Cortez, Calif., February 8, 1982.
26. Yanagisako, pp. 107–8.
27. Gene N. Levine and Colbert Rhodes, *The Japanese American Community, A Three-
Generation Study* (New York: Praeger, 1981), p. 57.

her own home, should her husband's family treat her too harshly. Many of the Issei escaped living with in-laws because of their immigration to the United States, but in the event of marital difficulties, thousands of miles of ocean removed the option of "going home to mother."

Impelled by a sense of duty and obligation but often worn by frustration and physical exhaustion, the Nisei women found themselves in a demanding new situation with few role models. Because the household tasks were their primary responsibility, it was they who had to deal most frequently and directly with the Issei. And for some, the feeling of being "outsiders" in a tightly knit community persisted for years.

A never-ending round of work awaited the Nisei daughters-in-law, most of whom were joining ready-made families with many needs. "My [five] brothers were all there," Ernest Yoshida related, "and she [Ruth] had to wash and cook for the brothers. Boy, I tell you, my wife went through a lot of hardship. We didn't have any luxuries like our electric washing machine or anything like that for quite a spell. Everything was sort of primitive, because [when] we came back here, we had to start over from scratch."[28] Ruth Yoshida, May Sakaguchi, and other Cortez women mentioned that during these years they became accustomed to preparing large quantities of food. "I had to learn differently," May said, "trying to feed so many people and trying to be economical about it. It was a big change because I came from a small family."[29]

For all, the daily schedule was a busy one. "Everything was like clockwork for me," Ruth explained.

> You get the babies fed in the morning, and you've got to go do the wash, and you have to use all that bath water [for the laundry]. You have to use a bucket and put it into the basin and start scrubbing. You have to get that out as soon as possible so it will dry. In the meantime, you're preparing for lunch, so you have to run back and forth to wash the rice, get the *okazu* ready, or whatever. Then you have to feed the kids again so they won't be noisy at noontime. . . . And then bath (*ofuro*) mistakes happened many a time when I let the water overflow, so the fire would go out. . . . I don't

28. Ernest Yoshida interview, Cortez, Calif., January 24, 1982.
29. May Kuwahara Sakaguchi interview, Cortez, Calif., March 10, 1982.

think I could do it now. And in between, when the kids were napping, pretty soon they'd start tying the vines—for eggplants—I went out and did that for an hour, and then I'd run back for fear the kids got up from their nap.[30]

Although Ruth weighed 120 pounds when she married, by the time her father came to visit, a year after she moved to Cortez, she weighed 78 pounds. When he returned to Chicago, he sent her a Maytag electric wringer-washer.

The presence of a daughter-in-law enabled some Issei women to shift their duties. One Nisei remembers that her mother-in-law preferred to do fieldwork. "That's all she wanted to do was to just work out, and so she wanted me to take over, even to teach her children. . . . That's when I said 'no.' That was her job." Even with the assumption of household responsibilities, the Nisei wives were also expected to do a share of the fieldwork. "When the kids were small, I was out there cutting apricots. . . . We had apricots on the other ranch—forty acres—and over here we had peaches that we dried, Lovells," said Miye Baba. "It was hard work, because Nesan [sister-in-law] and I used to go and pick all the nice-looking fruit that fell before the pickers came; we'd go ahead of them, so we had to work pretty fast."[31]

The different crops necessitated a variety of work for the people of Cortez. "I did everything," said another Nisei woman.

> There isn't a piece of ground that I haven't crawled over. . . . I would go out and help them plant trees—that means digging and planting, and then we would have to do the hoeing. . . . And we had twenty acres of grapes, and that takes a lot of work: We would have pruners, and I would go ahead and do the preliminary pruning, and then . . . I would do all the wrapping—the whole twenty acres by myself. . . . You wind the canes around the wire. . . . And then when we were harvesting almonds, we didn't do it mechanically in those days. We had to knock it by hand and gather it on canvas. We'd drag canvas through the field, and my husband and I did that. I went out in the field to work with him; then I'd come home a little bit earlier and do the cooking—everybody did that. All the women did that. And then we would take time off to take the kids to school or to go someplace, or we'd have 4-H.

30. Ruth Yoshida interview, Cortez, Calif., January 24, 1982.
31. Miye Baba interview, Cortez, Calif., July 18, 1982.

In addition to the stamina required by fieldwork, domestic arrangements required the daughters-in-law to be diplomatic and patient. The Nisei men worked hard, too, but they did not have the additional responsibility of domestic chores or the close contact with the Issei that their wives had. The delicate balance of power within the household was not always easily maintained. As one Nisei woman recalled,

> It was hard, but I got along real well with them [in-laws], simply because I was intimidated by her [mother-in-law], I guess. She was a very strong person, because I know that she ran the family. . . . [She] was very strait-laced, very "just-so" about things, very neat. . . . She was very kind. She never said an angry word to me . . . and she never scolded the kids. She would be a little rough with [my sister-in-law] sometimes, but she never said anything to displease me. But then, of course, at the same time, I never said anything to displease her either, and I really played up to her all the time. I would always listen to her. Because I decided, "We're going to live together, we just have to get along best, and if we said one unkind word to each other, that would just be the end."

Other women also made accommodations to try to please their in-laws. "I learned to can fruits when the children were small," explained another woman, "because Ojiichan [grandfather, referring to her father-in-law] would always mention how he used to like canned fruits before the war. . . . And it just made me feel I better be a good daughter-in-law and do it. So I used to do it after I put the kids to bed."

Many of the Cortez women had invalid Issei to care for—their husbands' and occasionally their own parents. Their acceptance and even their expectation of these and other responsibilities as the wives of oldest sons did not make them any easier. Their own parents, although sympathetic, felt bounded by the same sense of roles and could not help them. "At that time I started to tell my problems to my father," said a Nisei woman who had come from another community, "that I was having difficulty, and also I was trying to raise my children, and I was telling him it was just too hard, and then my father said, '*Gaman shinasai.*' You know—'bear it.' That 'you're young yet, and the father [in-law] is old, and so try to make the best of it.' And that's when I felt I needed religion, and it did help."

Having parents nearby did not necessarily lessen the problem. One woman remembered the crying sessions she would have with her father. Although her parents expressed concern for her, they were also old friends of her husband's parents. "They couldn't do anything; they didn't want to break up their friendship, and so all that they could do was to sympathize with me and tell me, 'You have a good husband . . . so stay with him and someday things will be different.'" This Nisei, however, was unusual in that she dared to take a step only dreamed about by her peers: When pregnant with their first child, she told her husband, "It's either your parents or me. I just can't go on living like this. So if you can't tell your parents that we're going to live separately [from them], I think I'm going to have to leave." After she spent two weeks with a relative, her husband made his decision. "He said, 'We can't have a nice place to live; we'll just have to live in that little house on the ranch,' which was a worker's house. But that," she agreed readily, "was fine to me."

In these three-generational households, the Cortez Sansei, unlike most of the Nisei, grew up knowing their grandparents. Their childhood and adolescent experiences were similar in some respects to those of their parents, however, particularly in the area of work. Like the Nisei, the third generation began to help with the family farmwork early in life. "My oldest daughter was only five years old when she would sit on the tractor during peach season as they hauled out the peaches, because we picked peaches in boxes those days," May Sakaguchi related. Having a child to handle the tractor, which only needed to be moved three or four times before the trailer was full, freed an adult to do picking and loading.

Like their parents, the Sansei had a wide spectrum of responsibilities. They hoed weeds, sorted and cut fruit, acted as "checkers" on harvest crews, helped with pruning and irrigation. "I recollect having to get up before school and having to work after school," said Sharyn Yoshida, echoing Nisei childhood memories. "It was survival. I mean, my father felt that if we wanted to have food and clothing, we had to participate, because we were all made to feel responsible for the development of that ranch."[32] Not only a matter of need, the Sansei's labor reflected a training in values. "My husband believes in working our kids real hard, just like the Isseis," Mae Kajioka explained. "We always had something for them to do when they came home from school, if they weren't in tennis or something. . . . Weekends, they always had to work. . . . Some people used to tell us, 'Gosh, why do

32. Sharyn Yoshida interview, Menlo Park, Calif., August 17, 1982.

Gail Taniguchi with eggs, in the 1950s. Photo courtesy of Alice Taniguchi.

you want to work your kids that hard?' But my husband is one of those that believe that hard work never hurts anybody. I think it's good for them to know that they have to work for what they want."[33]

Regarding the division of labor in the family, Japanese cultural practices dovetailed with those of the mainstream society in the 1950s and early 1960s. Sansei daughters, like their mothers, performed more of the domestic chores—like cooking and cleaning—than their brothers, who mostly did outdoor work and tasks like taking out the garbage. However, the exigencies of the small family farm continued to necessi-

33. Mae Kajioka interview, Cortez, Calif., January 16, 1982.

tate fieldwork for both genders. Said one Sansei woman, "I worked outside as well, but I was pressured more to develop other kinds of skills—cooking and sewing—so I could prepare to be supportive of a male. . . . But I never had this feeling that the man is the only one that does the physical labor. I felt that I was given as much responsibility as I was capable of doing, and when I was old enough to drive a tractor, I was driving a tractor and irrigating just like my brothers." Many of the teenaged daughters also worked for wages as part-time help at the CGA office during the harvest seasons, doing bookwork, or acting as weighmaster.

Even with the similarity of work experience, the Sansei's childhood and adolescent years differed significantly from those of their parents. Although the immediate postwar period presented economic difficulties, the Cortez families had their own farms and homes, and most enjoyed more material comfort than they had during the arduous years of the Great Depression. In addition, the Sansei grew up with parents who had had similar education and spoke English fluently. In fact, very few of the Sansei learned Japanese, beyond a limited childhood vocabulary. The completeness of their identification with English is illustrated in this Sansei's early misconception: "When I was a kid, I used to always think that you spoke American and then when you got old, you started speaking Japanese, because all the old people I knew spoke Japanese. . . . I used to just have a heartache when I saw my parents speaking a lot of Japanese, and I'd think, 'Oh no, they're getting old—pretty soon I won't be able to understand them.' . . . I just thought aging and Japanese went together, and when you got old, that's all you could speak—you gradually lost English."[34]

Because of their familiarity with public education, their driving skills, and English fluency as well as a gradually improving economic situation, the Nisei participated in their children's schooling in ways rarely possible for the Issei. They could also afford to encourage the Sansei's involvement in extracurricular activities that were luxuries for many Nisei before the war. Some activities previously considered improper also gained eventual sanction, which meant that the youngest of the Nisei could participate in events denied their older siblings, the women in particular. So the Sansei and the Nisei who attended the Livingston High School after World War II were able to engage in

34. Robin Yuge Alexander interview, Los Gatos, Calif., August 26, 1982.

In 1952 the passage of the McCarran-Walter Immigration Act permitted Asian immigrants to become naturalized citizens. These Cortez Issei took a preparatory class in 1953 and became citizens. Front row, from left: Sakuzaemon Kumimoto, Kazue Masuda, Maju Sakaguchi, Akio Yamamoto, Kikuyo Shiojiguchi, Masa Kajioka, Mai Yoshida, Masa Yamaguchi, Seitaro Yoneyama, Matsuichi Miyamoto, Yonezo Yoshida, and Jiro Yotsuya. Back row: Suye Sugiura, Sachiko Noda, Shizuka Asai, Shinjiro Sugiura, Riu Kajioka, Hachizo Kajioka, Chokichi Sakaguchi, Saburo Narita, Itsusaku Uyekubo, Yonehichi Sugiura, and Yakichi Kajioka. Photo courtesy of Ben Kumimoto.

a variety of teenage pursuits: sports, dances, cheerleading, music, speech, and art. They held positions in student body leadership, won awards for their accomplishments, and attended racially mixed social events.

As the Nisei began to assume leadership roles and establish families, they modified former social and organizational patterns to serve altered needs and position in U.S. society. This postwar change within the Cortez community was reflected in the formation of three new organizations: the Young Married Group, which coalesced in 1947; a Cortez chapter of the Japanese American Citizens League, organized in 1948; and in 1950, the Shinwakai—the Cortez senior citizens' group—which formed with fifty-five Issei charter members.

Relations between the Christians and Buddhists also underwent significant transformation. The majority of the Cortez Nisei regarded the old animosity as primarily an Issei one, exacerbated by the geographical division of Cortez, in which most of the Buddhists lived on one side of the Santa Fe's railroad tracks and the Christians on the other. Some of the Nisei attribute the change in relations, in part, to the dissolution of major differences during the years of internment. The two halves of the community came to see themselves as united in their experience of camp life, and the most evangelically minded of the Issei, mellowing with age, became more tolerant of differences in religious belief. "They found out in the war that it wasn't Cortez Buddhists or Cortez Christians anymore," speculated one Nisei, "but it was Cortez together as a community."

Another factor was the arrival in 1947 of a new Issei Christian minister, Nakamura Isamu, a man remembered with warmth and appreciation.[35] "After Reverend Nakamura came," said a Buddhist, "the members of this community got closer. . . . He respected what we [Buddhists] were doing and he didn't try to convert us. He used to encourage us." One way in which he did this was by writing a Cortez news column for the Japanese section of the *Nichibei Times* newspaper, published by Abiko's son Yasuo. After the passage of the McCarran-Walter Immigration Act in 1952, which eliminated race as a consideration in American immigration and naturalization laws,[36] Reverend Nakamura taught a naturalization class for the Issei, thirty of whom proudly received U.S. citizenship.

After their postwar return, the Cortez people—Buddhist and Christian alike—began to socialize together through organizations like the Young People's Club. Harry Kajioka was the first president and his future wife, Mae Taniguchi, secretary when the group was revived by the unmarried Nisei, who were attending, or who had just graduated from, high school. The club met once a month to plan activities: raffles, outings, dances, and community-service projects. Although many Issei had objected to dancing before the war, Mae Kajioka felt that having become accustomed to frequent dances in camp lessened their disapproval.

The three new organizations that formed in the early postwar years

35. For an oral-history interview of Reverend Isamu Nakamura, see *Issei Christians, Selected Interviews from the Issei Oral History Project*, ed. Michiyo Laing, Carl Laing, Heihachiro Takarabe, Asako Takuno and Stanly Umeda. (Sacramento: The Issei Oral History Project, 1977), pp. 158–88. This collection also includes a group interview of Cortez Issei.

36. In the words of historian Roger Daniels, "Nothing more clearly demonstrates the mixed effect of the cold war on American domestic legislation than the passage of the McCarran-Walter Immigration Act of 1952." This law, passed by Cold War conservatives over the opposition of President Harry Truman, continued the National Origins Quota System, expanded the bases for denying entry to the U.S. and enlarged the grounds for deportation, as well as eliminating racial, religious, or ethnic bars to immigration or naturalization. Daniels, *Asian America*, pp. 305–6.

The kitchen crew preparing for the thirtieth anniversary celebration of the founding of the Cortez Colony, held at the Educational Society Hall in Cortez, 1951. Around the table, left to right: Utako Kajiwara, Kiyono Morofuji, Nobuzo Baba, Yukihiro Yotsuya, and Saburo Okamura. Around the stove: Florice Kuwahara (in front), June Asai, May Sakaguchi, Kazumi Kajioka, and Mabel Yoneyama. Back row: Yonekichi Kuwahara, Chieko Sugiura, Shizue Asai, Albert Morimoto, Yeichi Sakaguchi, Saburo Narita, Ernest Yoshida, Helen Yuge, and Kiyoshi Asai. Photo courtesy of Nobuzo Baba.

reflected not only the community's continued solidarity but also the second generation's adoption of mainstream cultural pastimes. The emergence of these groups also marked a shift in roles within Cortez; the Nisei began to assume broader responsibility for community projects and leadership as the Issei increasingly reached retirement age.

The first of these organizations was the Young Married Club, founded in 1947, to which nearly all of the Nisei couples in Cortez belonged. A few of the Issei disapproved of the club, and its card parties and dancing, but the Nisei still remember with nostalgia the good times they shared. "One of the things we started was dancing lessons," May Sakaguchi recalled. "Hardly any of us danced in high school days, because our parents kind of frowned on it. Livingston people, I think, used to dance, but of the Cortez Japanese, very few danced. So this was really something. . . . We learned to waltz, and we learned to do the tango. . . . The Young Married Group was just fun!"[37] The Young Married Club met once a month for bowling, bridge lessons, and other activities. They also started an annual fishing derby; in its first year, the proceeds of the derby—$170—were donated to the Ballico School. The Japanese American Citizens League (JACL), the next new organization to form in Cortez, eventually took over sponsorship of the highly successful derby.

Although the national JACL had coalesced in the 1930s, the group did not garner large support or interest in Cortez until after World War II. At that time, the JACL devoted much of its energy to making the Issei eligible for U.S. citizenship, obtaining the reversal of the California alien land law, and enabling American servicemen to bring their Japanese war-brides into the country legally.[38] "The JACL was undoubtedly the most effective advocate in behalf of the 1952 Immigration and Nationality Act," Dillon S. Myer thought, "and the organization of course had strong backing from all over the United States as a result of the Nisei military record and the widespread support resulting from relocatees and their friends."[39] The thirty Cortez Issei joined a total of 46,041 Japanese aliens who became naturalized U.S. citizens between 1952 and 1964.

As the Nisei increasingly stepped into community leadership and as their families grew, the local JACL group shifted from serving a social function to a civic one. Initially, many of the Cortez Nisei thought that their branch of the JACL would serve the purposes of the Young Married Club, which eventually disbanded "after the JACL became active, because that was just too many clubs to support."[40] The JACL meetings, however, became primarily community business functions rather than social occasions. The several remaining social events sponsored by the JACL included a Valentine's Day meeting; a Christmas program (later to become—in deference to the Buddhists—the "End-of-Year" Program); and the community's annual picnic, held in May.

A major event in Cortez was the building of the JACL Hall, which

37. May Sakaguchi interview, Cortez, Calif., March 10, 1982.
38. Wilson and Hosokawa, pp. 257–85.
39. Myer, p. 288.
40. Mae Kajioka interview, Cortez, Calif., January 16, 1982.

has provided since its completion a meeting place for almost all of the groups in the community, from the Boy Scouts and past 4-H classes, to the CGA, the local Lions Club, and the Shinwakai, the senior citizens' association. The process that culminated in the construction of the JACL Hall illustrates both the longstanding familiarity with committee work in Cortez and the issues of intergenerational change within the community at that time.

The JACL Hall had its beginnings in controversy. By 1957 the annual fishing derby had amassed a considerable profit, and the people of Cortez began to discuss possible projects that might be funded. After return from Amache, as before the war, most community gatherings took place at the Gakuen—the Educational Society Building—which also housed the Buddhist church services. With the accumulated funds, some proposed that the first project be a community hall, to be dedicated to the Issei pioneers. Supporters of this proposal included a number of Buddhists who were not displeased with the idea of having the Gakuen become principally—and formally—their place of worship. Others, both Christian and Buddhist, who had the Sansei children in mind, spoke in favor of a community swimming pool.[41] Many discussions took place over a number of years regarding the projects. Although both proposals had their merits, the problems of maintenance and liability for a swimming pool and the attraction of a building that "would serve all ages at any time of the year" resulted in the decision to construct a hall with some recreational features. Architect Kay Kajiwara, the son of Cortez community members Hajime and Utako Kajiwara, designed the hall, dedicated in 1967, which stands next to the Buddhist Church. Thus, the construction of the hall has embodied the continuing commitment to community identity in Cortez.

The building of the JACL Hall resulted in several rearrangements in the status of local property. Subsequently, it was decided that the Gakuen would become the Buddhist Church. The Japanese Educational Society which handled Gakuen matters became the Japanese Service Society, and the front piece of Gakuen land was parceled out to the Buddhist Church, the Cortez JACL, and the CGA. The title to the JACL Hall's seven-acre piece is held in the name of the Japanese Service Society although the JACL farms it and has paid the insurance and property taxes for the past several years. This arrangement evi-

41. As of 1982, there were two private swimming pools in Cortez.

dences the strength of local identification and loyalties. If the Cortez people had chosen to hold the property in the name of the JACL and the Cortez community were to disband, the land would then revert to the national JACL. However, the people of Cortez preferred to set up their own title-holding organization and to include a stipulation in the title that, in the event of their disbanding, the JACL Hall would go to the county, ensuring that the local community would always be able to use it.

The running of the JACL Hall has also demonstrated the continuity of Cortez's community networks. In 1961, the JACL planted an almond orchard on the seven-acre piece with trees that came as a half-donation from local nurseries. Every year two cochairs are chosen to head a committee that handles the care of this orchard, which has been the primary source of funds for the Cortez JACL. They prepare a work schedule for the year and everyone in the community pitches in to help. The growth of the hall has also reflected that of the community. Since its dedication in 1967, the JACL Hall has been enlarged to almost twice its original size, and another project, a tennis court, has materialized beside it.

The third new organization to form in Cortez was the Shinwakai, the senior citizens' group. It began in 1950 with fifty-five charter members, all Issei. Although many Issei remained active on the family farms, the formation of this group acknowledged their retired status and the appropriateness of their now spending leisure time in social activities. Reflecting the prosperity of the past twenty years, these activities have come to include gambling trips to Reno as well as to the Monterey Aquarium. In the past ten or eleven years, the composition of the Shinwakai has altered with the addition of a substantial number of Nisei who have reached retirement age, even if they have not yet chosen to retire.

Cortez has had a long history of overlapping associations, from the CGA to the churches, to the Young People's Club, Young Married Club and the Shinwakai—as well as myriad specialized intragroup committees and local interracial group affiliations. The JACL has not become the predominant organization as it has in other Japanese American communities; rather, it constitutes but one thread in the fabric of community life. "The reason it is not very strong," said one farmer in 1982, "is there is really not a need for an organization like that. . . . When the Issei were trying to gain their citizenship rights, there was really a strong need for it. Evacuation claims—there was a strong need for it. But today there's no immediate need." The JACL continues to provide a useful umbrella for certain community interests, but in Cortez it has always been one among a constellation of institutions.

This inner network of support extends throughout the community, swinging efficiently into action whenever the need arises. The *toban* system of the Cortez Buddhist Church provides an example. This system consists of annually rotating committees that assume responsibility for both planned events and unexpected emergencies. The continual round of responsibilities expected of community members can sometimes be demanding, and many have sighed over the addition of committee work to their farm duties and family obligations. Yet all of the Cortez people—even those who consider themselves on the periphery of community affairs—feel a sense of security within the social web they have spun from their labor. Both informal and formal channels provide assistance. When the Sakaguchis' barn burned down, friends and neighbors immediately appeared to help. "Practically the whole community was there," May recalled. "They said, 'Let's just clean this up.' One post had gone down—an electric post with wires leading to the house where my in-laws lived—and by evening, the new post was up, all electrical lines were fixed, all the trash had been taken to the dump. Everything was cleaned up. . . . Where else can you get help like that, willingly?"[42]

In an agricultural community like Cortez where certain times of year require critical work, the support networks have proven invaluable. The farmers cannot control, or always predict, the weather or the markets, but at least they have been secure in the knowledge that, in the event of their death or illness, the community—primarily through the CGA—will handle the farm responsibilities until permanent arrangements can be made. At such times they can count on emotional and personal support as well. "When there's a death in the family, we usually just pitch in and try to take care of their meals right up to the funeral day," a Nisei woman explained. "And then on the funeral day, we take care of all of the out-of-town guests." She admitted that "There are times when it is *urusai* [bothersome]" living in a tightly knit community, "because you can't keep a secret—everybody knows everything." But she felt strongly that the kind of support Cortez offers is "something you just don't find everywhere."

42. May Sakaguchi interview, Cortez, Calif., March 10, 1982.

Living in such a small close community has entailed not only a certain sense of security but also a fair amount of public pressure. Hiroshi Asai expressed his view of the Nisei's perspective within the context of long-term residence:

> You've got a home, and this is your home, and you think you own it. . . . Because it's gone through one generation, you think it's going to keep on. . . . So when you feel that way, you've got to be careful how you act. You've got to face your community, whereas if you're not that tied down, and if you do something bad, you move and in the next place you've got a fresh start, you've got another chance. But over here [laughing], somebody will remember 50 years ago if you've done something, he'll still remember. So you've got that pressure on you.[43]

A number of Nisei felt this pressure most intensely as their children grew up. "It's hard being a parent in a small community," said one, referring to the way everyone knows about their friends' and neighbors' children and any problems that a family may be having. Another Nisei mentioned her son's discomfort in school and said, "I guess I always think the Japanese are . . . harder to get along with in school, in the sense that they're more critical." She also admitted that, regarding her own children, "I think we put too much pressure on them to do well academically."

The Sansei felt not only the pressure to excel in school but also the weight of the knowledge that their actions reflected on their families as well as themselves. "I felt like I was being watched, and I just said, 'I could give a damn. . . . I really don't care,'" one Sansei explained. "It was easy for me to say because I was just a kid. My parents were the ones who probably had to take any of that or feel any of that." Another Sansei perceived this pressure with more ambivalence: "I always felt uncomfortable because I felt that the community had these standards of what is a good Japanese citizen or participant, and you couldn't just go to the church bazaar and bring a dish. You had to bring a dish that was perfectly made; or you don't bring one dish, you bring two dishes, or something. And as I progressed through school, I felt like everybody was just trying to prove that they could do more and more and more." She described the complexity of simply taking food over to someone who was ill: "If they [the neighbors] brought over anything,

---

43. Hiroshi Asai interview, Cortez, Calif., February 23, 1982.

it was the best. . . . You don't bring over something that doesn't look like it wasn't a reflection of perfection. And that's nice, but it's a real pressure. . . . like you've got to prove yourself. It's no longer nice that you're being thoughtful. It's like somebody's going to grade you on the darn thing and evaluate you." The beneficial aspect to the community pressure, she felt, was that "of course we were a highly prosperous community. I mean, some very positive things were an outgrowth of that kind of determination to just improve and improve your skills and refine your expectations."

Given the weight of community pressure within such a small, close-knit society, individuals' needs for group acceptance and participation vie with the need for privacy and the assertion of self. The Nisei men and women of Cortez have balanced this tension in their lives between their activities and interests within and outside the community. One realm has provided cultural roots, security in the sense of belonging, and pride derived from a shared history. The world outside Cortez has offered the stimuli of different experiences, a measure of respite from community pressure, and affirmation of a personal identity outside the collectivity.

A major generational difference among the Japanese Americans is that the Nisei—and the Sansei—have had access to interracial social groups from which most of the Issei were barred. As economic conditions improved and orchard work became increasingly mechanized, the Nisei could devote more time to their children's education and family activities. Their and the Sansei's command of English and their American upbringing also gave them opportunities closed to the immigrant first generation. These factors as well as change in public opinion through the postwar years have enabled the second and third generations to participate in racially mixed groups more than ever before. They involved themselves not only as PTA members, Scouts and Scout troop leaders, and 4-H members, but also joined organizations like the Lions Club and California Women for Agriculture, Turlock civic groups, Merced County political associations, and many local agricultural boards. Almost every Nisei interviewed had several outside affiliations or interests. While continuing their commitment to a unified Japanese American community, the Cortez Nisei and Sansei have experienced much more interaction with the rest of society.

The Nisei have not only joined but have also acted as leaders within such racially mixed organizations and have received public recognition for their accomplishments. In 1982, a few months after George Yuge had been selected as the outstanding orchard man for Merced County and Kiyoshi Yamamoto had received the Turlock Chamber of Commerce award for agricultural production, Kiyoshi described it as "Something that we would have never dreamed of 25 years ago. We never dreamed that something like that would ever happen to any of us. And today, Niseis in our own community have taken their place in society or in the agricultural community and they hold quite a few positions."[44]

Their affiliations with friends and organizations that are neither located in Cortez nor predominantly Japanese American have also provided, on the one hand, a kind of escape valve from the intensity of Cortez community involvement and, on the other, an arena in which the Nisei truly feel themselves to be individuals separate from the collective whole. Developing outside interests has served as a means of exercising personal choice. As one Nisei explained, "Here in Cortez, you don't really choose your friends. You kind of fall on your friends. I mean, you just kind of go with people you see all the time." Much as the people of Cortez have appreciated their community, some have also found in their outside affiliations and friendships the satisfaction of yearnings for a bigger community, a larger world.

Although the Cortez community returned to California relatively intact, it was an altered one. The Issei had relinquished much of the responsibility of community leadership to the next generation, who had begun to establish their own families. Many households consequently contained three generations, which created shifts in family dynamics and concomitant adjustments. These alterations within the family, as well as an improving economic situation and a thaw in public opinion regarding Japanese Americans, changed the character of community institutions. They also allowed the Nisei and Sansei broader social horizons than they had had before.

Despite these changes, as in the prewar years, community support networks have continued to provide assistance and fellowship to the people of Cortez. They have become inextricably woven into the fabric of life. "I just like this comfortable feeling in Cortez—being close to my neighbors. We get along," explained a Nisei woman. Laughing, she

44. Kiyoshi Yamamoto interview, Cortez, Calif., February 10, 1982.

added that she and a number of Cortez people have neighboring cemetery plots. "In fact, when we die, we're going to be neighbors. . . . all that place is *nihonjins* [Japanese people]! So it will be a *nigiyaka* [bustling] place even when we die." For the most part, the Nisei and Issei of Cortez currently live in the comfort provided by their almond and peach orchards and vineyards. They have reached a level of financial security and acceptance by the surrounding dominant society. The questions that face them now are those regarding the choices of the Sansei, and the future of the community they have built.

CHAPTER 6

Rice and
Reflection

With each generation the cultural legacies that nourish the people of Cortez have undergone transformations. The impact of social, economic, and technological change on valued practices and individual choice appears even in time-honored staples. For example, as an integral part of life in Cortez—as among most Japanese Americans—rice exemplifies historic change and continuity. Whereas food preparation for Issei farm women entailed the lengthy rinsing of talc-coated rice and laborious cooking over an outdoor fire, their grandchildren wash rice touted as free of talc (thanks to consumer health awareness) and more often than not leave the cooking to the efficiency of an electric rice-cooker. Some, influenced by the dietary concerns of the 1970s, have mixed their consumption of short-grained white rice with brown rice.[1]

Simple and uncontroversial as rice may now appear as a staple, to the Nisei and Sansei it was both a cherished and embarrassing mark of ethnicity in school environments shared with Euro-American classmates who regarded potatoes and bread as the norm. Sansei Grace Yotsuya described with pleasure her oldest daughter's self-assurance and the receptivity of her non–Japanese American peers: "Denise will

---

1. David Mas Masumoto has described the cultural meaning of white rice and his introduction of brown rice sushi into a Del Rey Japanese community New Year's potluck in chap. 10: "*Gochisoo* (Good Foods) and Brown Rice *Sushi*," in *Country Voices, The Oral History of a Japanese American Family Farm Community* (Del Rey, Calif.: Inaka Countryside Publications, 1987), pp. 113–21.

take *nigiri* [rice balls] and she takes the *nori*—*ajitsuke nori* [flavored dried sea vegetable]—and she shares it with the *hakujin* [white] friends of hers, who *will* eat it. *I* would never have *dared* take *onigiri* to school!"[2] Her husband, Dennis Yotsuya, echoed this sentiment. The contents of their Yonsei (fourth generation) child's school lunchbox represent nothing less than the hearty fare of cultural affirmation, made possible by social change.

As research in Cortez revealed, not all cultural legacies were embraced with equal fervor. Some, in fact, met with ambivalence. For instance, when asked about other aspects of Japanese American tradition, Grace said, "You hold back—you hold back on everything. If you're angry at your friend, you don't confront them . . . You don't be aggressive." As an illustration, she mentioned a short-tempered relative who expresses anger quickly and forcefully if rubbed the wrong way. "To me," she admitted, laughing, "that's not very Japanese." What her parents instilled in her was that "you try to be congenial to everybody, you try to be friendly with everybody. You don't do anything to offend others."[3] Dennis explained that this was "a lot of that know-your-own-place kind of [attitude] that we used to fight with the Niseis about." While restraint and unassertiveness were not bad characteristics in and of themselves, they might not be conducive to success "in the modern capitalistic society."[4] Clearly, concern about adaptation to changing circumstances has necessitated reevaluation of the attitudes and behaviors that proved critical to survival in previous times.

A number of the Cortez Sansei, like Dennis and Grace, consciously select and maintain their heritage. Those who have returned to farm in Cortez help to shape the community by participating in a host of organizations and activities. They have become working members of the Cortez Growers Association (CGA) and the local chapter of the Japanese American Citizens League, as well as honorary members of the Shinwakai (senior citizens' group, now largely Nisei). They take their children to dance in the Buddhist *Obon* festival, and enroll them in a summer Japanese American cultural program that is organized in conjunction with Sansei from Livingston and Turlock. Steven S. Fugita and David J. O'Brien assert that the cohesiveness of the Japanese

2. Grace Yotsuya interview, Cortez, Calif., June 5, 1988.
3. Ibid.
4. Dennis Yotsuya interview, Cortez, Calif., June 5, 1988.

American community depends in large measure on participation in such flexible voluntary associations. In addition, they note that this group involvement has persisted throughout the Japanese American population even as more visible aspects of community have faded in the postwar period.[5] Voluntary organizations, they suggest, have shifted from addressing fundamental economic and social necessities before World War II, to a more recreational, social, and cultural focus. Associations in Cortez continue to meet a full panoply of needs, buttressed by their members' involvement in a wide range of outside groups. Even for those no longer resident in the farm settlement, the community still serves as a cultural base.

The shifting meaning and function of the Cortez community illustrate the concept of "emergent ethnicity" propounded by Fugita and O'Brien. Moving beyond a structuralist emphasis on an economic context as the primary determinant of the persistence of ethnicity, they suggest that "the reasons individuals have for maintaining ethnic identification and ethnic community involvement change with each succeeding generation."[6] Flexible adaptive responses to social, political, and economic conditions, as well as the impact of historic events in shaping a community are both manifested in the past processes of institutional and family development in Cortez.

In the last decade, the acceleration of external and internal changes have made it less clear how long Cortez can continue, and in what form. The population boom in the Central Valley has placed greater pressure on farmland. Fluctuations in global markets and new foreign competition, in addition to increasing costs of technology, have raised the stakes for farmers. These developments have created a widening gap between large farms and small operations like those in Cortez, increasingly dependent—as in the case of Dennis and Grace Yotsuya—on off-farm income.[7] Meanwhile, increasing prosperity and mobility within the larger society since the postwar return have significantly influenced the development of Cortez family dynamics, gender roles, marriage, and retention or rejection of cultural practices. As

5. Fugita and O'Brien, pp. 41, 95, 104.

6. Ibid., p. 21.

7. Harold O. Carter, Warren E. Johnston, and Carole Frank Nuckton, "Some Forces Affecting Our Changing American Agriculture," *California Agriculture* 33(January 1979):9–10; Kenneth R. Farrell, "Refining Goals and Priorities," *California Agriculture* 41(March–April 1987):2; UC Agricultural Issues Center, "Keeping the Valley Green: A Public Policy Challenge," *California Agriculture* 45(May–June 1991):10–14.

farming has become a harder choice, other options—to which the Issei and Nisei had little access—have opened to the Sansei and Yonsei. Examination of the development of community dynamics after World War II illuminates the complexity of choice and adaptation that will determine the future of Cortez.

This chapter first provides a historical profile of the Cortez community from the 1950s to the 1970s. The following sections principally draw on oral history interviews to examine in detail the shifts and continuities in family relations, gender roles, and individual expectations. A blending of oral history with a more sociological thematic approach makes it possible to explore the transformations over time in personal life in a way that the chronological treatment of earlier chapters could not. These voices of two generations of men and women reinforce the sense of community not only as a geographic place but also as a set of flexible relationships, changing over time. The Nisei and Sansei's discussion of cultural legacies, as well as personal decisions and concerns, illuminate the internal and external forces that continue to shape the community.

Despite the hardship of the immediate postwar years and crop shifts in the early 1950s, during this time the people of Cortez began to see expansion in the operations of their cooperative association and increasing acceptance by the surrounding society. After 1950, the Cortez farmers moved from row crops to vineyards and almond and peach orchards. Although all family members remained involved in farmwork, the labor became less arduous and time-consuming because of the increased use of machinery and the less labor-intensive nature of vineyard and orchard cultivation. Both sons and daughters helped with weeding, fertilizing, and harvesting, although boys often did more tractor work and girls were expected to shoulder a greater number of domestic duties. The facilities of the Cortez Growers Association (CGA) grew steadily to meet the needs of increasing production. In 1951, the CGA purchased its first almond pickup machine, and began bulk handling of almonds in 1953, at which time a bulk-handling system was also developed for the grape harvest. By 1959, rising almond production resulted in the enlargement of the hulling facility; by 1972, the size of the CGA warehouse and office complex had more than doubled.

The composition of the CGA also reflected changes in the Japanese

The Nisei encouraged their Sansei children to participate in a range of extra-curricular activities. Shirley, Bonnie, and Nancy Baba (from left) took dance classes and often performed together. They posed here in 1956. Photo courtesy of Nobuzo Baba.

Americans' relations with the larger society. In 1947, the Blaine brothers of Ballico joined the CGA as its first non-Japanese American members; in 1949, Hilmar Blaine became the first Euro-American to hold a position on the board of directors. In 1961, the CGA hired Dave Zollinger as its first non-Japanese American manager. By its fiftieth anniversary celebration in 1974, the CGA included sixty-two members, of whom fifteen were not Japanese Americans. At that time, the holdings of co-op members comprised 3,000 acres, all located within a two-mile radius of the CGA facilities.[8] The CGA has also mirrored other changes within the community. In the mid-1950s, economic

8. *The Modesto Sun*, March 24, 1974.

improvement and the influence of mainstream culture transformed the annual CGA dinner, begun in 1947, from an all-male function to one attended by wives and guests as well.

The increased participation by Japanese Americans in local interracial social, church, and school events heralded a growing measure of acceptance within the surrounding society during the late 1940s and 1950s. The Cortez Nisei began to take part in local and county agricultural associations, like the county grape growers' group and the Ballico Farm Center, and local civic organizations such as the Lions Club. By the 1950s, mention of interracial children's birthday and holiday parties appeared in the Ballico section of the *Livingston Chronicle* and demonstrated both the economic gains of Japanese Americans and their increasing interaction with non-Japanese American peers.

Generational changes also manifested themselves within postwar community organizations. In the late 1940s and early 1950s, the continuation of the Cortez Young People's Club and the coalescence of a Young Married Group evidenced both the wide age range among the Nisei (most of whom grew up during the 1920s and 1930s), and the maturation of a significant number of them. The 1950s witnessed the passage of community leadership from the first to the second generation with the transfer of Nisei energies from the social events of the Young Married Group to the primarily civic functions of the local chapter of the Japanese American Citizens League (JACL), in conjunction with the formation of the Shinwakai.

In the postwar period, the Nisei established their families, and the third generation, the Sansei, appeared. Although there exists a wide age range, as among the Nisei, the majority of the Cortez Sansei were born between 1940 and the mid-1960s and thus were part of the larger "baby boom" of 1947–1963. In the 1960s and 1970s, the economic gains of the community and the acceptance of the Japanese Americans in mainstream society meant that the Cortez Sansei could attain the college education that had remained beyond the reach of most of their parents. After graduation from Livingston High School, many pursued higher education, either close to home at Modesto Junior College and the California State University, Stanislaus, in Turlock, or farther away, at schools such as San Jose State University and the University of California at Berkeley.

During the 1970s, more and more of the Cortez Sansei began to settle and establish their own families, often in nearby towns and cities of the San Joaquin Valley and the San Francisco Bay Area. They entered a broad spectrum of jobs, including teaching, engineering, medical professions, automotive mechanics, law, produce distribution, and agriculture. And some of the third generation, notably oldest sons, began to return to Cortez to farm, usually with their parents. They had grown up with the expectation of farming the "home place." The prosperity of the Nisei's orchards and vineyards in the 1970s also made the prospect attractive. In 1982, the CGA included among its 62 members fourteen Sansei, listed singly like Daniel Kubo, Alan Osugi and Rodney Sakaguchi, or in partnership with Nisei, like Hiroshi and Gary Asai or the DMH Ranch of Dwight, Mae, and Harry Kajioka.

The return of the Sansei and the establishment of their families signaled both community continuity and generational change. By the end of the 1970s and the beginning of the 1980s, the number of Issei dwindled, and the ranks of the Shinwakai began to include a growing number of Nisei who were approaching retirement age. Despite a significant Sansei presence in the CGA, the Nisei continue to operate the majority of farms.

The future of Cortez as a cohesive ethnic minority community is by no means certain, for many reasons. Economic survival may preclude the choice of farming as a career for a number of Sansei. Farming has always been a gamble, as painfully evidenced when three days of rain robbed a Cortez family of an $80,000 raisin crop in 1982. Natural risks aside, modern farmers face the pressures of domestic and foreign market competition, steep costs of land and equipment, as well as the encroachment of urban workers who wish to commute to rural homes. Demographers have predicted that three million newcomers will swell the Central Valley's population by the year 2005.[9]

Agriculture in California has become a highly technological, highly capitalized industry, characterized by a growing gap between large-scale farming and small or part-time operations. In 1987, Kenneth Farrell, vice-president of Agriculture and Natural Resources of the University of California, observed that 14 percent of the nation's farmers accounted for 75 percent of its produce. The majority (70 percent) of the farms, contributing 10 percent of agricultural production, were small and their operators depended heavily on off-farm income.[10] This

9. "Keeping the Valley Green," pp. 10–14.
10. Farrell, p. 2.

pattern has emerged in Cortez as elsewhere. Even with a core group of Sansei maintaining farms, the trend toward consolidation of holdings may mean a smaller, more spread out, and possibly less cohesive community.

Conscious of the economic fragility of the small farm, many of the Sansei, who are able to parlay their education into a broader range of careers, have sought the opportunities and advantages of urban areas. The rise in interracial marriage also has caused alteration in family relations and community networks. Given these shifts within and outside the colony, the future of the community has become a major concern.

Oral history interviews with the Nisei and Sansei, some living away from their hometown, have revealed the interplay of intergenerational dynamics. Examining the areas of family relations, gender roles, marriage and intermarriage, cultural traditions, and perspectives on farming indicates the paths taken by the people of Cortez, and the direction of the community.

Child-rearing practices in the Nisei-Sansei family of the 1950s and 1960s offer an example. In some respects, the Nisei behaved very much like their own Issei parents; they too stressed the value of hard work, academic achievement, and respect for authority. As in the Issei-headed family, women cared for children and managed the household while men ran the farm. Upon later reflection, several Nisei men expressed the wish that they had been more involved with raising their children. "At that time, I was expanding my farm operation and I spent a lot of time working," said one father, "and I feel like I did neglect the kids when they were growing up. I kind of regret that I didn't spend more time with them. I have more time now; I feel a little more established."

Within the home, the mainstream middle-class cultural ideology of the 1950s and traditional Japanese patterns dovetailed. As Mary Ryan has observed, the prescribed female role was to socialize children and to "direct the emotional and psychological functions of the home."[11] Nisei women, like their Issei mothers and non-Japanese American peers, did most of the day-to-day disciplining, holding in reserve the ultimate threat of paternal displeasure. Echoing the recollections of

11. Mary P. Ryan, *Womanhood in America, from Colonial Times to the Present* (New York: New Viewpoints, 1975), p. 337.

several peers, one Sansei recalled, "My mother did all the disciplining, except when it was 'Wait until your father gets home,' and then we knew we were in *big trouble*. That was *the* threat. Otherwise, she'd handle it. . . . My mother really raised us kids." Another Sansei added that "there was more of a threat with my father. Mom was softer in the sense that she would repeatedly warn us before actually doing something, like taking away the toy or spanking us, whereas Dad—we knew that he would tell us a couple of times and then that would be it. Mom would give us a lot more slack."

Like their parents, the Cortez Sansei helped with farmwork from an early age. Girls and boys alike hoed weeds, tied vines, spread fertilizer, swamped boxes, and joined harvest crews, although boys generally did a greater share of tractor work and were often exempted from the domestic chores assigned to their sisters. "My Mom wanted me to stay home and clean house," remembered a Sansei woman, chuckling, "and I would sneak out and help my Dad, because it's more fun. . . . And then she couldn't yell at you because you were helping."

The Sansei, like their parents, grew up with a sense of their ties to community institutions. For instance, the Nisei expected regular church attendance by their children. And during their early years, the Sansei complied, although some—like their parents—regarded this as a strongly social as well as religious obligation. "I went there because the community built it," a Christian Sansei said. "The purpose it served, to me, was a place to socialize."

Along with these continuities in child rearing, considerable socioeconomic changes have occurred in both the Japanese American community and the larger society, changes that have rendered the Sansei's youth different from that of the Nisei. For one thing, "their parents could speak English," pointed out Mary Kamiya. "And in this community, we're in the social power group, the academic group and the leadership positions, liked by the teachers, outstanding in sports. . . . So they [the Sansei] grew up in a very different atmosphere than we did. I would say that they grew up financially secure compared to the Nisei."[12] The Nisei, with gratification, perceive their children as having more opportunities than they did, in terms of education, career goals, and social interaction. "We had dreams," Kiyoshi Yamamoto explained, "but knowing what we have been through, we knew that

12. Mary Noda Kamiya interview, Ballico, Calif., February 13, 1982.

they could not be fulfilled. Whereas the Sansei do not come from the background that the Nisei had, and so they're not handicapped. I honestly think that their dreams can be fulfilled. And we're happy for them."[13]

These factors have led to significant changes in parent–child relations across generations. The Nisei, being fluent in English and having grown up in this country, had a basis of common understanding with their children, which was rarely possible for the Issei. Kiyoshi Yamamoto expressed the sentiments of many Cortez Nisei in discussing his relationship with the Sansei: "I feel that I am much closer to our children than I was to my parents because I could joke with our kids, and talk about their problems, and talk about my problems, which I didn't have the opportunity to do with my parents. . . . I could help them with their homework."[14]

Another area of difference for many, if not all, is a greater breadth in communication. Certain subjects, while still sensitive, are less taboo than before. For instance, very few Nisei women received information about menstruation from the Issei. "My mother did not tell me a thing," said one Nisei. "My younger sister even said the same thing— that she thought she was bleeding to death, and she was afraid to tell anybody because she thought she was dying." This woman has taken a very different approach with her own children: "I guess it would shock my mother how open I am so far as talking about things like that with my daughters. I even talked with my sons. You have to. And they have always felt comfortable, even my sons have come and asked me, 'What exactly is a woman's cycle? . . . What's happening?' And so I sit and talk to them."

The expression of affection has been another arena of change within family interaction. The Issei parental style was one of reserve and restraint. Given the absence of grandparents "to counterbalance the severity of parental authority,"[15] public displays of affection among Issei spouses, or between the Issei and Nisei, rarely occurred. "That's what was kind of hard," said one Nisei. "You never saw them hug or kiss, or even touch each other in front of you. And they didn't hug us or anything." Their feelings about their children were conveyed in

13. Kiyoshi Yamamoto interview, Cortez, Calif., February 6, 1982.
14. Ibid. See also Fugita and O'Brien, p. 80.
15. Lyman, p. 60.

other, less direct ways. "You could see it sometimes when they were talking to their friends about what they were doing. Then you sensed some of the feeling of pride if we did well in something, and they would be telling friends." The Nisei knew that their parents cared about them, but the parent-child relationship often remained rather formal until the Nisei themselves became parents and discovered new bonds of understanding with the Issei.

The Nisei, armed like their contemporaries with Dr. Benjamin Spock's baby book, appeared far more demonstrative with their children. This, in turn, has spilled over into the Sansei's interaction with their grandparents. A number of Nisei remarked on their parents' adjustment to this expression of feeling. "At first it used to embarrass my mother," explained one, "when [my oldest daughter] would walk up to her and say, 'Hi, Grandma.' She'd always hug her and give her a kiss. But now my mother has gotten so she expects it. If you don't kiss her goodbye or give her a hug hi, she'll say, 'How come you don't kiss Grandma hello?' "

This kind of emotional expression has been more difficult for the Nisei men than their wives, who have spent more time in close interaction with the children. "I always kind of regret that I've never shown open affection to my daughter the way I should," mused one father. "I think I'm closer to them now than before. Occasionally I'll write to them and tell them [that] even though I don't tell them about it, I do love them a lot. As they get older, I think I better let them know that."

Although most of the Cortez Nisei considered their relationship with their children to be closer and less formal than their relationship with their own parents, a number felt that this closeness and openness developed gradually in recent years. As a Nisei woman explained, "When we were growing up, [and] as we were parents, there weren't all these books and all these talk shows about feelings, and how to raise your kids, and communication. That's all in the last ten, fifteen years that it's come about, really."[16]

The Sansei, as they grow older, have gained new insights about their parents. "I always thought when I was younger that my father was quiet and had no emotions," a Sansei woman said, "because he didn't express them. But in my adult life I realize that we didn't express or verbalize anything to my father. Now . . . we tell my father,

16. May Shirakawa Toyoda interview, Cortez, Calif., February 4, 1982.

'We love you,' and 'Dad, we're really appreciative of when you used to do this for us.' So he in turn relates to us on that level. So it didn't mean he never had those qualities; we [just] never had that interaction." One Nisei woman described the Issei and Nisei men as being pretty similar with regard to the expression of feeling and commented that "Nisei men may show more affection to the wife, but not to the children." She laughed and added, "By the next generation it might be better."

Indeed, the Sansei men and women from Cortez said they would like to be more open with their own children, real or hypothetical. Although major shifts have taken place between the Issei-Nisei and Nisei-Sansei relationships, some Sansei felt their parents were far less open than the parents of their non-Japanese American peers. One Sansei related how "[my mother] felt that we were being rebellious and outspoken, and one of the things she emphasized was that you just don't talk that way to your parents. And we, of course, were influenced by our peers in school—by non-Asians who were very verbal and were talking to their parents very openly." Fugita and O'Brien also found Japanese Americans making comparisons between their "cautious style of interpersonally relating" and the perceived greater frankness of Euro-Americans.[17]

As Nobu Miyoshi has observed, such openness is important to the Sansei because they rely on verbal communication more than their parents did. Miyoshi asserts that social restraint, considered a strength and a virtue in Japanese society, is, in everyday relations, regarded as "a social handicap if not an abnormality in the United States."[18] The Sansei, in their orientation to verbal communication, have been influenced by the surrounding society and their non-Japanese American peers.

The people of Cortez, like most Japanese Americans, have perceived gender roles as distinctly different, although farming has engaged the energies of all family members. Despite the overlap in farmwork and domestic tasks for women, it is the men—Issei and Nisei—who have been considered the farmers. They developed particular horticultural expertise and they make the major decisions regarding the ranches—a

17. Fugita and O'Brien, p. 46.
18. Nobu Miyoshi, "Identity Crisis of the Sansei and the American Concentration Camp," *Pacific Citizen*, Holiday Issue, December 19–26, 1980, p. 42.

pattern reflected in non-Japanese American farming as well.[19] And although both Sansei men and women grew up doing farmwork, the majority of the Nisei, like the Issei, expect or hope that a son—especially the oldest son—will eventually run the "home place." In the absence of sons or interested sons, some families have pinned their hopes on a daughter's marrying a man who will be willing to farm.

Today there still exist biases against women taking a primary role in farm operation. One Sansei woman described an incident involving a third-generation woman who runs a ranch while her husband holds an office job. When she went to the CGA for some spraying material, a Nisei man told her, "You can't spray!" "It's obvious that the reason he was saying that was because she was a woman. And that attitude is so prevalent, people don't even see what's wrong with it, or that it might not necessarily be so—that a woman can't spray." This Sansei added, "It's really funny, because some of the women, especially in the (Nisei) generation above ours, have not worked other than on the farm, and yet if there is a woman who's *really* involved in the farm, then they kind of look funny at that, too."

In the 1950s and 1960s, only a small number of the Cortez Nisei women held wage-paying jobs while their children were still in school. Like their non-Japanese American sisters, those who did so generally considered themselves "supplementary workers,"[20] taking jobs because of the desire and need to contribute to the family income. "I was responsible for clothing my mother-in-law," explained one. "She liked clothes, and to keep her dressed, I had to go to work." These women found jobs processing poultry at the Armour Company as well as in the local school system and in white-collar Turlock businesses. Several women said they would have liked to take such jobs if they hadn't been deterred by logistics or spousal disapproval. "I always envied people who worked out and had their own money," a Nisei admitted, "because I just felt like whatever came out of the ranch was [my

---

19. Orville E. Thompson, Douglas Gwynn, and Charlotte Sharp, "Characteristics of Women in Farming," *California Agriculture* 41(January–February 1987):16–17; Orville E. Thompson, Douglas Gwynn, and Charlotte Sharp, "Women on Commercial Farms," *California Agriculture* 39(May–June 1985):21–22. In their 1985 article, the authors reported that a review of 600 journal articles on women in agriculture revealed no data on women in California farming.

20. Ryan, p. 329.

husband's family's] money. My husband's father . . . felt like this was his *zaisan* [wealth]. Whenever we had any problem [with him], he would always bring out the fact that 'This is my *zaisan*, the ranch' . . . And so, all the more, I never felt like I could do anything I want with the money. So I always wanted to work out, but the children kept coming and then I was always helping out on the ranch, even when the children were small."

Although the Nisei hoped that at least one son would want to farm, they believed that all of their children should prepare for a career. As Darrel Montero has asserted, the Nisei, like the Issei, valued education and viewed it as a key to social mobility.[21] Because of the growing prosperity of the farms as well as growing acceptance of Japanese Americans, they could provide their daughters and sons with the college education unattainable for so many Nisei. As Sansei Candice Toyoda stated, "I always knew that I was going to go to college."[22] To my knowledge, every Cortez Sansei—and 88 percent of the Sansei studied by Gene Levine and Colbert Rhodes—had some college or university education, and several have attained advanced degrees.[23]

The Cortez Nisei expected their children to attend college, find work, and marry, in that order, and many Sansei have done so. However, some mothers had different dreams for their daughters, perhaps reflecting the fact that so many of the Nisei women had lived and worked away from their families during the wartime. "I expected them to work and earn, to be on their own for awhile before they got married," said one. "I didn't want them to get married right away. . . . I think all girls should be free for awhile." Several Nisei mothers suggested to their daughters, "Why don't you go to college, go to work, and then see the world?" Ironically, their daughters, influenced by their college peers in the early 1960s, felt differently. "I think my mother was sort of living through me, wanting me to do these things that she never did," a Sansei speculated with wistful hindsight, "so

21. Darrel Montero, *Japanese Americans, Changing Patterns of Ethnic Affiliation over Three Generations* (Boulder, Colo.: Westview Press, 1980), p. 64.

22. Candice Toyoda interview, Cortez, Calif., July 17, 1982.

23. Levine and Rhodes, p. 121. This study and that of Darrel Montero, cited in footnote 21, were both based on extensive material gathered by the Japanese American Research Project, carried out by UCLA in conjunction with the Japanese American Citizens League. The JARP data represents interviews conducted from 1963 to 1967 with 1,047 Issei (64 percent male), 2,304 Nisei (52 percent male) and 802 Sansei throughout the country.

she wanted me not to get married. I wanted to get married. . . . After I graduated from college, I started working and I also was getting ready to get married because that's what everybody I was going to college with was doing. . . . It was seldom that a girl established her career and went out and did the world."

Like their ancestors and middle-class non-Japanese American peers,[24] the Nisei assumed that they would marry and that marriage would naturally be part of their children's lives also. "I think in the end that a person married has more companionship, and . . . I consider myself very fortunate, that I am quite happy," said a Nisei woman. Like nearly all of the Nisei living in Cortez, she married another Japanese American and finds satisfaction in their shared experiences and background. "We have a lot in common. In some ways, we're like a brother and sister, in that our families are so similar, our heritage, in our outlook, in our feelings. . . . And so then I just feel that our children would be happier if they could marry." By 1985, of the Sansei and young Nisei children of the thirty-eight resident Cortez families, thirty-nine had married Japanese Americans, thirty-six had married interracially, and fifty-six were single. Of the latter, nine had been divorced.

Both the Nisei and Sansei discussed the changes they saw in current marriage patterns and their related concerns. Two trends in particular have received attention from the people of Cortez: the rising rate of interracial, or exogamous, marriage and an increase in divorce among the Sansei. The interviewees linked these trends to several interwoven elements, including changes in Sansei gender roles and opportunities, an alteration in the relationship between a couple and the community, and attitudinal shifts in the mainstream society.

A number of interviewees remarked upon the wider social and economic opportunities available to the Sansei, with particular emphasis on the change in women's roles. "You see the biggest change in the girls," said a Nisei woman. "They're just really independent." She felt that their broader opportunities and independence have placed them in a position of greater choice than that of the married Nisei women. "You know, a lot of us [Nisei women] would be divorced if it weren't for the fact that people didn't get divorces. We just stuck it out, regardless. And then, too, we knew that we couldn't go out and make

24. Kiefer, p. 179.

a living for ourselves and for our kids, too." Besides her approval of broader roles for women, her words also mirrored the ambiguity some Nisei feel regarding what they view as the Sansei's lesser ties to, and concern with, community. "I think the Sansei women know what they could do, and they could really do much more with their own lives [than the Nisei], if only to just fulfill themselves, do the things that they want to do, regardless of whether they think about other people or not, or the world outside their own life. They will live a much happier and more fulfilling life, I think, because of the strength they've gotten now."

A number of sociologists have noted the change in Sansei women and their widening opportunities. Christie Kiefer found in his study of Japanese Americans in San Francisco that consequently many Sansei women did not want the role of their mothers.[25] That role appeared both admirable and daunting to one Cortez Sansei who said, "I couldn't do the stuff my mother did or any of those women—take care of in-laws, and raise your kids, and be involved in community activities, and be a wife to your husband, and go out and work on the ranch. . . . Plus do the laundry. And in those days we had a wringer-washer. . . . You still hung all the clothes out, either outside or inside. They never had any dryers. I couldn't do all that. All I can do is take care of myself and my dog."

On the other hand, the Sansei men of Cortez seem to have changed less than their sisters, which also correlates with more general findings. A 1963 sociological survey showed that Japanese American men were more likely to hold "male-dominant views while there were no significant differences between Japanese-American females and Caucasian males and females."[26] In her study of married women's "second shift," published in 1989, Arlie Hochschild documented the pattern of "faster-changing women and slower-changing men" in the larger population.[27] One Cortez Nisei likened the Sansei men to their Nisei fathers in this respect: "I think they see their fathers and the way they kind of control their family," she said, "and . . . I think that they see that it's pretty nice, the way their fathers have lived; you know, their

25. Ibid., p. 225.

26. A. Arkoff, G. Meredith, and J. Dong, "Attitudes of Japanese-American and Caucasian-American Students toward Marriage Roles," *Journal of Social Psychology* 59(1963):11–15.

27. Arlie Hochschild with Anne Machung, *The Second Shift* (New York: Avon Books, 1989), p. 205.

mothers wait on them and have always done things for them, and they think that's the way of life: to have children, and let the mothers take care of them and maybe go out and earn a little extra money . . . not because they [wives] do this for themselves, but because that gives a little more income to the family." That is why, she concluded, "Sansei women are not marrying Sansei men."

Sansei men have also acknowledged the changes in women's roles but with considerably more ambivalence. One Cortez Sansei male expressed anger and alarm about women's increasing independence and economic opportunities. "You know, there's nothing holding a woman to marriage nowadays, it doesn't seem, except for her love for her husband"—a bond which in his view did not last beyond the honeymoon period. "Before, a woman usually halfway needed a man to protect her or support her, and she kept the house," he said. "But nowadays a woman is basically equal to a man and that means if they don't like each other, they just split. Because each party can take care of their own selves." He likened this change to alterations in community dynamics: "[Because of] the fact that they have a career, they're not as dependent on the man, and therefore it's the same analogy with the community. If everybody had to work together to survive, there'd be that bond. And that kind of bond is a real strong bond. But now everybody is big [in terms of acreage] and can survive on their own, basically. . . . That's just like a marriage. If my wife is just as strong as me, [and] we're both affluent, if we don't get along, she can just split without any problem at all, because she could support herself." Deepening the fear of divorce is the fear of losing farmholdings. "Especially me being a farmer, it complicates things a lot, because you can't give her half the farm. . . . If you've got cash, you can always split cash down halfway—you lose half. But you can't split a farm down halfway and lose half—you lose more than half. It just doesn't operate right. So the divorce would really hurt, as far as being able to farm."

Many Sansei—especially the men—perceive childcare as primarily a woman's responsibility. A 1987 study of farm women in northern California's Yolo County revealed the broader entrenchment of this attitude, finding that "women had virtually exclusive responsibility for meal preparation and childcare."[28] This expectation has proven to be a source of inner conflict for women who have grown up expecting

28. Thompson, Gwynn, and Sharp, p. 16.

to have families of their own and who have also attained a high degree of education and developed professional career goals. A Sansei man who has pursued a career away from Cortez expressed concern about married women working, because of the possible effects on their children: "When I get married, if at all possible, if I can survive and support a family, I would not like to have my wife working. Not from a chauvinistic standpoint, but because I feel in the first early years of a child's life the basic personality is formed, and I think I'd rather have his or her personality in the hands of either myself or my wife, rather than a day-care center, or at my mother's." While he felt that he had retained "a lot of the old-time morals and attitudes of the Issei," he also believed that "you have to be progressive, you have to keep on changing with society." He recognized the difficult decisions faced by two-career marriages and the negotiations they might necessitate: "As far as if one should forfeit their job to do it [childcare], I don't think that my wife would want to give up her job and I don't think I would either, but that's one of the choices you have to make when you do have a child. And I think that that's something you have to sit down and talk about, and see where your futures are going, what will happen if you quit and start up later." One Sansei woman who made such a decision to leave her job to have children is looking forward to going back to work when they are older, "because it's nice having your own money. I was on my own and worked before I got married, and so you get used to having your own money, being an independent person."

Even without children, married and wage-earning Sansei have had to grapple with the demands of the "second shift." Like the racially diverse couples examined by Hochschild, Japanese Americans have experienced the tensions of negotiating marital responsibilities.[29] A third-generation woman living away from Cortez said of her Sansei husband: "He liked the fact that I was working but he also seemed to want me to do these housewife things all the time to perfection like his mother did—have dinner ready at a certain time, on time, everyday; have his clothes all washed and all this—and I said, 'Hey, wait a minute. I can't both have a career and be there like I'm your servant.' So I started to rebel and he started to then realize that he was doing this . . . out of habit. Then we started to work together."[30] Despite their efforts, however, this couple eventually divorced.

29. Hochschild, pp. 1–10, 22–32, 173–215.
30. At the time of the interviews in 1982, there were five Sansei couples living in

As one might expect from the previous discussion, the Cortez Sansei have a much higher divorce rate than their parents, mirroring trends in the larger society. To my knowledge, although some of the Nisei who have moved away from Cortez have divorced, only one Nisei living within the community has done so. While changes in women's roles and opportunities have been cited as a factor in this trend, others have suggested additional reasons. Some Nisei attribute the higher divorce rate among the Sansei to the fact that they did not struggle through the Depression and experience hardship as did the Nisei, and therefore, as Hisako Asai said, "if something goes wrong, they say, 'Okay, that's it,' instead of saying, 'Well, let's try to stick it out.' "[31]

Some Nisei also have the sense that community pressure, definitely a factor in Nisei marriages, exerts less influence on the Sansei—most of whom reside away from Cortez—wherever they live. "It isn't that all Nisei were happily married," Hisako's husband Hiroshi expounded. "I think there's plenty of times when they wanted to split, but I think there was enough outside pressure that they didn't feel comfortable getting a divorce. They may have wanted it, but it isn't that easy to do because you had to worry about your folks, their feelings. You're not just thinking about your feelings but you had to worry about the public image."[32] Gary Asai, a Sansei, added, "That's the difference between the Nisei and the Sansei—the Sansei is less obligated to the family."[33]

Although the Sansei who were interviewed, both those living in and those living away from Cortez, do care very much about their parents and families, they seem less willing than the Nisei to live their lives in strict conformity to community standards. In general, they do not have the same degree of anxiety about "public image," although they acknowledge its importance in the lives of their parents. "I'm sure that it was much more a concern of my parents," one Sansei explained, "because this is where their home was, and I had pretty much always known I was going to college and probably not going to come back to

---

Cortez. In one instance the wife farmed and the husband worked as a lawyer; in another, the wife worked as a teacher and the husband both farmed and held a job as an accountant. Of the other three couples—one since divorced—the husbands farmed exclusively and two of the wives held part-time jobs in fields for which they had completed professional training. The last three couples also had children. At this time there were also a number of unmarried Sansei men farming in Cortez.

31. Hisako Asai interview, Cortez, Calif., February 23, 1982.
32. Hiroshi Asai interview, Cortez, Calif., February 23, 1982.
33. Gary Asai interview, Cortez, Calif., February 23, 1982.

Cortez." Even so, she also felt the force of community pressure as a teenager. "Just because the community is as small as it is, I remember my own paranoia around a young man I was seeing in high school that my parents didn't want me to associate with at all. Whenever I did meet him on the sly, somehow they always found out. I attribute that to our community." The Sansei still living in Cortez are aware of their neighbors' scrutiny, but feel less pressured by it. As one Sansei man said with equanimity, "Yeah, they're watching you, every move, and what's going on. . . . I really should think about it more, but I don't. You have to live your own life."

The sense of community pressure has decreased among the Nisei as well. As the Sansei have reached maturity, chosen a variety of career paths, married interracially or not, or remained single, their parents have become less concerned about what their neighbors might think. In this respect, they have mirrored the more pluralistic attitude of society at large during the 1970s. "Before, it was harder," explained a Nisei. "But now I came to the point where it's not going to bother me. . . . My children are all grown up now, so there's nothing to be afraid of; there's nothing for people to say. . . . Nowadays more and more [Cortez] people are having this attitude: You can't say anything about anybody because how do you know when something may happen within your own family, or your grandkids, or your children. So no one has the right to say anything about anybody else." A Sansei agreed, particularly with regard to interracial marriage, saying, "people are much less into pointing fingers and saying, 'Ha ha! Look what your son or daughter did!' because, I think, everyone feels a bit threatened."

The people of Cortez join a number of social scientists in expressing concern over the consequences of interracial marriage for the ethnic community. Gene Levine and Colbert Rhodes have called it the major indicator of assimilation into the larger society,[34] and Darrel Montero has agreed that, in general, the exogamous or outmarried Sansei have a greater tendency to move away from the Japanese culture and community than their endogamous peers. However, Fugita and O'Brien reported that the intermarried Japanese Americans in their sample maintained a significantly greater degree of participation in ethnic community institutional life than did the members of any other ethnic

34. Levine and Rhodes, p. 145.

group.[35] Nevertheless, a sense of intermarriage as a potential factor in weakening ethnic ties is evident among some Cortez Nisei, one of whom said, regarding her generation, "Once you get out of school, whether it's college or high school, you kind of find yourself drifting back to your own people. . . . But I don't know about the Sanseis, because there are so many mixed marriages now."

As mentioned by a number of scholars, the current trend among Japanese Americans in general is one of rising outmarriage, due to shifts in both the Japanese American and mainstream cultures.[36] Whereas 10 percent of all Nisei chose non-Japanese American marital partners, by the 1970s roughly 50 percent of all Sansei did so: In 1970, Hawaii—with the largest population of Japanese Americans in the United States—had an outmarriage rate of 47 percent; in the same year Fresno, California, had a rate of 49 percent. In 1971, San Francisco had an outmarriage rate of 58 percent, and in 1972 Los Angeles—with the second largest Japanese American population—had 49 percent.[37] In a more recent study of Asian American marriage, Larry Hajime Shinagawa and Gin Yong Pang also reported the increasing growth rate of interracial and interethnic unions among Japanese Americans. Shinagawa and Pang found interracial marriage occurring primarily among the most advantaged members of Asian American and Euro-American populations; thus, as a demarcator of class, they suggested that it serves better as a gauge of socioeconomic hierarchy than as an indicator of the fall of racial barriers to Asian Americans in U.S. society.[38]

Nearly all of the Cortez Nisei, like their Japanese American contemporaries, married other Japanese Americans. The first Nisei to marry interracially in the 1950s was disowned by her father, and a number of years passed before her parents would accept her marriage. Since then, only two of the Nisei still farming in Cortez have married non-Japanese Americans. A Nisei man noted the change between the second and third generations: "The Sansei kids, whether they're boys or girls, for them to go around with [a person of] a different race is

35. Fugita and O'Brien, p. 184.
36. Akemi Kikumura and Harry Kitano, "Interracial Marriage: A Picture of the Japanese Americans," *Journal of Social Issues* 29(1973):75.
37. Ibid., p. 74.
38. Larry Hajime Shinagawa and Gin Yong Pang, "Marriage patterns of Asian Americans in California, 1980," *Income and Status Differences between White and Minority Americans*, ed. Sucheng Chan, Mellen Studies in Sociology, vol. 3 (Lewiston, N.Y.: The Edwin Mellen Press, 1990), pp. 225–82.

nothing. And I think that's absolutely normal. But during my generation, that was an entirely different thing. Very few Nisei married white girls, and when a Nisei would marry a white girl, in most of the cases, [people would say] 'Ah, you know what kind of woman she was.' "[39]

The Nisei parents of Cortez would like their children to marry other Sansei but they have developed a pragmatic attitude. One father voiced the sentiments of many, saying, "I would prefer that they marry a Japanese person but I feel that if the person they choose to marry is a nice person and I feel they are going to be happy, I'll be happy for them too. Because our children have *hakujin* friends." His wife agreed, observing that nowadays a common ethnic background does not ensure a stable marriage: "I have too many friends who got married to other races and are doing beautifully, and then there are others that married Japanese kids and are losing it all. This is how it is. And so I'm leaving it up to the kids. They've got to live with them, not me. I would like to see that they marry *nihonjins*, but it doesn't have to be." The sentiments of this couple also reflect an Issei-Nisei generational shift in the meaning of marriage and family, from an alliance concerned primarily with obligation and survival to a union centered on the concept of individual happiness.

The Cortez Nisei also have preferences within the area of interracial marriage. "I think the overwhelming preference," said a Sansei, "would still be that everyone's sons and daughters marry other Japanese, first of all; then another Asian; and then perhaps Caucasian." Whereas most Nisei said they could accept—or had accepted—the marriage of their children to other Asian Americans or Euro-Americans, there still remains a strong stigma against marriage with African Americans. On a wider scale, Shinagawa and Pang found generally that, given controlled population size and composition, Asian Americans tended first to marry members of their own ethnic group, followed by other Asian Americans, then Euro-Americans, and last, Hispanics and African Americans.[40]

The rate of interracial marriage has increased dramatically between the second and third generations of Cortez as it has in the larger Japanese American population. As discussed earlier, this trend reflects changes in gender roles, alteration in the social climate, and the wider

39. The Nisei from Cortez who married interracially all chose Euro-American partners.
40. Shinagawa and Pang, p. 269.

educational and career opportunities that have taken the Sansei into areas where they meet few other Japanese Americans. A good number of the Sansei from Cortez, like other Sansei, have chosen non-Japanese American marital partners. And, as Kikumura and Kitano noted, although the rate of outmarriage has been higher for women, this trend appears to be changing with a substantial portion of men also marrying interracially. However, half of the third generation from Cortez who are already married have Sansei spouses. The five Sansei couples farming in Cortez in 1982 were all Japanese American.

Interracial marriage has also changed relations between in-law families, and thus signals potential alteration in the dynamics of community networks. While most of the Nisei in Cortez have come to like and respect their non-Japanese American sons- and daughters-in-law, there is a sense that they have a less close bond with their in-laws' families, some of whom also have had reservations about interracial marriage. "It's just that I think it's a lot easier to have family things with a Japanese [in-law] family," explained a Nisei who has both Japanese American and Euro-American in-laws. "Of course, my son-in-law's parents live in L.A., so we don't see them too much. But you know, we're brought up differently and we think differently. So we can do things socially, but I don't think we'll ever be close friends like we would be with a Japanese family." It is these ties of common experience and culture and shared activities that have kept the Cortez community close, and it is outmarriage that most clearly heralds change and the need for adjustment.

While interracial marriage does not inevitably precede the loss of ethnic culture, it does take a conscious agreement and effort on the part of the couple to maintain the elements that are important to them, as in the case of Larry Frice and Shirley Baba Frice. Shirley, who has tried to expose their children to Japanese art and cuisine, spoke of her hopes regarding their future: "I would want our daughter to marry somebody who recognizes that she is of a different culture and respects whatever interests she has in it. And if she continues to be a Buddhist . . . I hope he will support her in that, and if he doesn't join the church as Larry has, at least allow her to go and give her children the choice to go to Sunday School. I would like that. And the same with our son."[41]

41. Shirley Baba Frice interview, Atwater, Calif., April 26, 1982.

To the Nisei, the vast majority of whom never even considered marrying a non-Japanese American, the dynamics of such a relationship are often difficult to imagine. "Sometimes I wonder," mused a woman, "if they really get old—in their 60s and 70s—I wonder how they will feel . . . would they wish they had married their own race? . . . Because it's easy to sit across a table when you're both old and you're both Japanese, but if one of you is *hakujin* or Spanish or some other race . . . [I wonder] what the feeling would be. But . . . then I think to myself, 'Well, maybe it's because we're still racially conscious, whereas the Sanseis aren't.' "

While many of the Cortez Sansei socialize with and marry non-Japanese Americans, questions of culture and ethnicity remain important to them. They are not as blithe and unconcerned as the Nisei perceive them to be, perhaps because, although they feel they have greater opportunities than their parents did, they do not feel completely at ease within the dominant group.[42] For some, dating and marriage are highly sensitive issues. One Sansei man whose work has taken him to several different states and who has dated women of varied ethnic backgrounds said that his closest friends were Japanese American. "I think that that's . . . my own security blanket," he explained,

> because in some areas of the country . . . it's hard to tell if people are just patronizing you. . . . I've got some really good friends that are out in Oklahoma City, and I tell you, those guys—I'd trust my life with them. But on the same token, as far as the social standpoint, especially like going out on dates, you're not sure if they're doing it because they want to show their friends they have a unique boyfriend, or that they're patronizing you, or they feel sorry for you. Actually, some of those things shouldn't even come into mind, but I've seen it happen so often that you almost have to be a little—conscious, I guess.

A Sansei woman who spent a good deal of time with activist Asian Americans in the San Francisco Bay Area articulated additional concerns regarding interracial relationships. Having struggled with her parents over issues of interracial dating and marriage in high school and college, she found it ironic that some of her politically active Asian

---

42. Connor, *Tradition and Change*, p. 318.

American friends "argue more for separatism . . . argue that it's only been forty years since Tule Lake, and if we continue to intermarry, forty years from now there may be very few people who remember what [Executive Order] 9066 is, what the Tule Lake pilgrimages entail." She elaborated further on her conflicting feelings regarding separatism. "On one hand, I could see that having an Asian partner . . . can be seen as a reflection of ethnic pride, and accepting a lot and not rejecting things that you might project on other people. On the other hand, I don't think that any of us have the right to tell anyone else who we should or shouldn't associate with, marry or have children with, because it's a personal decision. I'm close to Asians and I'm close to non-Asians, and I don't want to invalidate the closeness I feel towards people who may not be Japanese, Chinese, Filipino." Such concerns about separatism have fueled ongoing debate among other racial ethnic and gay and lesbian communities.

It is the Sansei who must bridge the various groups that are important to them: the Japanese American farming community of their roots; largely non-Japanese American spheres of work and recreation; and, for some, Asian American urban organizations whose cultural pursuits the Nisei approve but whose radical politics they regard with suspicion. Not always easy, this bridging is a continual process. Montero has asserted that with the lessening of discrimination, the "temptations of greater economic and political opportunities inevitably pull" ethnic minorities into the current of the dominant society.[43] The Cortez Sansei certainly have more opportunities and choices than their parents or grandparents did, but they continue to live in a world where persisting inequities remind them of their status as an ethnic minority. John Connor has contended that these factors sustain the Sansei's need for a "periodic retreat into ethnicity" to escape the stress of dealing with the larger society.[44] In addition, as Fugita and O'Brien have suggested, Japanese American cultural interaction can provide satisfactions of fellowship and shared experience.

How much the Sansei have retained of "things Japanese" is a subject of interest and uncertainty for both the Nisei and Sansei. Naomi Yamamoto, a Nisei, considered the issue of ethnic identity "the greatest problem and the greatest asset" for the Sansei.

43. Montero, p. 88.
44. Connor, *Tradition and Change*, p. 318.

Because they do not have it, each person has to develop their own. And that is going to be one of the problems for each individual. And yet for those who do not want any [ethnic] identity per se, they don't need to worry about that. They would fall in with whatever majority group that they fit. But I notice that in my daughter's case, she is feeling that need of identity. That's why she took Japanese, that's why she wanted to go to Japan, that's why she is now writing a little story on evacuation. It's partly for a class, but also because she's interested.[45]

Tradition is a changing and selective process rather than a static body of customs and belief. Among the Cortez people, discussion of what constitutes "Japanese tradition" ranges from language to food to sense of community. In this respect, Fugita and O'Brien have argued persuasively that the aspects of ethnicity stressed by social scientists— language and religion, for example—are not as integral to Japanese culture as are the ways of structuring social relations.[46] While the Japanese American identity constructed by the Sansei would probably baffle their Issei grandparents, John Connor has suggested that the Issei themselves "subtly transformed many aspects of their traditional culture."[47] In this vein, one Sansei mentioned a discussion with several other Cortez Sansei regarding "how much of what we have is actually Japanese culture or how much of it is what the Niseis perceive as Japanese culture, from their parents." The differences she noticed between Japanese and Japanese Americans came as a surprise to her. "It was a long time before I realized how hard-drinking most Japanese are, and all this stuff, because you don't see it in the Niseis. . . . In the Niseis, you see this hard-work part of it come out, but you don't see the other part of it at all. So I'm not sure how much of what we see is really Japanese culture. . . . But it could be because they did have it so hard, and they didn't have time to relax."

There was variation in how much of the Japanese cultural heritage the Cortez Sansei felt they had retained. One Buddhist Sansei described his generation as "99.9 percent Americanized. We're just like the Caucasian next door." However, nearly all of the Sansei expressed interest in learning more about their history and cultural background.

45. Naomi Yamamoto interview, Cortez, Calif., February 6, 1982.
46. Fugita and O'Brien, p. 27; chap. 2, "The Structure of Social Relationships among Japanese Americans," pp. 29–46.
47. Connor, *Tradition and Change*, p. 318.

In part, changes in the social climate and the affirmation of ethnic pride generated by the movements of the 1960s and 1970s have facilitated this interest. "We [my family] didn't retain much," explained a Sansei, "and I think it's because after the war we really tried to be Americans. We really tried not to be Japanese—so much so that I really felt that I lost out. . . . Because I felt like it really encumbered my lifestyle, like it was really a handicap to me, so I really tried to push away from it, maybe more so than a lot of other kids my age. I really made a purposeful effort not to be that, to be white. So now I'm really trying to get it back—I never had it, but I'm . . . trying to learn it."

The Sansei from Cortez, as Levine and Rhodes have observed about Sansei in general, are virtually unanimous in wishing for the continuance of a Japanese American culture.[48] This has meant their engagement in an ongoing, if sometimes uneven, process that draws on both past legacies and present choices. What Dennis Yotsuya discovered about Asian American identity during his years of student activism pertains to Japanese American culture as well. He came to the conclusion that although examination of one's history remained important, "*we* were creating the new Asian American identity and it wasn't really something we could find. The things we were doing and the things we were experiencing were creating . . . that identity."[49] Along the way, some cultural elements have proven less durable than others.

Few of the Sansei can speak Japanese, although a number grew up communicating with Issei grandparents. "My Mom says that I didn't speak any English until I was about four," said Ann Kubo Osugi, "and we got some new neighbors next door. They were *hakujin*. They had a girl who was just a little bit older than I was, and I picked up English fast!"[50] In addition to Ann, Dan and Chris Kubo also understand Japanese, but not many of their peers do, even in Cortez, except those who have taken Japanese language courses in college. The Sansei are more likely to say, "I speak probably twenty words of Japanese, and at least half of them are food."

Food remains the major visible feature of Japanese culture that the third generation have retained; certainly many Cortez Nisei thought so. One Nisei father said he didn't know how much he had passed on to his children "because I can't differentiate what's tradition and

48. Levine and Rhodes, p. 109.
49. Dennis Yotsuya interview, Cortez, Calif., June 5, 1988.
50. Ann Kubo Osugi interview, Cortez, Calif., April 28, 1982.

what's not tradition, except that they eat *okazu* and rice and *tsukemono* and *ochazuke*. Those are tradition."[51]

In Cortez, the sharing of traditional foods has long been part of the events that still bring scattered family members and community together: church bazaars, funerals, holidays, and the annual picnic. The Sansei who were interviewed said they liked Japanese food, and most of the women have had experience in preparing it—on their own, with the aid of a cookbook, or in the company of family and relatives during holidays. Favorite recipes are often shared by Nisei women and handed from mothers to daughters; Sharyn Yoshida made a special effort to collect and preserve her grandmother's recipes. Also, all of the Cortez Sansei know how to eat with chopsticks, regardless of how regularly they may do so; it is assumed as a given in their lives. Several Cortez people recounted with amazement an anecdote regarding a Livingston Sansei who lacked this skill. One of his former classmates recalled, "We were talking in high school one time, and I remember him saying that he didn't know how to use chopsticks, and I thought, 'My gosh! What a thing to admit—being Japanese and not knowing how to use a pair of chopsticks!' "

Religion is another aspect of cultural heritage undergoing change in Cortez. Although the Buddhist Church and Presbyterian Church both serve almost entirely Japanese American congregations, they have not fared the same. Because of the smaller number of Issei and local resident Sansei, attendance has decreased in both, but more markedly in the Christian church. One Christian Nisei explained, "Church is not as important to people as it was 50 years ago. They didn't have this much social life. The reason why I went to church was because I met people there. . . . These kids go to church, they only see the same people that they see normally. And it's not a social function anymore. I think that's why our church is going to be dying. I think it's going to be dissolved into Delhi church or some other church. I hate to say that, simply because I think it's nice to have a church in a community, but the community is not growing in that direction." The Christian Sansei interviewed rarely attend church, except for holidays and when they are visiting in Cortez. At present, the Presbyterian Church has discontinued its Sunday School because no children attend.

On the other hand, the Buddhist Church—the more traditional

51. Ernest Yoshida interview, Cortez, Calif., January 24, 1982.

vehicle of Japanese culture—while not the size it once was, has a larger attendance and does offer Sunday School. A third-generation Buddhist, Shirley Baba Frice observed, "As Sansei kids are coming back into the area, more of them are coming back to the farms and enrolling the kids in the Sunday School. It's kind of funny, too, because for a while some of the kids tended to get away from things, wanted to get out of Livingston . . . or Cortez, go to the big cities and have their families. But now I think they're becoming more aware of their Japanese heritage, too. . . . there's more interest in starting things up again. So they want to keep the church going, and they want to keep the *Obon* going. . . . I think it's great." Shirley, a skilled dancer who leads the *Obon odori* [dance] practices, also commented on the positive response of the Yonsei to the revival of the *Obon* festival. "I'm glad we've started this up again because even some of the younger girls . . . at Sunday School are saying that it's something that they're not exposed to—wearing the kimono and dancing to Japanese music. It's some little bit of their culture that they're glad that they can hang on to, at least for now."[52]

Cortez itself provides a cultural linkage for many Nisei and Sansei who visit frequently. Some come from the Bay Area once or twice a month; others living closer in cities like Modesto and Merced visit more often. "There's a real sense of home base here that I'm sure other people just don't have," said one Sansei. As a "home base," Cortez provides visible roots, and a vision of close community. How long will it endure?

The Cortez community has reached a major transition period as the Nisei come to retirement age, more non-Japanese Americans join the CGA, and growing competition with large-scale corporate farming threatens relatively small family farms throughout the United States. The future of the Cortez Colony lies in the balance between the Sansei's professional training and the past decade of fluctuating fortunes in farming on one hand, and, on the other, the advantages of rural life within an ethnic community.

The complexity of the situation, as well as the lack of role models regarding retirement, have made some Nisei reluctant to face it. One Sansei expressed some frustration compounded by urgency over this hesitation: "It's really kind of been a sore point because so many of the

52. Shirley Baba Frice interview, Atwater, Calif., April 26, 1982.

people are coming up to retirement ages now, and instead of facing up to it and trying to figure out what's going to happen in the future, they've kind of ignored it and just figured it's always going to go on the way it is. There are more Sansei coming back, but I really don't know if there would be enough to take over farms and everything." Encompassed in that "everything" are the painstakingly woven networks of community interaction that have so long provided the people of Cortez with a sense of security and belonging.

For men whose lives have been intimately bound with the running of farms for many years, retirement can present a drastic change. "The thing about retirement," said one Nisei, "is that the adjustment period takes so long. All of a sudden, you're retired. . . . The thing is this: You've always felt responsible for seasonal chores, like the spray, and prune and spray, then get the farm ready for frost, and all that. Suppose you have all that taken away from you. All of a sudden." However, he did have activities in mind that he hoped retirement would allow him to pursue: "I'd like to do some fishing, travel with my wife, be able to not worry about coming home for awhile. Right now, wherever you go, you still worry about home, not because there's kids at home but there's farm chores that you have to come home and take care of. That's the main thing."

The prospect of retirement has been somewhat easier to face for Nisei who already have Sansei children farming in the area or planning to return. Other Nisei, lacking a definite successor, have delayed retirement in the hope that a son—or less frequently, a daughter and her husband—will decide to settle in Cortez. Those without children or whose children will definitely not farm would like to see a relative or neighbor buy their land. The question is most complicated, perhaps, when two or more children express an interest in farming, or wish to retain a monetary interest in the family place. A Nisei woman described her own family's deliberations: "[Our son] was brought up to believe that as the boy he should be the inheritor or the buyer of the farm, because we talked about a boy farming. Now I realize that is a mistake, because maybe [our daughter] might want to manage a farm. She knows she has a lot to learn if she's going to come back, but she says sometimes she thinks she would like to." The son has said he would welcome his sister as a business partner, but their mother is worried that if either of them married, spousal disapproval might jeopardize the partnership. Concerned lest any of their children feel badly about the disposal of the "home place," this Nisei couple have considered incorporation of the farm "so that nobody owns it, and that whoever works would have to draw wages. And it would be hard on [our son] because he's always been brought up to think that as the boy, he should get to buy it." Some parents also have a nagging anxiety that their expectations may be a burden to their children. At times, a father admitted, "I feel maybe I ought to sell it off and let my kids do what they want to do. Because the fact that the farm is here kind of limits his [my son's] choice."

The lives of the Sansei who farm in Cortez differ significantly from those of their parents, because of changes in both intergenerational expectations and agricultural practices. Farming is less grueling now, thanks to the postwar shift from row crops to orchards and vineyards, and the increasing mechanization of farmwork—for instance, sprinklers have replaced irrigation ditches, and machines do the most backbreaking work in harvesting the almonds. Also, the relative economic security of the Sansei and the accessibility of nearby cities allow them to pursue additional social interests and attend cultural events. Increased mobility has made rural life less isolated, with three colleges offering courses and programs within a thirteen-mile radius and San Francisco two-and-a-half hours away by car. "I don't think there is as much of a difference now as there used to be," said one Sansei—who plans to settle on the family farm—in comparing urban and rural lifestyles. "Farming is a little easier now. You still have to put in long hours but it doesn't have to be quite as long or quite as hard. You're not tied to it as much, I don't think, so much so that you can't take advantage of anything else. It used to be something really rare for us to go anywhere, just because my father was always busy."

Another difference lies in the pattern of household structure. "The Niseis' attitudes are entirely different from the Isseis'," explained Sam Kuwahara. "They would never expect the Sanseis to live with them. The Isseis figured the children were their insurance for old age. It's from the old country; it's been that way: that's what children are for. But the Niseis don't feel that way. They figure that their children have their own lives to lead."[53] His wife, Florice, agreed that this made the living situation easier: "There are quite a few Sanseis that have come back to Cortez and are farming with their folks, but then they still have

53. Sam Kuwahara interview, Cortez, Calif., January 25, 1982.

separate households now. They don't live in the same house under one roof, and that's a big help."[54]

Significantly, the Nisei view separate residences as a good thing for them as well as for their children. One does not have to go far to trace this attitude to their own experiences as young married couples sharing a household with parents and in-laws. "As much as possible, I do not want to live with my children," said one woman, "and I think most of us have the same feeling. I think it's going to be very hard if we have to, because we want to be independent, and we don't want to get on our children." Similarly, those with children living in other communities do not necessarily plan to move closer. "None of our friends would be there," remarked a Nisei whose children visit twice or more each month. "They [our children] go their way, and I don't expect to see them every Sunday . . . or to go around with them. Sometimes it's better not to know what your kids are doing!"

A large number of Nisei have planned to stay in Cortez. Not only do most of their friends reside there, but the prospect of life in other areas does not appear particularly attractive. "I've tried to think where would I like to live," said George Yuge. "I don't want to move to a metropolitan area. If I'm going to live in the country—a rural area— it's about as good as any place. . . . Also, I don't like the crime rate in the metropolitan areas. I'm getting old, you know, and I want to be where people are friendly, not always looking to mug you."[55] Life in Cortez offers not only a quality of personal warmth and relative safety, but also a sense of tranquility that Cortez residents do not expect to find in a city. "Life here is very quiet and real good," Naomi Yamamoto said. "And this is one place where I don't have to feel harassed or rushed."[56]

Despite the headaches and uncertainties of farming—"a gambler's business"—and the fluctuations of various crops in the postwar decades, many Cortez residents value their life style. "I would never do otherwise," said Sam Kuwahara. "I enjoy the challenge—so many things can go wrong on a farm. There are so many things you have to know. Your decisions have to be right. There's such a wide variety of knowledge that you have to have—maybe not be an expert in any one,

54. Florice Morimoto Kuwahara interview, Cortez, Calif., January 25, 1982.
55. George Yuge interview, Cortez, Calif., February 8, 1982.
56. Naomi Yamamoto interview, Cortez, Calif., February 6, 1982.

but you have to know enough of any one subject so you can make the right decisions. . . . I find it an interesting challenge. That's why I won't retire. . . . It will keep you younger."[57]

Sansei Dan Kubo also relished the challenge of farming, although he had a clear view of the uncertainties involved. "It's hard because costs are always going up and the price that you get for your commodities just isn't stable. I mean, everybody thought that almonds were real great, and they still are good, but this past year just kind of showed everybody that, yes, the almond market could go down. . . . It took a drastic drop. It makes the future look uncertain. But I think if you have to do it, you can do it." In trying times, he has been bolstered by a sense of the Issei spirit: "I think they went through a lot tougher time and they made it. And I figure that this land . . . [is] our family land, and I would like to keep it that way. I think that my grandparents and my parents worked so hard for it that I should do that also, in order to keep it going."[58]

Although the Sansei are returning to farm, there remains some question as to whether there will be enough of them to sustain an active community, and whether they can survive as small farmers, even with the cooperative association. In 1982, five third-generation couples and four unmarried men were engaged in farming. By 1991, Sansei were operating nine family farms and managing six with parental help; a handful had worked out arrangements with parents or siblings to cultivate pieces of land separate from the family's "home place." Despite the increased Sansei presence, one Nisei felt that there were strong forces arrayed against the perpetuation of the community. "It's getting more difficult to make a living on a small farm and a lot of Sanseis aren't coming back, and for anyone to buy a farm now would take so much capital. Who can buy a farm now except for a big farmer or some conglomerate or some corporation? . . . And if it were a doctor or a dentist, they're not going to come and farm."

Two trends seemed inevitable to many: the consolidation of farm-holdings and an increasing number of non-Japanese Americans in the CGA, which would mean major changes in the community. "The trend of all farming is fewer and larger farms," Sam Kuwahara observed. "I think that will be a part of this area too. Part of it is eco-

57. Sam Kuwahara interview, Cortez, Calif., January 25, 1982.
58. Daniel Kubo interview, Cortez, Calif., February 27, 1982.

nomical—as the profits per acre go down, you have to have larger farms. . . . That's the trend all over the United States." In 1820, seventy-five percent of the United States population lived on farms. By 1985, this number had dwindled to three percent.

With fewer and larger landholdings, and a CGA with a growing Euro-American membership, Cortez's composition as a closely knit ethnic community will change. One male Sansei farmer expressed particular concern about the future role of the third generation. "The next five years is when everything will roll over. The only thing that scares me is that the Sanseis aren't doing stuff together. . . . I think we should have picnics, go out to the lake and have dinner, bring the kids. . . . When we were growing up, we always used to go . . . fishing and go to the beaches together." Such shared activities, he felt, proved important in building the kinds of ties on which the Nisei and Issei relied for support. "What bothers me is that, okay, we're going through this transition period, but Nisei run the Co-op. We're [the Sansei] going to have to be able to work together ourselves. And that's the whole thing—the transition's going to come over and we don't know each other. . . . That's what's really scary." It is well to keep in mind that, as an unmarried man, this Sansei seemed less likely to be involved in the activities that bring together Sansei parents and Yonsei children in Cortez. On the other hand, the pressures of combining off-farm jobs with the duties of orchard cultivation, housework, and community service have also decreased the time that might be spent in joint recreation.

Like the people of Cortez, social scientists have debated the future of the Japanese American community. Researchers like Connor, Levine and Rhodes, and Montero have predicted its eventual disappearance, perhaps as early as the fourth generation. One of the most ominous signs, they contend, is the fact that the majority of Sansei lack familiarity with "the kind of Japanese American world characterized by intimate, primary, communal association and by close social control."[59] From this perspective, the Sansei of Cortez constitute part of the dwindling minority who retain such linkages. Scholars with different interpretations of what defines and sustains community, however, have projected other outcomes. Fugita and O'Brien have identi-

59. Levine and Rhodes, p. 195.

fied affiliation with voluntary organizations as the key to community continuity and point to the proliferation of such groups as evidence of vigor. They suggest that the maintenance of ethnicity offers valuable economic and political resources in a society stratified by race and class. Ethnic identity can also provide a basis for bonds of fellowship in an increasingly impersonal and complex world.[60]

Cortez as a community faces many challenges. Externally, the increasing concentration of California agriculture as well as a metropolitan population shift to rural areas in the Central Valley have subjected small farmers to growing stress. Wider socioeconomic opportunities have drawn many Sansei into urban spheres and increased the likelihood of outmarriage, both of which might weaken their ties to the community. While it appears that the majority of Nisei-run farms will pass into the hands of Sansei kin or neighbors, it also seems clear that the ethnic cultural core of Cortez will grow smaller as farmholdings become consolidated and more non-Japanese Americans join the CGA.

Yet the preservation of collectivity retains powerful attractions. For the men and women of Cortez, it provides personal affirmation and cultural grounding as well as an intimate sense of connection with a larger history. The Sansei value their community, even those who live elsewhere. "I like the rural area," said Robin Yuge Alexander, a nurse in the Bay Area. "It's beautiful out there. The pace is slow. . . . I love going down there on the weekends or whenever I get time off. . . . My mother cooks up a storm, and it's really fun. It's a real holiday for me."[61]

The cooperative system embodied in the CGA still offers a measure of security to those who wish to continue the family farm. "You're not alone here because everybody works together," said Lester Yamaguchi. "If I need help, I can always go to Cortez Growers and ask them what I should do. . . . Everybody helps each other out."[62] In its existing institutions and informal networks of friends and kin, Cortez continues to provide much-appreciated emotional and material support.

Sansei parents also feel that Cortez can provide a stable and positive environment for their children, and a sense of belonging that they would like to pass on. "I feel close to family, close to my neighbors,"

60. Fugita and O'Brien, pp. 77, 184.
61. Robin Yuge Alexander interview, Los Gatos, Calif., August 26, 1982.
62. Lester Yamaguchi interview, Cortez, Calif., April 29, 1982.

said one Sansei woman. "Everyone grew up together. There's just a closeness there that I really value, and I hope I can pass it on to my kids, familywise and communitywise, because I think it's important. Otherwise you're just kind of like a drifter."

Cortez has been both an anchor and springboard for the third generation and it remains the "home base" many Nisei and Sansei visit periodically. While a number of Sansei have returned to farm, the current trend of the 1980s has been toward larger, more spread-out holdings, and fewer families. It will be up to the Cortez Sansei, like other third- and fourth-generation Japanese Americans, to decide what they wish to retain of their cultural legacies and institutions. The future of Cortez as an ethnic community lies in their hands.

Sustaining Fruit

On a warm day in May 1991, nearly a decade after beginning my research, I left Davis, California, heading south on Interstate 99 to attend the annual Cortez community picnic. When I arrived, dozens of cars and vans lined the road in front of the JACL Hall, surrounded by well-tended almond orchards. Outside, children shrieked and aimed water guns at each other. Inside the hall, the people of Cortez, relatives from nearby towns and the Bay Area, friends and neighbors sat on folding metal chairs at long tables. They sipped soda and tea while scanning their raffle tickets (a staple of Japanese American social functions) as winning numbers were called.

Miye Baba led me into a side room where tables groaned under the weight of a dizzying array of potluck offerings: *somen* salad, pasta salad, *makizushi*, chicken, chow mein, and fresh vegetables. Everyone else had already tackled desserts ranging from finger jello and strawberry pie to chocolate cake, melon, and exquisite homemade *manju*, a Japanese confection. This bounteous and well-organized *gochiso* (a feast; good things) brought to mind the generous hospitality I had enjoyed when pursuing research in Cortez. It also illustrated the mixture of influences that have shaped Japanese American community life and culture, some elements lovingly retained, others carefully adapted.

While the adults chatted and prepared to play bingo, tossed horseshoes, or spiked a volley ball, Yonsei children trooped in and out as they eagerly waited for the planned races—ranging from three-legged races to a chopstick race and a marshmallow-on-a-spoon event—to begin. In these competitions, supervised by Sansei parents, all who participated won squirt guns, crayons, soap bubbles, and other small toys. Nearly all the adults, too—even me—departed with a raffle prize: a Hauck's Pharmacy bag filled with handy items like raisins, Scotch tape, plastic storage containers, notepaper, and Japanese instant noodles. Nisei and Sansei vigilance ensured that no one left empty-handed and that balance prevailed. In this "everyone wins" collective spirit, the Cortez picnic reflected the ethos of many Japanese American community events, whether celebrations or fund-raisers.

The picnic illustrated growth and continuity in the community, as well as its flexibility. There were some absences at the tables; at least eleven of the people I interviewed had passed away, and others had moved away after retirement. The new faces included two recent Japanese women immigrants living nearby, and the swelling ranks of Yonsei, some of them the children of interracial marriages. The picnic brought together five generations: Issei, Nisei, Sansei, Yonsei, and Shin Issei (new Japanese immigrants). Perhaps 150 people had gathered to celebrate and renew community ties.

Contrary to its snug secure appearance, however, rural life in the Central Valley is neither static nor complacent. Both economic and population growth have encroached on agriculture. While California's population began to mushroom in the 1950s, the Central Valley did not experience the boom until the 1980s, when the soaring cost of urban housing, on one hand, and the emergence of local high-technology companies, on the other, drew more and more residents. Commuters, retirees, technicians, Latin American and Southeast Asian immigrants swelled the population by 30 percent, a trend predicted to continue into the next century.[1] Increased pressure on the land has given rise to a host of long-term concerns—termed by the UC Agricultural Issues Center a "growth-induced environmental crisis"—involving not only "land use, transportation and housing, but also air pollution, water resources, wildlands and open space—and, in conjunction with all of these, the future of the agricultural system."[2]

Contrary to dire forecasts, the number of California farms has actu-

---

1. UC Agricultural Issues Center, "Keeping the Valley Green: A Public Policy Challenge," *California Agriculture* 45(May–June 1991):10–12.
2. Ibid.

ally increased (from a low of 67,674 farms in 1974 to 83,217 in 1987), as has the market value of agricultural products sold, nearly $14 billion in 1987.[3] However, the amount of total farm acreage has declined steadily. And the gap between large farms and small operators has widened because of increasing concentration in the agricultural and food-processing industries, along with the costs of keeping pace with scientific advances in cultivation. Small farms have not, to be sure, disappeared. Eighty percent of the California farms recorded in the 1987 Agricultural Census were under 180 acres in size; 62 percent had fifty acres or less. Such farmers depend increasingly on off-farm income; just over 50 percent listed farming as their principal occupation. These figures may reflect an increase in the numbers of part-time farmers—a trend already visible in Cortez where some Nisei and Sansei split their time between town jobs and orchard care.

Shifting national and international markets and competition have challenged California's predominance in specialty-crop agriculture, the mainstay of the Cortez economy. The rapid transfer of agricultural technology and the emergence of contenders in countries like Mexico, Brazil, and Turkey have placed pressure on farmers to stay abreast of the latest scientific research and to increase their reliance on well-organized, innovative marketing strategies. Of the specialty crops that comprise Cortez's major crops—almonds, grapes, and peaches—the first two have retained a strong position among the state's primary export crops, due to sophisticated marketing by large cooperatives. Nevertheless, market fluctuations and the unpredictability of nature have fostered a highly cautious attitude among the farmers of Cortez.

The dynamics of gender-role negotiation and change have affected the Sansei somewhat more than the Nisei. Change is especially striking among married Sansei women who work in urban environments and struggle, like their contemporaries, with the demands of "the second shift." These alterations are less apparent within Cortez, as in other farming communities. Female contributions to agricultural operations seldom receive the recognition accorded to those of men, who still make many of the major production decisions. However, small ranches like those in Cortez rely on the valuable labor of women, both on and off the farm.

3. U.S. Bureau of the Census, *1987 Census of Agriculture*, vol. 1, part 5, California State and County Data (Washington, D.C.: Government Printing Office, 1989), p. 7.

Despite the tensions and uncertainties, the Cortez community persists because it meets a range of needs. The functions of its organizations have changed over time, demonstrating the flexibility deemed critical to survival by Steven Fugita and David O'Brien. In the 1920s and 1930s, the Cortez Growers Association, the churches, and other organizations provided fundamental economic and social services. During the World War II incarceration and the resettlement period that followed, this high degree of cooperative organization proved crucial to the continuity of the three Abiko colonies. In the past two decades, while the number of farmers has dwindled, Cortez has remained a touchstone for Nisei, Sansei, and Yonsei living outside its geographical boundaries. Community ties have stretched throughout and beyond the Central Valley, and continue to convey a cherished sense of belonging and of shared heritage.

In a postmodern world, fast paced and demanding, where each individual must puzzle out his or her own identities, where a media explosion inundates us with bewildering choices but where racial and class inequities linger, living in a small personal community retains considerable appeal. Beneath this vision of cozy collectivity, however, lies a much more complicated reality. For the people of Cortez, as for other Japanese Americans, the maintenance of ethnic ties has two dimensions: the web of support and affirmation remains interwoven with the bonds of duty and obligation. Being part of a community entails active engagement—networks require energy in order to give support. Examining the lives of the Issei, Nisei, and Sansei reveals that a community means not so much a group sharing a fixed site but an ongoing process. At the heart of this *nigiyaka* place are the four generations whose work, choices, conflict, strategies, and affection have produced, as a mature orchard does, sustaining fruit.

Notes on Research

The scholar's relationship to the subject of his or her research has itself increasingly become a focus for examination. Such "positionality" calls into question the assumption of objectivity and lays bare the power dynamics, the intricate human negotiations, involved in conducting a scholarly study. In this spirit, I offer the following thoughts on how I came to explore the history of Cortez, the nature of interviewing, and some of the personal legacies of this experience. In order to avoid one of the major pitfalls of "positionality"—an emphasis on the consciousness of the researcher that ironically may displace the subject of study—I have chosen to append my reflections at the end.

I had long wanted to study a Japanese American community, but choosing one proved daunting. The Central Arizona, Salt Lake City, and Orange County enclaves where I had friends or relatives were far larger and more spread-out than the rural settlement I hoped to find. In June 1982, I met anthropologist Sylvia Yanagisako at Stanford. She had just completed her study of the Issei and Nisei in Seattle, Washington. She passed on to me a letter of inquiry from a San Joaquin Valley agricultural community that was seeking a scholar to conduct a history project for them. A few days after I wrote expressing interest, Scottie Hagedorn—an anthropologist at Merced College and the community's liaison—called me. Her description of Cortez piqued my curiosity: I had not known that there existed any surviving planned settlements among Japanese Americans, nor had I heard of any economic cooperatives enduring after World War II. The persistence of three generations in one place and their active interest in finding a chronicler of their past appeared to be a stroke of serendipity, especially since I wanted to base my study, in part, on extensive oral-history interviews. After sending off my curriculum vitae and writing sample to them, I set about convincing my professors that such a study would be a viable project and a contribution to U.S. social history. No sooner had I done so than a call came informing me that the people of Cortez could not agree on the final form of the history project—film, book, photographic display, or slide show—and had abandoned the idea of hiring a researcher. My heart sank. About ten minutes into the beginning of deep despair, it occurred to me that the Cortez residents had not said they did not want a history project, only that they were not going to carry one out themselves. When I talked to Scottie about the possibility of conducting an independent study, she put me in touch with Nisei who could further advise me.

At this point, two families proved particularly instrumental and subsequently became my "home bases" in Cortez: the Babas and the Yuges. The first people I contacted were Nobuzo and Miye Baba, who invited me to visit the community. My journey there, about two hours longer than it should have been, was a comedy of errors stereotypical of a suburbanite's visit to the countryside: misjudged distances, shortcuts that ended in pastures, and rural roads that my map did not reveal as dead ends. My confusion gave me an unexpected opportunity to appreciate the diversity of San Joaquin Valley agriculture as well as the helpfulness of local farmers. I also gained a sense of how hidden a community's history can be. A number of the people I met in my quest had never heard of Cortez, located only a few miles away.

By the time I had turned my dusty Mustang onto Linwood Avenue, however, I could see a smiling woman waiting at the side of the road, and waving. Miye Baba, an insightful, diplomatic woman radiating cheerful efficiency, and her quiet thoughtful husband Nobuzo immediately made me feel at home. They showed me the Growers Association building, the JACL Hall, and the two churches, and then commenced calling their neighbors to see who would agree to be interviewed. Their membership in the Buddhist Church and familiarity with its networks made them particularly helpful in first contacts with other Cortez Buddhists. The initial telephone survey revealed that quite a few men and women welcomed the prospect of a study of Cortez and were willing to meet with me.

Equally helpful were George and Helen Yuge. Tall, lean George with his ready laugh and gracious, energetic Helen, a whirlwind of ideas and projects, introduced me to many members of the Christian side of the community. Their house was always a center of activity; a welcoming pot of coffee or a cold drink awaited any who might drop by. It seemed that hardly a day passed that neighboring farmers or town friends—Japanese Americans and others—did not stop in to chat. So that I could make contacts and set up interviews, the Yuges and the Babas took me on a round of events, from the Boy Scouts' fund-raising pancake breakfast to a local JACL installation banquet.

Because of the demands of the seasonal farm schedule, it became clear that the best time to do interviews would be in the winter, after the fall harvest and before spring activities. I spent the fall reading secondary materials and then in January began traveling to Cortez where I stayed alternately with the Babas and the Yuges for a week or two at a time to conduct interviews. Acutely aware of time constraints, I carried out two and sometimes three interviews per day and, on days when no appointments could be arranged, I visited the offices of the *Livingston Chronicle* and the *Turlock Journal*. Occasionally the intensity of the interviewing process, much as I enjoyed it, left me so drained that some evening interviewees, no doubt, found me dazed and sluggish. They were all, every one, patient and generous.

My undergraduate work with historian Mary Rothschild at Arizona State University had introduced me to the richness of oral history as a primary source. It is especially valuable in documenting the experiences of those less likely to leave extensive written records: women, ethnic minorities, the working class. Interviewing twelve Nisei women for an undergraduate honors thesis had hooked me on the process. Readings ranging from Willa K. Baum's nitty-gritty hints for local historical societies to primers like that of James Hoopes had provided a broad sense of the methods and philosophies of oral-history interviewing. In designing a format for the life-history questionnaires that I used in Cortez (Appendix B), I also found the issues of *Frontiers* on oral history particularly valuable.

Among oral historians there are different schools of thought on giving questions before the interview. Those in favor assert that prepared interviewees can provide greater detail; those opposed argue the merits of spontaneity and warn against the potential for more self-censorship or manipulation. I prefer to send questions ahead of time, in order to demystify what can be an anxiety-producing event. This approach gives the interviewee more control over the interview as well as time to look through photograph albums or to double-check family milestones. On rare occasions, if an interviewee expressed discomfort with a particular question, I simply omitted it from the taped interview. While interviews varied somewhat, according to the age, sex, and generation of each interviewee, the questionnaire provided a strong common framework.

My experiences in Cortez reinforced my sense of the importance of reciprocity in oral-history interviewing. A case in point is the day I went to interview Mark Kamiya. A farmer, social activist, and animal lover, he sat with one of several rescued cats curled in his lap, fixed a stern eye on me, and asked, "What is your *Weltanschauung?*" For a humbling half hour I struggled to articulate the familial and educational training that had influenced my worldview. Then, over the course of two or three hours, Mark candidly and humorously shared *his* memories and concerns. This interaction mirrored the general format of the interviews, each of which actually consisted of two interviews: a first friendly interrogation of me, and then the tape-recorded history of my subject. Nearly all the interviews took place in the interviewees' homes, usually in front of a warming aromatic fire of almond branches, and fueled by cups of green tea. The interview often began or ended with a meal, during which more tantalizing reminiscences would surface. I tried to interview several members of every family in Cortez, as well as a number of Nisei and Sansei who had moved away. Whatever their feelings and degree of connection to the community, all were hospitable; even those who declined to be interviewed were supportive of the project. Being allowed glimpses into so many lives, seeing how linked individuals strive both to fulfill their dreams and to honor commitments to others made manifest the strength and persistence needed to maintain a flexible, coherent community.

My perspective on Cortez has, no doubt, been influenced by the fact that, for me, its history and hospitality were intertwined. Because of the extensive social networks and the collective interest in my project, because of my upbringing as a Japanese American woman aware (even partially) of the work involved in preserving the delicate balance of obligation and support, and because I was in age and generation much like the children of the majority of people I interviewed, I always remained conscious of the bonds of responsibility and affection.

While squabbles and friction have punctuated life in Cortez as they do wherever people congregate, on the whole, I was more struck by the effort made to negotiate and resolve differences, a willingness (at least in the post–World War II period) to "live and let live." Particularly in such a small community, where everyone is bound together by a shared history and mutually invested in a common economic enterprise, the ability to "get along" with others remains essential. In addition to their social and religious ties, the fact that the residents of Cortez own land with approximately the same-sized holdings has also contributed, I think, to the cooperative ethos that differentiates them from the more factionalized Japanese American farmers in Timothy Lukes and Gary Okihiro's Santa Clara study. My emphasis has, I hope, not downplayed the existence of conflict, clearly present in the prewar period in Livingston–Cortez relations and between Buddhists and Christians, as well as more recently, in the inception of my own project. Rather, I aimed to draw attention to what I think is the predominating tenor of community relations: the value placed on flexibility, negotiation, and tolerance.

Community members also value the ability to share—the manifestation of material and spiritual bounty. The giving of recipes, vegetables, nuts, stories embodies the ongoing renewal and affirmation of ties. For those who feared that their best culinary efforts might not be good enough, such giving could create pressure. However, this interaction is instructive *because* it is multilayered and suggestive of simultaneous different meanings. On one of my last visits to Cortez, I stood admiring the Yuges' vegetable garden, lush with Japanese eggplant, green beans, tomatoes, and other delicacies. In the evening dusk, I could see a cottontail rabbit hopping from the peach orchard toward a small pile of corn culls and leaves outside the fenced garden. George chuckled, admitting that he never thought he'd see the day, after the hard early years of protecting young trees and plants from voracious rabbits, that he would leave food for them. "Must be getting soft," he said, smiling.

Doing research on a living community entails consideration of individual feelings and vulnerabilities, in addition to concerns regarding factual accuracy and incisive analysis. One must examine one's priorities as a scholar, and weigh the implications of one's work for the women and men whose history has formed its bedrock. There exist no easy, perfect, or formulaic methods for reaching balance among these concerns, but interaction with the Cortez community has underlined for me the importance of trying. Perhaps scholars should be reminded that we, no less than those we study, are actors in history, making choices that affect the lives of others.

Oral History
Interview Questions

Nisei

1. Please state your full name, place and date of birth, and current address.
2. From what part(s) of Japan did your parents come? Did they come from farming families? What were their names?
3. How many were there in your mother's/father's family? What did your parents tell you about life in Japan? How much education did they receive?
4. When did your parents immigrate from Japan? Did your father come to the United States first? Where did they settle?
5. How did they decide to move to Cortez? What did they tell you about their early pioneering days? What crops did they farm?
6. How many children in your family? What was your birth order in relation to your brothers/sisters? (oldest child, youngest child, etc.)
7. What kinds of chores and responsibilities did you have when you were young?
8. Where did you go to school? How did the Japanese American kids get along with the non-Japanese American kids? Did the Cortez kids feel rivalry with those from Livingston? What was your school like?
9. What did you like/dislike about high school?
10. What types of extracurricular activities did you participate in?

11. Did you work and/or go to Nihongakko [Japanese language school] after regular school?
12. What kinds of occasions and holidays did your family celebrate? Did you celebrate with neighbors?
13. Do you feel you and your brothers and sisters were treated equally by your parents?
14. What kinds of rules of behavior did you feel obligated to follow as a child? As a teenager? What kinds of values did your parents emphasize?
15. Who made the key decisions in your family? (regarding moving, property, approval of marriage, etc.) Was one of your parents more dominant than the other?
16. Who disciplined the children, and how?
17. With what religion were you raised? What were the services like at your church when you were young? Do you attend a church in Cortez? How has it grown and/or changed over the years? Do most of your friends attend the same church?
18. What community activities did your family participate in?
19. What were the daily schedules of family members?
20. What was considered "success" for different members of the family?
21. What were your activities as a teenager? Were you allowed to date? Did you generally socialize with other Japanese Americans?
22. What were your expectations for the future? Did you expect to go into farming? Did you expect to marry?
23. After you completed your formal education, did you farm with your parents?
24. Were you a member of the Growers Association? How did it work?
25. What crops did you raise?
26. How and when did you meet your spouse? Was he/she from this area? Please describe your wedding.
27. I'd like to jump to the World War II years, now. Can you remember what you were doing on Pearl Harbor Day? How did you and your family react to the news?
28. How were you and your family notified that you would have to go to the Assembly Center? What was it like?
29. Did the Growers Association manager take care of making arrangements for your farm? Who rented it?

30. When were you sent to Amache? What was your first impression of it?
31. What were the living conditions at Amache? Were you and the other Cortez people assigned to the same area?
32. Did you work in camp? How much were you paid?
33. How did the Issei react to camp life? How about the Nisei?
34. What camp activities—classes, clubs, religious meetings, etc.— did you participate in?
35. Did you and your family eat in the mess hall? Did you eat with your family or with your friends?
36. Did anyone in your family serve with the Armed Forces during the war?
37. When did you return to Cortez? Where did you stay? What kind of work did you do?
38. What kind of attitude did you encounter from your non-Japanese American neighbors when you returned?
39. Did anyone help you when you got out of camp? Did you continue farming?
40. How many children do you have, and when and where were they born? What are their names?
41. Do you think you raised your children the way you were raised? What kinds of values and ideals have you stressed to them?
42. Do your children speak Japanese? How much of the Japanese tradition have they retained? Do they like Japanese food?
43. Is your relationship with your children different from your relationship with *your* parents?
44. Where did your children attend school? What kinds of school and extracurricular activities did they participate in?
45. What kinds of holidays did you celebrate together? Do you still?
46. What are your children doing now? Are they married? Did they marry other Japanese Americans?
47. What are your views on interracial marriage?
48. Do you have any grandchildren? Where do your children and grandchildren live?
49. Do you still farm? What kinds of crops do you grow? Would you please describe what kinds of work have to be done each season?
50. What kinds of activities have you been engaged in since your children have grown up? What are your interests?

51. Do you plan to stay in Cortez?
52. What was the happiest time of your life? What was the most exciting event?
53. If you had your life to live over, would you do anything differently?
54. Is there anything you have not yet done that you would like to do?
55. Is there anything I haven't asked that you would like to add?

Sansei

1. Please state your full name, place and date of birth, and current address.
2. What are your parents' names?
3. How many children in your family? Are you the oldest, youngest, etc.?
4. What kinds of crops did your family farm when you were growing up?
5. What kinds of chores and responsibilities did you have, growing up?
6. What was Ballico School like? Were there many Japanese American kids in your class? Did the Japanese American kids get along with the non-Japanese American kids?
7. What did you like/dislike about high school?
8. What kinds of extracurricular activities did you participate in?
9. Do you speak Japanese? If so, where did you learn?
10. Who made the key decisions in your family (concerning moving, property, etc.)? Is one of your parents more dominant than the other?
11. Who disciplined the children, and by what means?
12. Do you feel you and your brothers/sisters were treated equally by your parents or did they expect more of the oldest?
13. What kinds of rules of behavior did you feel obligated to follow as a child? As a teenager?
14. What kinds of values have your parents emphasized? Do you think your values are different from those of your parents?
15. With what religion were you raised?
16. What kinds of occasions and holidays did your family celebrate?
17. What community activities did your family participate in?

18. What did you and your friends do in your free time when you were growing up?
19. What were your social activities as a teenager? Were you allowed to date non-Japanese Americans?
20. Were your friends mostly Japanese Americans, or non-Japanese Americans, or both?
21. As a teenager, what were your expectations for the future?
22. Did you go to college? What was your major field?
23. Were you involved in any extracurricular activities or groups there?
24. What did you like/dislike about college?
25. What is your occupation/occupational goal?
26. How often do you see your parents/relatives in Cortez?
27. How much have they told you about their experiences during World War II? How do you feel about the redress and reparations movement?
28. What do you admire most/least about the Issei? the Nisei?
29. How much of the Japanese cultural traditions have you retained?
30. Do you eat/prepare Japanese food?
31. Have you experienced any prejudice? How did you handle it?
32. How do you feel about interracial marriage? Do your parents feel the same way?
33. What proportion of your friends are non-Japanese American?
34. How frequently do you get together with other Japanese Americans?
35. Are you married? Do you have children? Would you like to raise them the way you were raised?
36. What organizations do you belong to?
37. What do you like to do in your free time?
38. If you live in Cortez, do you plan to stay? If you don't live in Cortez, would you like to move back someday?
39. What do you think will happen to Cortez?
40. What are your dreams/ambitions for the future?
41. What issues in today's world concern you most?
42. Is there anything I haven't asked that you would like to add?

APPENDIX C

Recipes from Cortez,
with List of Terms

Food plays an important role in nearly all family and community events in Cortez, as I happily discovered. Recipes represent another legacy, adapted and passed on from generation to generation. Nearly every Japanese American church has a fund-raiser cookbook of its members' specialties, ranging from traditional holiday dishes like *makizushi* and *nishime* to increasingly eclectic offerings like tamale pie, persimmon cookies, and chow mein. Many of the Cortez women have contributed recipes to such cookbooks, but Cortez does not yet have its own compilation. With clear memories of many wonderful meals, I am pleased that a number of Nisei women agreed to share, potluck-style, some of their favorite recipes. (Rather than standardizing the format of these recipes, I have instead chosen to present them as they were written down, with some concessions to uniformity in measurement.)

Recipes are beginning to receive scholarly attention as keys to the past, providing insights with regard to available resources and technology, notions of nutrition and presentation as well as clues to cultural persistence and adaptation. How these elements change over time affords food for thought as well as for gustatory consumption. The confluence of ethnic cultures in the United States is nowhere more apparent than in the area of cuisine, as the following dishes illustrate.

List of Terms

ajinomoto (*aji-no-moto*)	monosodium glutamate
ajitsuke nori	flavored dried seaweed
an	sweetened red bean paste
azuki	red beans
chasu (*char siu*)	Chinese barbecued pork
futo-udon	thick noodles
hiya mugi somen	thin noodles served cold
kamaboko	steamed fish cake
katakuriko	potato starch
kinako	soybean flour
makizushi	seasoned rice rolled in seaweed sheets, with vegetable or other filling
mame	beans
manju	confection filled with sweetened bean paste
mirin	sweet rice wine, used for cooking
miso	fermented soybean paste
mochi	cake made of sweet rice (glutinous rice) flour
mochiko	sweet rice (glutinous rice) flour
nigiri	rice ball
nori	dried seaweed, used in sheet form to prepare makizushi
ochazuke	rice eaten with green tea
okazu	a dish eaten with rice
omochi manju	confection made with sweet rice flour
ozoni	mochi soup eaten on New Year's
saifun	mung bean-thread noodles
sato imo	taro root
shiitake	dried black mushrooms
shiso-no-furikake	condiment for rice, made with shiso (a fragrant plant with red and green varieties, related to mint and basil)
shoyu	soy sauce
somen	thin white noodles
suribachi	earthenware bowl (mortar) for grinding with pestle
sushi	vinegar-seasoned rice
teriyaki	broiled meat cooked with soy sauce, wine, and ginger
tsukemono	pickled vegetables
udon	noodles
umeboshi	pickled plums

Chinese Chicken Salad—from Evelyn Yamaguchi

½ pound white chicken meat, cooked and shredded
2 ounces saifun (bean thread), deep fried with light oil
1 small head lettuce, sliced
4 green onions, julienne-sliced
2 tablespoons chopped roasted almonds or peanuts
2 tablespoons toasted sesame seeds
Dressing:

¼ cup salad oil	2 tablespoons sugar
3 tablespoons vinegar	1 teaspoon salt
½ teaspoon black pepper	1 teaspoon ajinomoto

Combine ingredients and mix just before serving. Garnish with Chinese parsley (optional).

Somen Salad—from Susie Asai

1 package hiya mugi somen
Garnish:
   shredded lettuce
   ham, chasu, kamaboko
   2 eggs—beaten, fried thin, and sliced in strips
   3 green onions
Sauce:

2 tablespoons sesame oil	3 tablespoons vinegar
2 tablespoons sugar	2 tablespoons shoyu
1 teaspoon salt	ajinomoto
¼ cup salad oil	

Mix all the sauce ingredients and refrigerate. Follow directions for boiling the somen (crack the somen in half or in thirds first). Rinse and drain well. Put in large bowl and mix a little of the sauce. Mix somen with lettuce and some of the garnish, then put in flat salad bowl and garnish with ham, chasu, kamaboko, eggs, and onions. Pour rest of the sauce on top. Mix when ready to eat.

Futo-Udon Salad—from Toshi Kubo

2 halves chicken breast	3 tablespoons mirin
3 tablespoons sugar	4 or 5 shiitake, softened
3 tablespoons shoyu	2 teaspoons cornstarch

Cut chicken breast into bite-size pieces. Brown in little oil and add sliced shiitake. Add sugar, shoyu, and mirin to flavor. Dilute cornstarch in shiitake water and add to thicken. Set aside to cool.

Cut 1 package futo-udon or any size udon in half and boil till done. Wash in cold water and cool.

Meanwhite, cut 4 stalks celery in thin slices and chop 2 or 3 green onions. Leave about 2 tablespoons green onion for topping. Just before serving make the sauce and add to layered noodle and chicken and vegetable in serving dish. Toss and garnish with green onion and serve.

Sauce:

¼ cup shoyu
2 or 3 tablespoons vinegar
1½ teaspoon sugar
ajinomoto

This will make enough to fill a 9×13-inch pan.

Blueberry Jell-O—from Mary Kamiya

Mix:

2 cups boiling water
1 large package of dark Jell-O (blackberry, raspberry, or black cherry)

Add:

15 ounce can of blueberries
8 ounce can of crushed pineapple

Put all ingredients in a 9×13-inch pan, and set in the refrigerator until mixture is firm.

Topping:

8 ounces cream cheese
8 ounces sour cream

Mix the cream cheese and sour cream, and spread over the Jell-O just before serving. Sprinkle nuts on top of the cream mixture if you wish.

Instead of the cream mixture, sometimes I use only whipped cream.

Cranberry Jell-O Salad—from Mary Kamiya

Mix:

1 3-ounce package raspberry Jell-O
1 package Knox unflavored gelatine
2 cups boiling water

Add:

> 1 can whole cranberries
> 1 small can crushed pineapple
> 1 cup celery, chopped
> juice of one orange and rind if you wish

Pour mixed ingredients into a 9×13-inch pan. Refrigerate.

Rice Pilaf—from Edna Yamaguchi

2 cups uncooked rice	5 cups chicken broth
1 cup vermicelli (break in small pieces)	½ teaspoon salt
	½ teaspoon black pepper
¼ cup margarine	1 small can mushrooms

Melt margarine in skillet. Add vermicelli and brown. Wash rice, add vermicelli, mushrooms and broth. Mix well and cook in rice cooker.

Sweet and Sour Chicken—from Mickey Yoshida

1 chicken	oil
2 eggs	crushed peanuts or chopped walnuts or finely
¼ teaspoon salt	chopped green onions
cornstarch	

Sauce:

salad oil	2–3 teaspoons vinegar
pinch salt	1 cup sugar
2 cups water	⅔ or ¾ cup catsup
cornstarch	1 clove garlic

Cut chicken into bite-sized pieces. Break egg in bowl, add salt and cornstarch to make sticky dough. Mix in chicken. Stir until well coated. Deep fry in oil. Arrange neatly on platter.

To prepare sauce: Heat a little oil in pan. Add pinch of salt and garlic, water, vinegar, sugar, and catsup. Add more vinegar if too sweet. Thicken with cornstarch dissolved in water. Bring to boiling point.

Pour sauce over chicken. Garnish with chopped nuts or green onion.

Apricot-Glazed Chicken—from Edith Yotsuya

1 cup bottled Russian salad
    dressing
¼ cup vegetable oil
1 package (1¾-oz.) dry
    onion soup mix

1 cup apricot preserves
3 tablespoons lemon juice
1 teaspoon salt
2 whole fryers (chicken),
    cut into pieces

Mix together salad dressing, oil, soup mix, preserves, lemon juice and salt. Arrange chicken pieces in shallow baking dish. Pour preserve mixture over chicken. Bake for one hour at 350°F or until chicken is tender. Baste twice while baking. Serves 6–8.

Chow Mein—from Helen Yuge

(This recipe also appeared in the Livingston High School Band Cookbook, date unknown.)

1 pound pork, chopped
3–4 slices ginger root
1 clove garlic, chopped
1 onion, sliced
1 pound noodles, boiled
    and deep-fried or
    pan-fried

1 small can water chestnuts,
    sliced
1 small can mushrooms (ends
    and pieces)
½ pound Chinese peas
3–4 stalks celery
½ pound bean sprouts

Brown pork with ginger and garlic, add onion. Add 1 cup water, salt lightly and simmer 10 minutes. Thicken stock with cornstarch and season with monosodium glutamate. In another pan, saute bean sprouts in butter or oil and season with salt and monosodium glutamate. Again, separately saute celery, Chinese peas, water chestnuts and season each lightly. Spread fried noodles on platter. Cover with pork mixture and layer with rest of vegetables. Garnish with egg strips, if desired. Serves 4 to 6.

Beef Kabob Marinade—from Haruko Narita

½ cup soy sauce
1 large clove garlic
1 teaspoon ground ginger
2 tablespoons brown sugar

2 tablespoons lemon juice
2 tablespoons salad oil
1 tablespoon chopped onion
¼ teaspoon pepper

Marinate 4 hours or longer. Skewer beef alternately with mushrooms, onions, bell peppers, or zucchini squash which has been marinated with the beef. Cook over hot charcoal.

Barbecued Spareribs—from May Sakaguchi

5 pounds spareribs, cut into 3 × 5-inch pieces
1 piece fresh ginger, crushed

Put spareribs in large pot; cover with water. Add ginger and boil (low heat) 45 minutes to 1 hour.
Sauce:

¾ cup sugar	¼ cup oyster sauce
¼ cup honey	¾ cup shoyu
1 cup catsup	a little water

Pour sauce over spareribs and let stand for 2 hours or longer. Brown over charcoal or bake in oven until brown on both sides.

Tamale Pie—from Evelyn Yamaguchi

2 pounds ground meat	¼–½ cup cornmeal
1 onion, chopped	2 eggs, slightly beaten
1 teaspoon salt	1 cup milk
1 medium (10 oz.) can corn	1 tablespoon chili powder
1 medium can tomatoes	2 tablespoons Worchestershire
1 can olives, sliced	sauce
	¼ teaspoon Tabasco sauce

Cook beef, onion; add salt, corn, tomatoes, olives and cornmeal. Cook slowly 15 minutes. Remove from fire. Add milk, eggs, chili powder and sauces. Bake in greased pan at 350°F for 1 hour.

Shiso-No-Furikake—from Toshi Kubo

¼ cup salt	2 tablespoons ajinomoto
¼ cup shoyu	12 umeboshi, ground with
	suribachi or blender

Wash and drain a 5-gallon bucketful of red shiso leaves. Mix the 4 ingredients and stir into shiso. Weight down with pressure and after 3 days lay it out to dry in shady area. Crush by rolling pin or blender.

Almond Macaroons—from Alice Taniguchi

Preheat oven to 300°F. Line baking sheets with parchment.

1 cup whole blanched almonds	¼ teaspoon almond extract
1 cup sugar	2 egg whites at room temperature

In food processor or grinder, grind almonds with sugar to a powder. Transfer the mixture to a bowl and blend in almond extract and egg whites, one at a time, until mixture is combined well. Drop batter by teaspoons 2 inches apart onto the baking sheets and bake in the middle of the oven 20–25 minutes or until lightly golden. Let macaroons cool and peel off the paper.

Royal Rusks—from Irene Yamamoto

2 cups sugar	1 teaspoon almond flavoring
1 cup butter	1 teaspoon baking soda
2 eggs	2 cups ground almonds
1 cup sour cream	5½ cups flour

Cream butter and sugar, add eggs, sour cream, flavoring. Mix dry ingredients together and add to cream mixture. Roll out dough into long roll (like a rope), flatten to about ½-inch high and 2 fingers wide. Bake at 350°F for 20–30 minutes, then cut on bias while warm and turn onto sides and dry in oven 15 minutes or more until golden brown and dry.

Butterscotch Squares—from Florice Kuwahara

This was one of Sam's [my husband's] favorite cookies. He got the recipe from a fellow worker in 1944 when he was working for Kelly Fruit at the Denargo Market in Denver during the war.

¼ cup melted butter	1 teaspoon baking powder
1 cup brown sugar	½ teaspoon salt
1 egg	1 teaspoon vanilla
1 cup flour	¼ cup chopped nuts

Mix together the butter and brown sugar. Add eggs and beat thoroughly. Sift flour, baking powder, and salt, and mix thoroughly. Stir in vanilla and nuts. Spread out batter in greased 12-inch square pan. Bake in moderate hot oven (375°F) for 15 minutes. Cut in squares.

I melt my butter and add the sugar, then the rest of the ingredients. Double the recipe and use a 9 × 13-inch pan.

Omochi Manju with Automatic Rice Cooker—from Mae Kajioka

1 cup mochiko—Set aside in bowl. Put ⅓ cup sugar and 2 tablespoons Karo syrup into 1 cup measuring cup, add water to 1 cup mark. May add color if desired. Pour into mochiko and mix well.

Pour about 2 cups or more water into rice cooker. Put any type of rack into the cooker to hold the batter away from the water. (A vegetable steamer rack will work, or some rice cookers come with racks.) Put wet rag over the rack and pour mochiko in. Steam about 12 minutes or longer.

Check to see if cooked by testing with butter knife. Take out onto board covered with cornstarch. (Should look evenly cooked with no uncooked area in the middle.) Fill with "an." Will make about one dozen manju.

Jell-O Mochi—from Miye Baba

3¼ cup mochiko   2 cups water

Mix mochiko and water thoroughly. Line wet cloth (wrung out) over steamer and pour mixed mochiko into wet cloth. Steam for about 20 minutes.

Syrup for Jell-O Mochi:

In medium sized pan, dissolve 2 to 2½ cups sugar in ¾ cup water, adding 2–3 tablespoons of any flavor Jell-O and simmer for about 20 minutes until syrupy.

Mix steamed mochiko and syrup together and mix thoroughly in electric dough mixer or mix with wire whisk. Pour into 9 × 13-inch pan sprayed with Pam. Leave over night until firm enough to cut. Slice to desired size, dipping cut sides into cornstarch or katakuriko to dry. Brush the sliced Jell-O mochi of all the powder and it will look beautiful.

Note: When steaming, check to see if mochiko has steamed enough by cutting into the middle with wet chopstick or butter knife. It should look evenly cooked with no uncooked area in the center.

Pink Mochi (Baked)—from Mae Yotsuya

4 cups mochiko	1 can (12 ounce) coconut milk
2½ cup sugar	1¾ cup water
	½ teaspoon miso

Mix together until smooth the dry and liquid ingredients, then add a drop of red food coloring. Bake in 7½ × 11¼-inch greased pan, covered with foil at 350°F for 1 hour. When done, remove foil, then let stand for 12 hours. Dust with kinako or katakuriko (potato starch) when cutting.

Coffee Azuki Jell-O—from Susie Asai

Mix in large bowl 4 envelopes Knox unflavored gelatine with ½ cup water. Then add 4 teaspoons instant coffee dissolved in 2 cups of hot water.

Combine 1 can Borden's condensed milk with 1 can *tsubushi an* and add to rest of the ingredients. Mix well.

Pour in 9 × 9-inch pan, which is sprayed with Pam. Refrigerate at least overnight and cut into eating size.

Regular or decaf coffee may be used, more or less to your own taste. *Tsubushi an* could be made with less sugar, then it won't be so sweet like the canned *an*.

Lemon Cloud Pie—from Mae Yotsuya

Filling:

1 cup sugar	1 teaspoon grated lemon rind
¼ cup cornstarch	⅓ cup lemon juice (scant)
1 cup water	2 eggs, separated
4 ounces cream cheese	

Combine in sauce pan ¾ cup sugar, cornstarch, water, lemon rind, lemon juice, and slightly beaten egg yolks. Cook over medium heat, stirring constantly until thick. Remove from heat, add cream cheese, blend well. Cool. Beat egg whites until soft mounds form. Gradually add ¼ cup sugar, beat until stiff peaks form. Fold into lemon mixture. Spoon into 9-inch pie shell. Chill at least 2 hours. May be topped with whipped cream or Cool Whip.

Covered Lemon Pie—from Helen Yuge

Mix: 1¼ cup sugar
2 tablespoons flour
⅛ teaspoon salt

Blend in:
  ¼ cup soft margarine or butter
Add:
  3 eggs well beaten
  1 teaspoon lemon rind
  1 lemon sliced (⅓ cup) after removing skin
    and white membrane
  ½ cup water

Put into unbaked crust; put on top crust, slash a few vent holes on top and bake at 400°F for 30–35 minutes.

Zucchini Bread—from Haruko Narita

3 eggs	1 cup oil
2 cups sugar	1 cup grated zucchini
2 teaspoons vanilla	3 cups flour
1 teaspoon soda	¼ teaspoon baking powder
1 teaspoon salt	3 teaspoons cinnamon
½ cup walnuts	

Beat eggs until light and foamy; add oil, sugar, zucchini, and vanilla. Mix lightly but well. Mix flour, soda, baking powder, salt, and cinnamon in a bowl. Add flour mixture to first mixture and blend. Add nuts. Bake in 2 greased 9 × 5-inch loaf pans at 325°F for 1 hour or until done. Remove from pan at once. Cool on rack.

Best way to use surplus zucchini.

Bibliography

Unpublished Sources

Cortez Berry Growers Association. Minutes, 1928–1933.
Cortez Growers Association. Minutes, 1924–1959. Miscellaneous correspondence and business records, 1942–1945.
Cortez Growers Association, 1924–1974. Fiftieth anniversary *Commemorative Pamphlet*, 1974.
Cortez Presbyterian Church Fiftieth Anniversary, 1927–1977. *Commemorative Pamphlet*, 1977.
Cortez Young People's Club. Minutes, 1923–1942.
Yuge, George. *History of the Cortez Growers Association*, Pamphlet.

Matsumoto, Valerie J. *Taped Interviews* (Tapes in Author's Possession)

Robin Yuge Alexander, August 26, 1982.
Gary Asai, April 27, 1982.
Hiroshi Asai, February 23, 1982.
Hisako Asai, February 23, 1982.
Shizue Asai, February 5, 1982.
Shizuka Asai, interviewed with the assistance of Shizue Asai, February 10, 1982.
Franklin Baba, July 18, 1982.
Miye Baba, July 18, 1982.
Nobuzo Baba, February 18, 1982.
Lena Date, February 7, 1982.
Takashi Date, February 7, 1982.
Shirley Frice, April 26, 1982.
Haruka Ishihara, April 25, 1982.

Eugene Kajioka, July 16, 1982.
Harry Kajioka, January 16, 1982.
Kazumi Kajioka, January 25, 1982.
Mae Kajioka, January 16, 1982.
Mary Kajioka, January 25, 1982.
Masa Kajioka, interviewed with the assistance of Umeko Yotsuya and Helen
    Yuge, February 24, 1982.
Hajime Kajiwara, February 10, 1982.
Utako Kajiwara, February 10, 1982.
Joe Kamiya, July 1, 1982.
Marcia Kamiya, August 19, 1982.
Mark Kamiya, February 8, 1982.
Mary Kamiya, February 13, 1982.
Christine Kubo, February 26, 1982.
Daniel Kubo, February 27, 1982.
Lucille Kumimoto, February 22, 1982.
Florice Kuwahara, January 25, 1982.
Sam Kuwahara, January 25, 1982.
Haruka Ishihara, April 25, 1982.
Grace Kimoto, February 12 and 24, 1982.
Frances Kirihara, February 5, 1982.
Kaoru Masuda, February 8, 1982.
Yuriko Masuda, February 24, 1982.
Tsune Matsushige, interviewed with the assistance of Lily Takahashi and
    Helen Yuge.
Ken Miyamoto, February 10, 1982.
Takako Miyamoto, February 10, 1982.
Albert Morimoto, January 27, 1982.
Lois Morimoto, January 27, 1982.
George Morofuji, August 25, 1982.
Kohei Nakashima, interviewed with the assistance of Caroline and Tom
    Nakashima, April 7, 1982.
Carole Narita, August 17 and 20, 1982.
Haruko Narita, January 26, 1982.
Leona Narita, August 17 and 20, 1982.
Saburo Narita, January 26, 1982.
Jack Nishihara, August 27, 1982.
Takako Nishihara, August 27, 1982.
Ada Nose, August 17 and 20, 1982.
Alan Osugi, April 28, 1982.
Ann Osugi, April 28, 1982.
Maju Sakaguchi, interviewed with the assistance of May Sakaguchi, March 11,
    1982.
May Sakaguchi, March 10 and 11, 1982.

Rodney Sakaguchi, April 29, 1982.
Yeichi Sakaguchi, March 10, 1982.
Edward Sugiura, July 15, 1982.
Suye Sugiura, interviewed with the assistance of Miye Baba, February 9, 1982.
Grace Tanaka, August 26, 1982.
Alice Taniguchi, March 9, 1982.
Howard Taniguchi, March 9, 1982.
Kumekichi Taniguchi, January 26, 1982.
Candice Toyoda, July 17, 1982.
Candice Toyoda, July 17, 1982.
Don Toyoda, August 5, 1982.
May Toyoda, February 4, 1982.
Edna Yamaguchi, February 9, 1982.
Lester Yamaguchi, April 29, 1982.
Akio Yamamoto, interviewed with the assistance of George and Helen Yuge,
    February 22 and April 4, 1982.
Kiyoshi Yamamoto, February 6, 1982.
Michael Yamamoto, October 23, 1982.
Naomi Yamamoto, February 3, 1982.
Ernest Yoshida, January 24, 1982.
Ruth Yoshida, January 24, 1982.
Sharyn Yoshida, August 17, 1982.
Dennis Yotsuya, June 5, 1988.
Edith Yotsuya, January 26, 1982.
Ernest Yotsuya, March 14, 1982.
Grace Yotsuya, June 5, 1988.
Mae Yotsuya, January 15, 1982.
Takeo Yotsuya, January 26, 1982.
Yukihiro Yotsuya, January 15, 1982.
George Yuge, February 8, 1982.
Helen Yuge, February 10 and March 14, 1982.

Matsumoto, Valerie J. *Untaped Interviews* (Notes in the Author's Possession)

Yoshi Kubo, 1982.
Takeshi "General" Sugiura, April 29, 1982.

Parker, J. Carlyle. *Taped Interviews* (Tapes at the Library of California State
College at Stanislaus in Turlock, California)

Hugh Griswold, January 25, 1975.
Kazuo Masuda, March 27, [ca. 1970].

Newspapers and Periodicals

Current Life: The Magazine for the American Born Japanese, 1940–1942.
Granada Pioneer (Amache Camp newspaper), 1944–1945.
Livingston Chronicle, 1919–1949, 1982.
Merced County Bee, 1919–1920.
Merced County Sun, 1919–1920.
The Mercedian (Merced Assembly Center newspaper), 1942.
Modesto Bee, 1971, 1974.
Modesto Sun, 1974.
New York Daily News, 1945.
Nichi Bei Times, 1980.
Pacific Citizen, 1971, 1980.
Turlock Daily Journal, 1919–1921, 1942, 1972, 1977, 1982.

War Relocation Authority Publications, Government Documents, and Amache Relocation Center Materials

Amache Senior High School. *1944 Onlooker*. Yearbook, 1944. (Copy in possession of Mitsuko Morimoto.)
California. Legislature. Senate. *Reports of Senate Fact-Finding Committee on Japanese Resettlement*. Sacramento: Senate of the State of California, 1944.
Kusaba, Henry, James C. Lindley, and Joe McClelland. *Amache*, a report. Amache, Colo.: Documentation Section, Reports Office [ca. 1944].
U.S. Bureau of the Census, *1987 Census of Agriculture*, Vol. 1, Pt. 5, California State and County Data. Washington, D.C.: Government Printing Office, 1989.
U.S. Congress, House. Committee on Immigration and Naturalization. *Japanese Immigration: Hearings before the Committee on Immigration and Naturalization*. 66th Cong., 2d sess., July 19–21, 1920.
U.S. Congress. Senate. Commission on Wartime Relocation and Internment of Civilians, *Personal Justice Denied*, a report. Washington, D.C.: Government Printing Office, 1982.
U.S. Department of the Interior, War Relocation Authority. *The Evacuated People: A Quantitative Description*. Washington, D.C.: Government Printing Office [ca. 1946]; New York: Arno Press, 1978.
U.S. Department of War. *Final Report: Japanese Evacuation from the West Coast, 1942*, by Lieutenant General John L. DeWitt. Washington, D.C.: Government Printing Office, 1947.
U.S. War Agency Liquidation Unit (formerly War Relocation Authority). *People in Motion: The Postwar Adjustment of the Evacuated Japanese Americans*. Washington, D.C.: Government Printing Office, 1947.
U.S. War Relocation Authority. *California and Her Less Favored Minorities: A Study in the Background of the Evacuation of Persons of Japanese Ancestry From the*

Pacific Coast, by Ruth E. McKee. Washington, D.C.: Government Printing Office, 1944.

———. Granada Relocation Center. *Historical Report, Operations Division—Agricultural Section, Granada Relocation Center.* Undated [ca. 1945]. Republished: Amache Historical Society (P.O. Box 4199, Torrance, Calif. 90510), 1978. [Copy in possession of Mitsuko Morimoto].

———. Granada Relocation Center. *Resettlement Handbook.* Amache, Colo.: Evacuee Information Center, Granada Project, undated [ca. 1945].

———. "A Message from the Director of the War Relocation Authority," by Dillon S. Myer. Pamphlet, undated [ca. 1945]. [Copy in possession of Yuriko Masuda].

Books

Adams, Ansel. *Born Free and Equal: Photographs of the Loyal Japanese-Americans at Manzanar Relocation Center.* New York: U.S. Camera, 1944.

Asian Women United of California, ed. *Making Waves: An Anthology of Writings by and about Asian American Women.* Boston: Beacon Press, 1989.

Baum, Willa K. *Oral History for the Local Historical Society.* Nashville, Tenn.: American Association for State and Local History, by special arrangement with the Conference of California Historical Societies, 1971.

———. *Transcribing and Editing Oral History.* Nashville, Tenn.: American Association for State and Local History, 1977.

Baum, Willa K., and David K. Dunaway, eds. *Oral History: An Interdisciplinary Anthology.* Nashville, Tenn.: American Association for State and Local History in cooperation with the Oral History Association, 1984.

Bethel, Elizabeth Rauh. *Promiseland: A Century of Life in a Negro Community.* Philadelphia: Temple University Press, 1981.

Bloom, Leonard [see also Broom, Leonard], and Ruth Riemer. *Removal and Return: The Socio-Economic Effects of the War on Japanese Americans.* Berkeley: University of California Press, 1949.

Bonacich, Edna, and John Modell. *The Economic Basis of Ethnic Solidarity: Small Business in the Japanese American Community.* Berkeley: University of California Press, 1980.

Borchert, James. *Alley Life in Washington: Family, Community, Religion, and Folklife in the City, 1850–1970.* Urbana: University of Illinois Press, 1980.

Bosworth, Allan R. *America's Concentration Camps.* New York: W.W. Norton, 1967.

Broek, Jacobus ten, Edward N. Barnhart, and Floyd W. Matson. *Prejudice, War, and the Constitution.* Berkeley: University of California Press, 1968.

Broom, Leonard [see also Bloom, Leonard], and John I. Kitsuse. *The Managed Casualty: The Japanese-American Family in World War II.* Berkeley: University of California Press, 1973.

Camarillo, Albert. *Chicanos in a Changing Society: From Mexican Pueblos to Ameri-*

can Barrios in Santa Barbara and Southern California, 1848–1930. Cambridge: Harvard University Press, 1979.

Chafe, William H. *The American Woman: Her Changing Social, Economic, and Political Roles, 1920–1970*. New York: Oxford University Press, 1972.

——. *The Paradox of Change: American Women in the 20th Century*. New York: Oxford University Press, 1991.

——. *Women and Equality: Changing Patterns in American Culture*. New York: Oxford University Press, 1977.

Chan, Sucheng. *Asian Americans: An Interpretive History*. Boston: Twayne, 1991.

——, ed. *Income and Status Differences between White and Minority Americans*. Mellen Studies in Sociology, vol. 3. Lewiston, N.Y.: Edwin Mellen Press, 1990.

——. *This Bittersweet Soil: The Chinese in California Agriculture, 1860–1910*. Berkeley: University of California Press, 1986.

Cheng, Lucie, and Edna Bonacich, eds. *Labor Immigration under Capitalism: Asian Immigrant Workers in the U.S. before World War II*. Berkeley: University of California Press, 1984.

Cinel, Dino. *From Italy to San Francisco: The Immigrant Experience*. Stanford: Stanford University Press, 1982.

Connor, John W. *Acculturation and the Retention of an Ethnic Identity in Three Generations of Japanese Americans*. San Francisco: R & E Research Associates, 1977.

——. *Tradition and Change in Three Generations of Japanese Americans*. Chicago: Nelson-Hall, 1977.

Conrat, Maisie, and Richard Conrat. *Executive Order 9066: The Internment of 110,000 Japanese Americans*. Cambridge: MIT Press, 1972.

Conroy, (Francis) Hilary, and Scott T. Miyakawa, eds. *East across the Pacific: Historical & Sociological Studies of Japanese Immigration and Assimilation*. Santa Barbara, Calif.: American Bibliographical Center, Clio Press, 1974.

Daniels, Roger. *Asian America: Chinese and Japanese in the United States since 1850*. Seattle: University of Washington Press, 1988.

——. *Concentration Camps North America: Japanese in the United States and Canada during World War II*. Malabar, Fla.: R.E. Krieger, 1981.

——. *Concentration Camps USA: Japanese Americans and World War II*. New York: Holt, Rinehart & Winston, 1972.

——. *The Politics of Prejudice: The Anti-Japanese Movement in California and the Struggle for Japanese Exclusion*. Berkeley: University of California Press, 1962, 1977.

del Castillo, Richard Griswold. *The Los Angeles Barrio, 1850–1890: A Social History*. Berkeley: University of California Press, 1979.

di Leonardo, Micaela. *The Varieties of Ethnic Experience: Kinship, Class, and Gender among California Italian Americans*. Ithaca: Cornell University Press, 1984.

DuBois, Ellen Carol, and Vicki L. Ruiz, eds. *Unequal Sisters: A Multicultural Reader in U.S. Women's History*. New York: Routledge, 1990.

Duus, Masayo Umezawa. *Unlikely Liberators: The Men of the 100th and the 442nd.* Honolulu: University of Hawaii Press, 1987.

Erikson, Kai T. *Everything in Its Path: Destruction of Community in the Buffalo Creek Flood.* New York: Simon & Schuster, 1976.

Fugita, Stephen S., and David J. O'Brien. *Japanese American Ethnicity: The Persistence of a Community.* Seattle: University of Washington Press, 1991.

Garcia, Mario T. *Desert Immigrants: The Mexicans of El Paso, 1880–1920.* New Haven: Yale University Press, 1981.

Gardiner, C. Harvey. *Pawns in a Triangle of Hate: The Peruvian Japanese and the United States.* Seattle: University of Washington Press, 1981.

Gee, Emma, ed. *Counterpoint: Perspectives on Asian America.* Los Angeles: Asian American Studies Center, University of California, 1976.

Genovese, Eugene. *Roll, Jordan, Roll: The World the Slaves Made.* New York: Vintage Books, 1974, 1976.

Girdner, Audrie, and Anne Loftis. *The Great Betrayal: The Evacuation of the Japanese-Americans during World War II.* New York: Macmillan, 1969.

Glenn, Evelyn Nakano. *Issei, Nisei, War Bride: Three Generations of Japanese American Women in Domestic Service.* Philadelphia: Temple University Press, 1986.

Gregory, James Noble. *American Exodus: The Dust Bowl Migration and Okie Culture in California.* New York: Oxford University Press, 1989.

Gutman, Herbert. *The Black Family in Slavery and Freedom, 1750–1925.* New York: Pantheon, 1976.

Handlin, Oscar. 1951. *The Uprooted.* Boston: Little, Brown, 1973.

Harrington, Joseph D. *Yankee Samurai (The Secret Role of Nisei in America's Pacific Victory).* Detroit: Pettigrew Enterprises, 1979.

Hartmann, Susan M. *The Home Front and Beyond: American Women in the 1940's.* Boston: Twayne, 1982.

Hata, Donald Teruo, Jr. *"Undesirables": Early Immigrants and the Anti-Japanese Movement in San Francisco, 1892–1893, Prelude to Exclusion.* New York: Arno Press, 1978.

Hatch, Elvin. *Biography of a Small Town.* New York: Columbia University Press, 1979.

Hine, Darlene Clark. *When the Truth is Told: A History of Black Women's Culture and Community in Indiana, 1875–1950.* Indianapolis: National Council of Negro Women, 1981.

Hochschild, Arlie, with Anne Machung. *The Second Shift.* New York: Avon Books, 1989.

Hohenthal, Helen Alma, et al. *Streams in a Thirsty Land: A History of the Turlock Region.* Ed. John Edwards Caswell. Turlock, Calif.: City of Turlock, 1972.

Hoopes, James. *Oral History: An Introduction for Students.* Chapel Hill: University of North Carolina Press, 1979.

Hosokawa, Bill. *Nisei: The Quiet Americans.* New York: William Morrow, 1969.

Hosokawa, Bill, and Robert A. Wilson. *East to America: A History of the Japanese in the United States.* New York: Quill, 1982.

Houston, Jeanne Wakatsuki, and James D. Houston. *Farewell to Manzanar.* Boston: Houghton Mifflin, 1973.

Ichihashi, Yamato. *Japanese in the United States: A Critical Study of the Problems of the Japanese Immigrants and Their Children.* Stanford: Stanford University Press, 1932.

Ichioka, Yuji. *The Issei: The World of the First Generation Japanese Immigrants, 1885–1924.* New York: Free Press, 1988.

Irons, Peter. *Justice at War: The Story of the Japanese American Internment Cases.* New York: Oxford University Press, 1983.

——. ed. *Justice Delayed: The Record of Japanese American Internment Cases.* Middleton, Conn.: Wesleyan University Press, 1989.

Ishigo, Estelle. *Lone Heart Mountain.* Los Angeles: Anderson, Ritchie & Simon, 1972.

Ito, Kazuo. *Issei: A History of Japanese Immigrants in North America.* Trans. Shinichiro Nakamura and Jean S. Gerard. Seattle: Executive Committee for the Publication of *Issei: A History of Japanese Immigrants in North America,* 1973.

Jackson, Clarence W. *A Study of the Japanese Population of the City and County of Denver.* Denver: The Denver Bureau of Public Welfare of the City and County of Denver, 1944.

James, Thomas. *Exile Within: The Schooling of Japanese Americans, 1942–1945.* Cambridge: Harvard University Press, 1987.

The Japanese Agricultural Association. *The Japanese Farmers in California.* San Francisco: The Japanese Agricultural Association, 1918.

Jelinek, Lawrence J. *Harvest Empire: A History of California Agriculture.* 2d ed. San Francisco: Boyd & Fraser, 1982.

Kiefer, Christie W. *Changing Cultures, Changing Lives: An Ethnographic Study of Three Generations of Japanese-Americans.* San Francisco: Jossey-Bass, 1974.

Kikumura, Akemi. *Promises Kept: The Life of an Issei Man.* Novato, Calif.: Chandler & Sharp, 1991.

——. *Through Harsh Winters: The Life of a Japanese Immigrant Woman.* Novato, Calif.: Chandler & Sharp, 1981.

Kitagawa, Daisuke. *Issei and Nisei: The Internment Years.* New York: Seabury Press, 1974.

Kitano, Harry H. L. *Japanese Americans: The Evolution of a Subculture.* 2d ed. Englewood Cliffs, N.J.: Prentice-Hall, 1976.

Kogawa, Joy. *Obasan.* Boston: David R. Godine, 1982.

Laing, Michiyo, Carl Laing, Heihachiro Takarabe, Takuno Asako, and Stanley Umeda, eds. *Issei Christians: Selected Interviews from the Issei Oral History Project.* Sacramento, Calif.: The Issei Oral History Project, 1977.

Leighton, Alexander Hamilton. *The Governing of Men: General Principles and Recommendations Based on Experience at a Japanese Relocation Camp.* Princeton: Princeton University Press, 1945.

Levine, Gene N., and Colbert Rhodes. *The Japanese American Community: A Three-Generation Study.* New York: Praeger, 1981.

Levine, Lawrence. *Black Culture and Black Consciousness.* New York: Oxford University Press, 1977.

Light, Ivan H. *Ethnic Enterprises in America: Business and Welfare among Chinese, Japanese, and Blacks.* Berkeley: University of California Press, 1972.

Lukes, Timothy J., and Gary Y. Okihiro. *Japanese Legacy: Farming and Community Life In California's Santa Clara Valley.* Local History Studies, vol. 31. Cupertino, Calif.: California History Center, 1985.

Lydon, Sandy. *Chinese Gold: The Chinese in the Monterey Bay Region.* Capitola, Calif.: Capitola Book Company, 1985.

Majka, Linda, and Theo Majka. *Farm Workers, Agribusiness, and the State.* Philadelphia: Temple University Press, 1982.

Masumoto, David Mas. *Country Voices: The Oral History of a Japanese American Family Farm Community.* Del Rey, Calif.: Inaka Countryside Publications, 1987.

Matsumoto, Toru. *Beyond Prejudice: A Story of the Church and Japanese Americans.* New York: Arno Press, 1978.

Maykovich, Minako K. *Japanese American Identity Dilemma.* Tokyo: Waseda University Press, 1972.

McWilliams, Carey. *Brothers under the Skin.* Rev. ed. Boston: Little, Brown, 1964.

——. *Factories in the Field: The Story of Migratory Farm Labor in California.* Boston: Little, Brown, 1939.

——. *North from Mexico: The Spanish-Speaking People of the United States.* New York: Greenwood Press, 1968.

——. *Prejudice: Japanese Americans: Symbol of Racial Intolerance.* Boston: Little, Brown, 1944.

Miyamoto, S. Frank. *Social Solidarity among the Japanese in Seattle.* Seattle: University of Washington Press, 1984.

Modell, John. *The Economics and Politics of Racial Accommodation: The Japanese of Los Angeles, 1900–1942.* Chicago: University of Illinois Press, 1977.

Montero, Darrel. *Japanese Americans: Changing Patterns of Ethnic Affiliation over Three Generations.* Boulder, Colo.: Westview Press, 1980.

Morin, Raul. *Among the Valiant: Mexican-Americans in World War II and Korea.* Alhambra, Calif.: Borden, 1966.

Murphy, Thomas D. *Ambassadors in Arms.* Honolulu: University of Hawaii Press, 1954.

Myer, Dillon S. *Uprooted Americans; The Japanese Americans and the War Relocations Authority During World War II.* Tucson: University of Arizona Press, 1971.

Naka, Kaizo. *Social and Economic Conditions among Japanese Farmers in California.* San Francisco: R & E Research Associates, 1974.

Nakano, Mei. *Japanese American Women: Three Generations, 1890–1990.* Berkeley: Mina Press; San Francisco: National Japanese American Historical Society, 1990.

Nee, Victor G., and Brett de Bary Nee. *Longtime Californ': A Documentary Study of an American Chinatown.* Stanford: Stanford University Press, 1986.

Nelson, Douglas W. *Heart Mountain; The History of an American Concentration Camp.* Madison: The State Historical Society of Wisconsin for the Department of History, University of Wisconsin, 1976.

Nettler, Gwynne. *The Relationship between Attitude and Information concerning the Japanese in America.* New York: Arno Press, 1980.

Noda, Kesa. *Yamato Colony: 1906–1960.* Livingston, Calif.: Livingston-Merced JACL Chapter, 1981.

Nomura, Gail, Russell Endo, Stephen Sumida, and Russell C. Leong, eds. *Frontiers of Asian American Studies: Writing, Research, and Commentary.* Pullman: Washington University Press, 1989.

O'Brien, Robert. *The College Nisei.* Palo Alto, Calif.: Pacific Books, 1949.

Okada, John. *No-No Boy.* Seattle: University of Washington Press, 1979.

Okihiro, Gary. *Cane Fires: The Anti-Japanese Movement in Hawaii, 1865–1945.* Philadelphia: Temple University Press, 1991.

Okimoto, Daniel. *American in Disguise.* New York: Walker/Weatherhill, 1971.

Okubo, Mine. *Citizen 13660.* Seattle: University of Washington Press, 1983.

Rice, Richard B., William A. Bullough, and Richard J. Orsi. *The Elusive Eden: A New History of California.* New York: Alfred A. Knopf, 1988.

Romo, Ricardo. *East Los Angeles: History of a Barrio.* Austin: University of Texas Press, 1983.

Rothman, Sheila M. *Woman's Proper Place; A History of Changing Ideals and Practices, 1870 to the Present.* New York: Basic Books, 1978.

Ryan, Mary P. *Womanhood in America from Colonial Times to the Present.* New York: New Viewpoints, 1975.

Sarasohn, Eileen Sunada, ed. *The Issei: Portrait of a Pioneer: An Oral History.* Palo Alto, Calif.: Pacific Books, 1983.

Saxton, Alexander. *The Indispensible Enemy: Labor and the Anti-Chinese Movement in California.* Berkeley and Los Angeles: University of California Press, 1971.

Sone, Monica. *Nisei Daughter.* Seattle: University of Washington Press, 1979.

Spicer, Edward, Asael T. Hansen, Katherine Luomala, and Marvin K. Opler. *Impounded People: Japanese-Americans in the Relocation Centers.* Tucson: University of Arizona Press, 1969.

Strong, Edward K., Jr. *Japanese in California.* Stanford University Publications, University Series, Education-Psychology, 1:2. Stanford: Stanford University Press, 1933.

Tachiki, Amy, Eddie Wong, Franklin Odo, with Buck Wong, eds. *Roots: An Asian American Reader.* Los Angeles: Asian American Studies Center, University of California, 1971.

Takaki, Ronald. *Strangers from a Different Shore.* Boston: Little, Brown, 1989.

Thomas, Dorothy Swaine, Charles Kikuchi, and James Sakoda. *The Salvage: Japanese American Evacuation and Resettlement During World War II.* Berkeley: University of California Press, 1975.

Thomas, Dorothy Swaine, and Richard Nishimoto. *The Spoilage: Japanese Amer-*

ican Evacuation and Resettlement During World War II. Berkeley: University of California Press, 1974.

Tilly, Louise, and Joan Scott. *Women, Work, and Family.* New York: Holt, Rinehart & Winston, 1978.

Tsuchida, Nobuya, ed. *Asian and Pacific American Experiences: Women's Perspectives.* Minneapolis: Asian/Pacific American Learning Resource Center and General College, University of Minnesota, 1982.

Uchida, Yoshiko. *Desert Exile; The Uprooting of a Japanese American Family.* Seattle: University of Washington Press, 1982, 1984.

———. *Picture Bride.* New York: Simon & Schuster, 1987.

Weglyn, Michi. *Years of Infamy; The Untold Story of America's Concentration Camps.* New York: William Morrow, 1976.

White, Deborah Gray. *Ain't I a Woman? Female Slaves in the Plantation South.* New York: W.W. Norton, 1985.

Wilson, Robert A., and Bill Hosokawa. *East to America: A History of the Japanese in the United States.* New York: Quill, 1982.

Yanagisako, Sylvia Junko. *Transforming the Past: Tradition and Kinship among Japanese Americans.* Stanford: Stanford University Press, 1985.

Yatsushiro, Toshio. *Politics and Cultural Values: The World War II Japanese Relocation Centers and the United States Government.* New York: Arno Press, 1978.

Articles and Pamphlets

Ano, Masaharu. "Loyal Linguists: Nisei of World War II Learned Japanese in Minnesota," *Minnesota History* 45(Fall 1977):273–87.

Arkoff, A., G. Meredith, and J. Dong. "Attitudes of Japanese-American and Caucasian-American Students toward Marriage Roles." *Journal of Social Psychology* 59(1963):11–15.

Befu, Harumi. "Contrastive Acculturation of California Japanese: Comparative Approach to the Study of Immigrants." *Human Organization* 24(Fall 1965):209–16.

"Bitter Harvest." *Newsweek*, February 18, 1985, pp. 52–60.

Bloom, Leonard [see also Broom, Leonard]. "Familial Adjustments of Japanese-Americans to Relocation: First Phase." *American Sociological Review* 8(October 1943):551–60.

———. "Transitional Adjustments of Japanese-American Families to Relocation." *American Sociological Review* 12(April 1947):201–9.

Bogardus, Emory S. "Culture Conflicts in Relocation Centers." *Sociology and Social Research* 31(May–June 1943):381–90.

———. "Current Problems of Japanese Americans." *Sociology and Social Research* 25(July–August 1941):562–71.

———. "The Japanese Return to the West Coast." *Sociology and Social Research* 28(January–February 1947):226–33.

——. "Relocation Centers as Planned Communities." *Sociology and Social Research* 28(January–February 1944):218–34.

Bonacich, Edna. "Small Business and Japanese American Ethnic Solidarity." *Amerasia Journal* 3(Summer 1975):96–113.

Carter, Genevieve W. "Child Care and Youth Problems in a Relocation Center." *Journal of Consulting Psychology* 8(July–August 1944):219–25.

Carter, Harold O., Warren E. Johnston, and Carole Frank Nuckton. "Some Forces Affecting Our Changing American Agriculture." *California Agriculture* 33(January 1979):9–10.

Colorado Council of Churches. "The Japanese in Our Midst." Pamphlet. Undated.

Connor, John W. "Family Bonds, Maternal Closeness, and the Suppression of Sexuality in Three Generations of Japanese Americans." *Ethos* 4(Summer 1976):189–222.

——. "*Joge Kankei:* A Key Concept for an Understanding of Japanese-American Achievement." *Psychiatry* 39(1976):266–79.

——. "Persistence and Change in Japanese American Value Orientations." *Ethos* 4(Spring 1976):1–46.

Endo, Russell, and Dale Hirokawa. "Japanese American Intermarriage." *Free Inquiry in Creative Sociology* 11(November 1983): 159–62, 166.

Farrell, Kenneth R. "Refining Goals and Priorities," *California Agriculture* 41(March–April 1987):2.

Fugita, Stephen S., and David J. O'Brien. "Economics, Ideology, and Ethnicity: The Struggle between the United Farm Workers Union and the Nisei Farmers League." *Social Problems* 25(December 1977):146–56.

Fujita, Michinari. "The Japanese Associations in America." *Sociology and Social Research* 13(1928):211–28.

Gee, Emma. "Issei: The First Women." *Asian Women* (Asian Women's Journal). Berkeley: University of California Press, 1971, pp. 8–15.

Glenn, Evelyn Nakano. "The Dialectics of Wage Work: Japanese-American Women and Domestic Service, 1905–1940." *Feminist Studies* 6(Fall 1980):432–71.

"Go for Broke." Exhibition brochure. San Francisco: Presidio Army Museum, 1981.

"Go for Broke; A Pictorial History of the Japanese American 100th Infantry Battalion and the 442nd Regimental Combat Team." *Pacific Citizen*, January 1–8, 1982.

Hansen, Arthur A., and David A. Hacker. "The Manzanar Riot: An Ethnic Perspective." *Amerasia Journal* 2(Fall 1974):112–57.

Higgs, Robert. "Landless by Law: Japanese Immigrants in California Agriculture to 1941." *Journal of Economic History* 38(March 1978):205–25.

Hirabayashi, James. "Nisei: The Quiet Americans?—A Reevaluation." *Amerasia Journal* 3(Summer 1975):114–29.

Hirata, Lucie Cheng. "Chinese Immigrant Women in Nineteenth-Century

California." In *Women of America: A History,* ed. Carol Ruth Berkin and Mary Beth Norton. Boston: Houghton Mifflin, 1979.

——. "Free, Indentured, Enslaved: Chinese Prostitutes in Nineteenth Century America." *Signs: A Journal of Women in Culture and Society* 5:1(1979):3–29.

Ichioka, Yuji. "*Amerika Nadeshiko:* Japanese Immigrant Women in the United States, 1900–1924." *Pacific Historical Review* 69(May 1980):339–57.

——. "Ameyuki-san: Japanese Prostitutes in Nineteenth Century America." *Amerasia Journal* 4:1(1977):1–21.

——. "The Early Japanese Immigrant Quest for Citizenship: The Background of the 1922 Ozawa Case." *Amerasia Journal* 4:2(1977):1–22.

——. "Japanese Associations and the Japanese Government: A Special Relationship, 1909–1926." *Pacific Historical Review* 46(August 1977):409–37.

——. "Japanese Immigrant Response to the 1920 California Alien Land Law." *Agricultural History* 58(April 1984):157–78.

——. "The 1921 Turlock Incident: Forceful Expulsion of Japanese Laborers." In *Counterpoint: Perspectives on Asian America,* ed. Emma Gee. Los Angeles: Asian American Studies Center, University of California, 1976.

Ikeda-Spiegel, Motoko. "Concentration Camps in the U.S.A." *Heresies* 2(1980):90–7.

"Issei, Nisei, Kibei." *Fortune,* April 1944, pp. 8, 22, 32, 74, 78, 84, 94, 106, 112.

Iwata, Masakazu. "The Japanese Immigrants in California Agriculture." *Agricultural History* 36(April 1962):25–37.

Johnson, Colleen L. "Authority and Power in Japanese-American Marriage." In *Power in Families,* ed. Ronald E. Cromwell and David H. Olson. New York: John Wiley, 1975, 182–96.

——. "Interdependence, Reciprocity and Indebtedness: An Analysis of Japanese American Kinship Relations." *Journal of Marriage and the Family* 39(May 1977):351–63.

Kawakami, Kiyoshi K. "Japanese on American Farms." *The Independent* 59(July–December 1905):961–67.

Kikumura, Akemi, and Harry Kitano. "Interracial Marriage: A Picture of the Japanese Americans." *Journal of Social Issues* 29:2(1973):67–81.

Kitano, Harry H. L., and Akemi Kikumura. "The Japanese American Family." In *Ethnic Families in America,* ed. C. H. Mindel and R. W. Habenstein. New York: Elsevier, 1976, pp. 41–60.

Kitano, Harry H. L., Wai-Tsang Yeung, Lynn Chai, and Herbert Hatanaka. "Asian American Interracial Marriage," *Journal of Marriage and the Family* 46(1984):179–90.

Levine, Gene N., and Darrel M. Montero. "Socioeconomic Mobility among Three Generations of Japanese Americans." *Journal of Social Issues* 29:2(1973):33–48.

Lyman, Stanford M. "Japanese-American Generation Gap." *Society* 10(January–February 1973):55–63.

Mass, Amy Iwasaki. "Asians as Individuals: The Japanese Community." *Social Casework* 57(March 1976):160–64.

Matsumoto, Valerie. "Japanese American Women during World War II." *Frontiers* 8:1(1984):6–14.

Maykovich, Minako K. "Political Activation of Japanese American Youth." *Journal of Social Issues* 29:2(1973):167–85.

McVoy, Edgar C. "Social Process in the War Relocation Center." *Social Forces* 22(December 1943):188–90.

McWilliams, Carey. "What about Our Japanese Americans?" Pamphlet. American Council, Institute of Pacific Relations, May 1944.

Miyamoto, S. Frank. "The Forced Evacuation of the Japanese Minority during World War II." *Journal of Social Issues* 29:2(1973):11–31.

Miyoshi, Nobu. "Identity Crisis of the Sansei and the American Concentration Camp." *Pacific Citizen*, Holiday Issue, December 19–26, 1980, 41–42, 50, 55.

Montero, Darrel, and Ronald Tsukashima. "Assimilation and Educational Achievement: The Case of the Second Generation Japanese-American." *Sociological Quarterly* 18(Autumn 1977):490–503.

Naske, Claus-M. "The Relocation of Alaska's Japanese Residents." *Pacific Northwest Quarterly* 74(July 1983):124–32.

Nomura, Gail. "Issei Working Women in Hawaii." In *Making Waves: An Anthology by and about Asian American Women*, ed. Asian Women United of California. Boston: Beacon Press, 1989, pp. 135–48.

Oka, Seizo. "Biography of Kyutaro Abiko: Issei Pioneer with a Dream." *Pacific Citizen*, Holiday Issue, December 19–26, 1980, pp. 1, 61, 63–66.

Okihiro, Gary Y. "Fallow Field: The Rural Dimension of Asian American Studies." In *Frontiers of Asian American Studies*, ed. Gail Nomura, Russell Endo, Stephen Sumida, and Russell Leong. Pullman: Washington State University Press, 1989, pp. 6–13.

——. "Japanese Resistance in America's Concentration Camps: A Re-Evaluation." *Amerasia Journal* 2(1973):20–34.

Osumi, Megumi Dick. "Asians and California's Anti-Miscegenation Laws." In *Asian and Pacific American Women's Perspectives*, ed. Nobuya Tsuchida. Minneapolis: Asian/Pacific American Learning Resource Center and General College, University of Minnesota, 1982, pp. 1–37.

"A Pilgrimage Guide to the Temporary Detention Centers." *Pacific Citizen*, Holiday Issue, December 19–26, 1980, pp. 56–59.

Poli, Adon, and Warren M. Engstrand. "Japanese Agriculture on the Pacific Coast." *Journal of Land & Public Utility Economics* 21(November 1945):352–64.

Rosaldo, Renato. "Others of Invention: Ethnicity and Its Discontents." *Voice Literary Supplement*, no. 82, February 1990: 27–29.

Rouse, Roger. "Mexican Migration and the Social Space of Postmodernism." *Diaspora* 1(Spring 1991):8–23.

Ruiz, Vicki L. "Oral History and La Mujer: The Rosa Guerrero Story." In

Women on the U.S.–Mexico Border: Responses to Change, ed. Vicki L. Ruiz, and Susan Tiano. Boston: Allen & Unwin, 1987, pp. 219–31.

Saloutos, Theodore. "The Immigrant in Pacific Coast Agriculture, 1880–1940." *Agricultural History* 49(January 1975):182–201.

Shimano, Eddie. "Blueprint for a Slum." *Common Ground* 3(Summer 1943):78–85.

Shinagawa, Larry Hajime, and Gin Yong Pang. "Marriage Patterns of Asian Americans in California, 1980." In *Income and Status Differences between White and Minority Americans,* ed. Sucheng Chan. Mellen Studies in Sociology, vol. 3. Lewiston, N.Y.: Edwin Mellen Press, 1990, pp. 225–82.

Smith, Bradford. "The Great American Swindle." *Common Ground* 7(Winter 1947):34–8.

Takahashi, Jere. "Japanese American Responses to Race Relations: The Formation of Nisei Perspectives." *Amerasia Journal* 9:1(1982):29–57.

Taylor, Frank J. "The People Nobody Wants." *The Saturday Evening Post,* May 9, 1942, pp. 24–25, 64, 66.

"They Work for Victory: The Story of Japanese Americans and the War Effort." Pamphlet. Edited by the Japanese American Citizens League. Salt Lake City: Japanese American Citizens League, undated.

Thompson, Orville E., Douglas Gwynn, and Charlotte Sharp. "Characteristics of Women in Farming." *California Agriculture* 41(January–February 1987):16–17.

———. "Women on Commercial Farms." *California Agriculture* 39(May–June 1985):21–2.

Tinker, John N. "Intermarriage and Ethnic Boundaries: The Japanese American Case." *Journal of Social Issues* 29:2(1973):49–66.

U.C. Agricultural Issues Center. "Keeping the Valley Green: A Public Policy Challenge." *California Agriculture* 45(May–June 1991):10–14.

Uchida, Yoshiko. "Evacuation: The First Five Months." *California Monthly* 77(November 1966):4–8.

Vecoli, Rudolph J. "*Contadini* in Chicago: A Critique of *The Uprooted.*" *Journal of American History* 51(December 1964):404–17.

Yamada, Mitsuye. "Invisibility Is an Unnatural Disaster: Reflections of an Asian American Woman." In *This Bridge Called My Back: Writings By Radical Women of Color,* ed. Cherrie Moraga and Gloria Anzaldua. Watertown, Mass.: Peresphone Press, 1981, pp. 35–40.

Yanagisako, Sylvia Junko. "Two Processes of Change in Japanese-American Kinship." *Journal of Anthropological Research* 31(Autumn 1975):196–224.

———. "Variance in American Kinship: Implications for Cultural Analysis." *American Ethnologist* 5(February 1978):15–29.

———. "Women-Centered Kin Networks in Urban Bilateral Kinship." *American Ethnologist* 4(May 1977):207–26.

Unpublished Papers, Dissertations, and Theses

Bridges, Noriko Sawada. "To Be or Not to Be: There's No Such Option." Broadside, undated.

Brown, Betty Frances. "The Evacuation of the Japanese Population from a California Agricultural Community." M.A. thesis, Stanford University, 1944.

Hanawa, Yukiko. "The Several Worlds of Issei Women." M.A. thesis, California State University at Long Beach, 1982.

Hayashi, Brian Masaru. "For the Sake of Our Japanese Brethren: Assimilation, Nationalism, and Protestantism among the Japanese of Los Angeles, 1895–1942." Ph.D. diss., University of California, Los Angeles, 1990.

James, Thomas. "Life Begins with Freedom: The Making of the College Nisei, 1942–45." Paper presented at the International Conference on Relocation and Redress: The Japanese American Experience, Salt Lake City, Utah, March 10–12, 1983.

Mossman, Robert Alan. "Japanese-American War Relocation Centers as Total Institutions with Emphasis on the Educational Program." Ed.D. diss., Rutgers University, 1978.

Nettler, Gwynne. "The Relationship between Attitude and Information concerning the Japanese in America." Ph.D. diss., Stanford University, 1945.

Sanchez, George Joseph. "Becoming Mexican American: Ethnicity and Acculturation in Chicano Los Angeles, 1900–1943." Ph.D. diss., Stanford University, 1989.

Shimada, Koji. "Education, Assimilation, and Acculturation: A Case Study of a Japanese-American Community in New Jersey." Ed.D. diss., Temple University, 1974.

Wong, Morrison Gideon. "The Japanese in Riverside, 1890 to 1945: A Special Case in Race Relations." Ph.D. diss., University of California, Riverside, 1977.

Index

Library of Congress Cataloging-in-Publication Data

Matsumoto, Valerie J.
   Farming the home place : a Japanese American community in California, 1919–1982 /
Valerie J. Matsumoto.
     p. cm.
   Includes bibliographical references and index.
   ISBN 0-8014-2074-1
   1. Japanese Americans—California—Cortez—Social life and customs. 2. Farm
life—California—Cortez. 3. Cortez (Calif.)—Social life and customs. I. Title.
F869.C815M38 1993
979.4'58—dc20
                                       92-56774